DANTE'S DAUGHTER

DANTE'S DAUGHTER

Kimberley Heuston

FRONT STREET
Asheville, North Carolina

Lyrics found on pages 131-134 are translations of Bertrand de Born,
Peire d'Alvernhe, and Arnaut Daniel and may be found in
Troubadour Lyrics: A Bilingual Anthology by Frede Jensen.
Reprinted here with permission from Peter Lang Publishing.

Library of Congress Cataloging-in-Publication Data

Heuston, Kimberley Burton
Dante's daughter / Kimberley Heuston.—1st ed.
p. cm.
Summary: In fourteenth-century Italy, Antonia, the
daughter of Dante Alighieri, longs for a stable family and home while
developing her artistic talent and seeking a place for herself in a
world with limited options for women.
ISBN 1-886910-97-9 (hardcover: alk. paper)
1. Alighieri family—Juvenile fiction. 2. Dante Alighieri,
1265-1321—Family—Juvenile fiction. [1. Alighieri family—Fiction.
2. Dante Alighieri, 1265-1321—Family—Fiction.
3. Family life—Italy—Fiction. 4. Sex role—Fiction.
5. Italy—History—1268-1492—Fiction.] I. Title.
PZ7.H443Dan 2003
[Fic]—dc21   2003005483

For Mark
This is a song for you ...

DANTE'S DAUGHTER

PROLOGUE

Abbey of San Galgano, Italy, the Year of Our Lord 1330

I've never cared much for Florence. I don't know if my father would be pleased or saddened if he knew. He's with God now, so I suppose he does know. I doubt that he's surprised.

My mother is a different story. Every time she visits, she pleads with me to leave this godforsaken place and come back with her to Florence. I laugh and tell her that I have never felt God's presence more strongly and I have no desire to leave, but she does not listen. I take her hands and tell her to look into my face and see if it is that of a prisoner. She looks and, smiling, admits that no, it is not. But that knowledge is more than she can sustain, so I compliment her new wimple or ask her for tidbits of city gossip, and soon enough she has forgotten me and remembers only that her life is as she has wished it to be for many years. Her name is an honorable one, worthy of respect and invitations, and she believes that it will live on beyond her death.

I have no such ambition, which is just as well, since I cannot imagine that my name will be remembered by anyone a hundred years hence. But anonymity is no grief to me. I have always preferred silence to speech, just as I have always preferred image to narration. Some things are too big to be put into words; others, too tender. So if, two lifetimes hence, the world knows me only as Dante's daughter, or even if that much is lost, what care I? Some kinds of understanding come only in the patient reaches of silence.

"And other ways of knowing," I can hear my father saying with an edge to his voice, "can only be achieved from the more strenuous disciplines of speech and action. Don't be lazy, Antonia. You have some time, so use it well."

He's right. I do have time, more than I can fill with the few duties the Brothers have allotted me. So in this season of waiting I will set my pen to parchment and summon the words that for many years I was careful not to speak, and perhaps between me and thee something new will be born.

I asked, "If the pope … is so good … why wouldn't he … want to help … against the Black Guelfs? … Doesn't he know … about the bad things they've done?"

Finished with my hair, Smerelda picked up her rag and began to clean my face and neck. "Boniface VIII is good only when it suits him to be. And he has no use for either the White Guelfs or your father."

"Why not?" I asked. My father was one of the best-known men in Florence. He'd been elected prior the summer before, a post so important he hadn't been allowed to leave the town hall for the whole two months of his term. And he was a famous poet. "Oh," I said, suddenly understanding. I dropped my voice. "Did the pope read the *Vita Nuova*?" The *Vita Nuova* was a collection of my father's poems, and, according to my mother, the source of every trouble that visited our house.

Smerelda snorted. "I doubt very much Boniface has read anything but accountings of his wealth in the ten years since he tricked Celestine V of blessed memory out of the papacy."

"The pope tricked someone?" I wondered uneasily if Smerelda was blaspheming. Before she could reply, however, the door to the room was flung open.

We both jumped, but it was just my seven-year-old brother, Jacopo, looking unusually clean. "Hurry up!" he said. "Our father is biting his fingers!"

"She's ready," said Smerelda, pushing me out into the courtyard.

I saw that the eight-year-old twins, Giovanni and Pietro, were dressed and crouching over the lizard cage they kept under the stiff, spiny branches of the pomegranate tree in the courtyard. Mother was ready, too, rustling down the staircase that led to the bedchambers and *sala* upstairs. She sketched a cross over my head as she reached me, whispered a few words of blessing, then

13

kissed me. Her lips felt cool on my forehead, her breath was sweet from the parsley she often chewed, and her gown held the scent of the dried flowers she strewed over it, but I knew enough not to put my arms around her shoulders and crush her dress.

She turned away to bless the boys, and I realized my father had been just behind her, coming from the little studio off my mother's chamber that had served as his office and sleeping room since the publication of the *Vita Nuova* shortly before my birth. I stepped back warily until I could judge his expression, but saw that, as usual, Jacopo had exaggerated. Babbo didn't look at all angry as he slapped a pair of leather gloves against his arm, just preoccupied. I hesitated, but Smerelda's words had troubled me. "Smerelda says you're going to see the pope," I said as he reached the bottom.

He came back from whatever he was thinking about and looked down at me. "Smerelda is, as usual, well informed. You look very pretty today, Antonia. Like a luscious strawberry."

"You mean a raspberry," I said.

"What?"

"My gown is raspberry-colored," I explained. "Not straw-berry."

"A luscious raspberry, then." He swung me up in his arms as the bell at the abbey church of the Badia began to call the monks to Compline. "Come along, my beautiful lady of the raspberries, whose kisses taste of summer's sweetness and whose eyes kindle the fires of autumn."

I giggled. I loved it when he talked poetry, whatever my mother said. My father was a thin, slightly stooped man, and most of the time his narrow face was closed and remote, like a monk who has drawn a veil between himself and the rest of the world. But when he talked poetry, the veil fell away, and he looked as young and eager as Jacopo.

Thinking about his poetry reminded me about the pope. "Is it true the pope doesn't like you?" I asked.

"Who told you that?" my father asked as he locked the front door.

"Smerelda."

Babbo gave his brief dry laugh and pocketed the key. "Of course." He settled me more comfortably on his arm and set off for the baptistery. "I think that's probably true."

I smoothed the thick pelt of his hair behind his ears. "Why doesn't he like you? Is it because he read your poems?"

"Is that what Smerelda said?" he asked.

"No. I thought of that myself."

"That's very clever of you, but I doubt very much whether Boniface knows or cares about my poetry. He doesn't like me because I want him to concentrate on being pope instead of trying to make money by ruling cities like a prince."

I was silent. It was what Smerelda had said, but I still wasn't sure I believed that a holy man like the pope would care about money. "Isn't he afraid of what God will think of him?" I asked.

"That's exactly why I'm going to Rome, Antonia. To help remind him that God is watching."

I was still unconvinced. "You're sure he's not just angry about the poetry?" I asked as we stepped out of the side street into the brightness of the cathedral square.

He laughed again, and swung me down onto the street.

But almost before my slippers touched the ground, I felt him grab me and pull me roughly against his chest, his fingers biting painfully into my arms. Behind me came the hard, loud clatter of shod horses' hooves against the paving stones of the street, so close I braced for impact. But although I felt the beasts' hot breath on my neck and smelled their sweat, my father's quick movements had prevented a collision. A moment later I felt myself half set, half dropped on the pavement. As soon as I had regained my balance I spun around to see what had happened. Two Black Guelfs, a neighbor of ours named Bocaccino and his wealthy kinsman Filippo Argenti, had evidently tried to run us down. I saw my brother Jacopo's scared face peering out from behind one of the stone tombs that dotted the baptistery's grounds, but there was no sign of Pietro, Gian, and Mother, who were probably already inside.

The men were half turned in their stirrups, yelling at my father and making the sign of the fig at him while they fought to control their beautiful horses. Silver bridles and shoes flashed gold in the late afternoon sun. Then the men settled back in their saddles, spurred their horses over the tomb where Jacopo had taken refuge, missing his head by inches, and wheeled around and galloped out of the square in the direction of the Badia.

I heard my mother calling sharply to Giovanni and saw that the commotion had drawn her and my brothers out of the baptistery. She was holding Pietro's hand, but Gian had broken away and was running after Bocaccino and Filippo, throwing cobblestones and yelling a stream of obscenities.

"Giovanni!" my father said.

Gian hesitated, lofted one last stone after the trouble-makers, then turned and came back into the square. "*Porca miseria,* those *stronzi!*" he said.

I gasped. My father strode toward him and in one quick movement clouted him on the side of his face so hard that he fell. "Go home." my father spat at him. "You are not fit to enter a Christian church with those filthy words on your lips. You debase yourself, and you debase me."

Jacopo started crying, but Gian scowled and opened his

mouth to argue. My mother moved quickly to him on the pretext of helping him up and brushing him off, but when he would have spoken, she shook her head with tight lips. "Surely you don't mean to prevent him from praying for your safety, my lord," Mother said to Babbo.

They locked eyes, and it was my father who shrugged and looked away. "As you wish," he said shortly. He looked down at me, his face gentling. "Are you all right, my lady of the raspberries?"

I tried to say yes but felt my face crumpling, so I merely nodded. Babbo seemed to understand that I didn't want him to make a fuss, though, and just patted my shoulder. "Good girl," he said. "Let's go see how Jacopo is."

Jacopo, although crying as usual, said he was fine. But my mother kept brushing him off and smoothing his hair until my father finally said, "Let be, Gemma."

"Some of your political friends?" my mother said in a thin, high voice. "Such charming manners."

If my father had looked like that at me, I would have known I was getting a beating, but he never beat my mother. He never even quarreled with her. "Let's go inside and get off the street," he said.

We entered the baptistery just as the bells calling people to mass began to ring. I shivered, partially from reaction, partially because I didn't like San Giovanni. The afternoon light slanting in through the open doors and down through the lantern on top of the dome was a muted version of the gold that had danced on the Argenti horses' hooves. More of that gold flashed bright and alive above my head in the mosaics of the dome, but I kept my eyes planted firmly on the floor. I wasn't going to look up. I was not. Giovanni said the devils glittering on the ceiling had no power over devout parishioners who were pious enough to look only at the mosaics of Christ and his prophets. But if you looked at the mosaics of Satan and his demons devouring the sinners, you were practically calling to the devils to come get your soul. Only bad people thought about evil things when they were at church.

I moved a little closer to my father, who picked me up again. His hair was all messy. I began to smooth it back for him, but he touched my wrist and I stopped.

The service started. I tried to be reverent, but it was in Latin and I couldn't understand the words. If we had been where the priests were, in the apse, I could have looked at the ceiling all I wanted to. That mosaic didn't have any devils, just the Hebrew prophets circling around the Lamb of God. Probably the priests were so holy the devils didn't even try to trick them.

I covered my eyes so I wouldn't be tempted to look at the devils that waited above my head, but, safe in my father's arms, I couldn't help one quick peek. A demon in the shape of a lizard was stuffing a boy into a serpent's mouth. The sight reminded me of Giovanni's lizards, and I wondered, not for the first time, if Giovanni had a demon inside him.

Smerelda said he did. When I was being christened in this very church on Holy Thursday with all the other children who had been born in Florence that year, Smerelda had been in charge of the four-year-old twins. When the priest dipped me under the water, two-year-old Jacopo had thought he was throwing me away and had begun to scream. In the confusion, Giovanni escaped and somehow managed to climb on top of the huge, eight-sided marble font without anyone's noticing until he toppled head-first into one of the basins. The basins were designed for babies, not powerfully built little boys, and he had almost drowned before my father was able to break away part of the stone frame and free him. You could still see the place where they mended the font.

I shivered again and snuggled against my father's shoulder. Bad things happened in San Giovanni. I didn't know why Babbo liked it better than comfortable, dark San Martino, just down the street from our house. That was where my mother and Smerelda usually took me.

"You are a wiggle worm today, my luscious lady of the raspberries," Babbo whispered to me. "Why don't you look at the mosaics?"

I closed my eyes and shook my head. "They scare me," I whispered back.

Mother would have just told me not to be silly, but I felt Babbo's head move as he looked at the dome above our heads. After a minute he whispered, "I never thought about that. When I was a little boy, they had finished only the circle of the angels. I used to twirl around underneath them until it looked like they were flying out of a beautiful golden rose to come and bless me."

I opened my eyes and saw Mother scowling at us for making noise. Babbo put his finger to his lips and set me down on the floor. I moved slightly away and looked at the circle of angels sparkling above the smoke of the incense. I noticed that they were all stooped forward as if they were bending down to watch over me. I squinted my eyes and wiggled my head a little until they were flying. Then I closed my eyes until I could almost feel their wings beating around me, brushing away the power of the devils. I opened my eyes and saw that two of the angels—the Virtues—were driving demons away from two scared-looking men. I liked not being the only one that the demons scared. And I liked knowing that the builders had made God and his angels before they made Satan and his demons.

Gian poked me and made a stupid face with his mouth hanging open, as if he were me looking at the ceiling. I stuck my tongue out at him, but I stopped looking. Instead, I pretended I was one of the angels flying out of a golden rose with a sword to drive off any demons who might be scaring little girls or big men on their way to see the pope. *Smack!* to Gian and his stupid face. *Smack!* to Smerelda for pulling my hair. *Smack!* to Bocaccino and Filippo Argenti for making Jacopo cry. I thought about smacking Boniface VIII for not liking my *babbo*, but hesitated. Probably God would not be happy about angels fighting the pope.

When the service finally ended and the big doors opened, my brothers went outside to meet the friends of their *brigade* while my mother greeted her friend Monna Beatrice Cavalcante. Monna Beatrice was always sad because her husband, Guido, had died last summer. He had been one of my father's poet friends, but he made too much trouble for the commune so my father and the rest of the government had had to send him away. Then a mosquito bit him and it made him sick and he died. Monna Beatrice didn't like my *babbo* anymore because of that.

I was sad about her husband, of course, but I thought it was his fault for making trouble. Mostly I liked to look at her son Andrea (we all called him Farinata, after his famous grandfather), who had the prettiest hair I had ever seen, long and curly and the color of chestnuts. No one else in Florence had hair that color, and I didn't care that Gian thought he was a nancy-boy, I thought he looked beautiful. I looked for his hair, but the light had fallen too much and tonight it looked like everyone else's.

My father was talking with Ser Dino, his friend who had shared the priory with him the previous year. I looked around for Silvana, but she wasn't there. I started to follow my brothers outside but hesitated at the door. The boys were playing hide-and-seek around the old Roman sarcophagi that dotted the square between the baptistery and the partially completed walls of the new *duomo*, and I wondered if dead spirits might be hiding out there in the gathering dusk. I turned back to the glowing candlelight of the baptistery and went to visit the animals.

There were two great wheels of animals made of inlaid marble on the baptistery floor. The one close to the door showed earthly animals. The one next to it, which was my favorite, was the wheel of the zodiac, with a sun in the middle. Sometimes, when he was tired of Gian, my brother Pietro would point out his and Gian's Goat, Jacopo's Water Bearer, and my Crab, and then would read me the magic words that chased each other around the sun in the middle and which said the same thing backward and forward. I visited the animals, then I found the place where the words began. But although I spent a long time looking at the letters, without Pietro's help I could not make them fall into the words I knew were there.

"Do you want to know what that says?" Babbo said over my shoulder.

"Yes, please."

"*En giro torte sol ciclos et rotor igne,*" he said, pointing out each word. "Behold, I the sun turn the orbits at an angle and am turned by the fire."

That was what Pietro always said, but, magic words or not, they made no sense to me. "Oh," I said.

"Don't you know what that means?"

I looked at the floor and shook my head. I hated not understanding.

"Orbits are the paths the sun, the moon, and the planets

21

follow around the Earth," he explained. "Each planet is part of a separate crystal circle, tucked inside each other like the layers of an onion. All the layers rub against each other, so when the sun layer turns, it makes the layer next to it move, too, like when I roll a quill pen between my fingers. The fire—the glory of God—turns the sun. So whoever made this wheel wants to remind the people who see it that God's glory and his love for us make the planets and stars move in the heavens."

He squatted down next to me. "Can I tell you a secret?"

I nodded.

"When I am far away from my beautiful lady of the raspberries and missing her, I think about the stars God put up there for us to see, and it makes me feel less lonely. They may look like they are moving away from Earth, but they always come back, just as I will always come back to you."

I loved my *babbo*.

"Come on," he said. "Your mother is waiting."

Night had fallen by the time we left the church, and a cold breeze was blowing. I put my arms up to be carried, and Babbo picked me up with a sigh. "You're getting too big for me to do this much longer," he said.

"Dante!" my mother called. "There is something you should see!"

I was surprised. My mother almost never talked to my father, yet there she was, her face excited and young-looking, calling to him from the new cathedral's construction site. The boys were with her, looking as excited as she was.

"Do you know what this is about?" my father asked me. I shook my head. "Well, we'd better go and find out."

The boys had climbed up onto the partially built walls and were pointing up at the sky. "Look, Babbo! What is it?"

I followed their pointing fingers and saw a huge star with a big long red cloud following behind it.

Babbo put me down next to one of the boys so he could look at it more carefully. His face was as young and excited as my mother's. "It looks like a comet."

"What's a comet?" Jacopo asked.

Babbo put on his teaching voice. "Aristotle says that a comet marks a dry exhalation from the earth, which is then ignited by the heat of the sun. The better question, Jacopo, is what does a comet *mean*. History teaches us that comets are important signs or portents. Many scholars, for example, believe that the Star of Bethlehem was a comet, and the Book of Revelations suggests that the Second Coming of Christ will be heralded by the appearance of comets."

"Is it the Second Coming?" Jacopo breathed.

"I don't think so," my father said. "Comets have very specific characteristics. *Dimmi*, Pietro, what is the color of that comet?"

"Red," Pietro answered.

"Gian, what planet is associated with the color red?"

"Mars," Gian said promptly. "The planet of war."

"That's right," my father said. "Red comets are associated with wind, storms, famine, fever, fire, war, and revolution." He looked across the heads of the boys to my mother. "Sounds like Florence these days, doesn't it?" he said. "But remember, boys, chaos can also lead to creation."

"That's enough stargazing," Mother said abruptly, and turned away. "No, Bice, you don't need to be carried. Your father has a long day tomorrow."

Babbo reached out to take her arm, but she pretended not to see, and walked ahead of the rest of us all the way home.

SILVER AND BLACK

Florence, 1301

All three of my brothers started grammar school about the time my father left for Rome. Normally I would have spent at least an hour with my mother every morning visiting her father, who lived around the corner, but my *nonno* was in France on business until after Christmas, so I was left alone with Smerelda for much of each day. It was a trying autumn for us both. I was a well-meaning child but clumsy, and my efforts to help her with her work were littered by crumpled linens and broken bowls. What patience Smerelda may once have possessed had long since worn away through the combined efforts of my brothers, and the top of my head was often sore from the raps she gave me when I failed to please her.

So when I awoke the day after All Saints' Day to the whistle of the wind through the closed shutters and the patter of the rain on the stone pavement outside, I didn't even open my eyes, just burrowed farther under the covers. Smerelda was always especially cross on rainy days—she said the damp settled in her joints—and I knew that this reminder of the cold, dreary winter to come would put her in a foul temper.

Sure enough, while the thought still echoed in my mind, I heard the bedroom door open and felt my bedclothes flung off me. "Out of bed, you lazy cat," Smerelda scolded. "Your lady mother wants us to clean out the storage room so there's room for the supplies from the farm at Fiesole." The harvest was over, but my father had not yet had time to arrange for the transportation of our crops from the farms we owned in the *contada*.

I dressed while Smerelda complained about her arthritis, then obediently ate my porridge, even though it was cold and had coagulated into a leaden mass. Another morning I might have fussed about how it stuck in my throat, but not when Smerelda's arthritis was acting up. Even at five years old, I had learned that the least painful strategy at times like this was compliance. I wiped out my bowl without being asked, and wordlessly followed Smerelda into the storeroom.

The work was easy enough—not even I could break a barrel of grain or a cask of wine by dusting it too energetically—but every time we came across some rancid oil or moldy onions, Smerelda would send me up to the kitchens to warm a new poultice for her to try. Judging by her temper, none of them worked, and my legs quickly tired of the climb up and down two flights of tall stone steps. When the knock came at the door, I was pleased by the interruption.

"I'll get it!" I said quickly. Smerelda just grunted and sank down on one of the chests, as grateful as I was for a reason to stop.

I pushed back the bolt and slowly dragged open the heavy front door. My Tio Teruccio, Mother's brother the priest, stood on the steps, shifting uneasily from foot to foot.

I gawked at him, so surprised to see him at our home instead of at the church where he belonged that I forgot my manners. But he forgot his, too, pushing past me into the house and asking, "Quickly, child, is your mother at home?"

"I think so," I started. "She's—"

But he didn't wait. He hurried past me and yelled her name just like a peasant fighting with his wife, and me with the door to the street wide open so everyone could hear. If he didn't remember how Mother was about the proprieties, I did. I shut the door and then ran after my uncle, who was bounding up the stairs to her chamber two at a time, calling, "Gemma! Gemma! For God's sake, Gemma!"

She came to the door of her chamber still unfastening the turban that protected her hair while she cleaned, an annoyed look on her face. "Teruccio, really," she began, but he paid no attention, just grabbed her elbow and walked her backward into her chamber, saying urgently, "Gemma, I have news …" and closing the door sharply behind him.

I stopped halfway up the staircase and turned to make my way down again. Smerelda was standing at the door of the storeroom. She looked from me to the closed door and then back again, and said abruptly, "Get your cloak, Bice. We've got laundry to do."

"But I thought we were …"

She was already dumping piles of linens in the big laundry basket. "You heard me."

"Why do I need my cloak?"

"It's cold down by the river."

I started to ask her why we were taking our laundry to the river on a wet day instead of just doing it over a fire in the courtyard, but then I looked at her big, square back and thought better of my words. I ran to fetch my cloak.

To my surprise, Smerelda was not the only woman who had decided to bring her laundry to the Arno that dreary day. A group of children, including my friend Silvana and her cousins, had already assembled around the old, cracked statue of Mars while their mothers and nurses scrubbed their laundry on the riverbank below. The old women said it was shameful that the city still kept the statue of the pagan god that had once protected Roman Florence, but the young men laughed at them and said it was Mars who kept our armies strong. The brigade Gian ran around with agreed with the men, and I saw some of the boys too young or too poor to go to school stockpiling stones from the riverbed beside the statue, the way they always did when tensions were running high between the Blacks and the Whites.

"Is there fighting?" I asked Silvana in greeting. She and her father had lived in a tavern near the bridge since the death of her mother, and they knew all the gossip.

"*Ciao*, Bice," she said. "Not yet, but soon." She nodded at the Frescobaldi palace across the river by the Ponte Santa Trinità, from whose tower the banner of Charles of Valois fluttered. He was the younger brother of the French king, invited by the pope to help win Tuscany for the church. I noticed that the women below us were casting glances at the closed gates of the palace, and that each had positioned herself so she could see it clearly. So that was why Smerelda had taken the laundry to the river.

A trumpet blared. I looked at the Frescobaldi palace, expecting to see the gates opening and the army pouring out. But nothing happened. The trumpet blared again, and I realized the noise was coming from the city behind me. A church bell began to ring, and then another. A distant clamor grew.

Silvana's aunt called sharply to her, and then Smerelda had me by the arm and we were making for home as fast as her arthritic feet could take her. I saw that the basket she balanced on her head was only half full, and I tried to stop. "The laundry! You've left some of the laundry!"

But she didn't stop, didn't even pause, just yanked at my arm until I thought she would pull it from its socket.

"You're hurting me!"

"Shut your beak!" she snapped. "They've opened the gates to the Black Baron."

I looked around and realized that the crowd that pressed around us included more than the women and children from the river. A merchant cursed as a length of gold and scarlet Lucchese silk slipped from under the box of books he was loading on a broken-down donkey and fell billowing to the muddy ground. A woman and her son were trying to hoist an elderly man up a ladder into one of the old towers that dotted the cityscape. A pile of their goods lay on the sidewalk beside them, and while I was watching two of the bulging packages were picked up and coolly carried away by a pair of beggars, one of whom saw me watching and brandished his teeth at me, waving a cudgel threateningly. I looked around, but no one had seen the theft except me—everyone else was too busy closing and locking shutters, loading donkeys, or herding children.

No one spoke, but the noise grew louder by the minute, pierced by screams. In the distance a cloud of smoke was forming and drifting toward us down the Via del'Corso.

We turned off the Via del'Corso into our *vicino*. The old gentleman who lived two houses down from ours was trying to fit his key into the lock on his door, but he was shaking so violently that even with two hands he couldn't make it slip into the hole. His mouth was forced into a sickly, shamefaced grin. As we passed, I smelled the stink of urine and saw the small pool by his feet.

My mother was evidently waiting behind our door, because as soon as we called to her it opened. "Do you have the boys?" she asked Smerelda urgently as we entered.

"No, Monna Gemma, they are at school."

Mother gave Smerelda a hard slap. "What were you thinking, taking Bice out on such a morning? Anything might have happened. The French are here!"

"I know," I said. "We went down to the river and saw them."

Smerelda pinched me hard, but Mother had already heard. She gasped, and slapped Smerelda again. "Get out of my sight, *puttana!* And don't come back until you have my boys with you. I mean it! Go!"

Smerelda hesitated, but my mother was in no mood to be defied. With a sour look at us both, Smerelda stepped back into the street.

My mother shut and bolted the door behind her, then knelt in front of me, her face white and drawn. "You are going to have to be very brave, Bice," she said, her cold hands nervously patting at my hair, my cheeks, my dress. "Your Tio Teruccio thinks there will be fighting, and we have no man to protect us."

Someone started beating on the door, and we heard Jacopo and Pietro calling. Mother opened the door, and the boys fell inside, both talking.

"They've let the prisoners out of the *stinche*—"

"The Blacks are on the march!"

"—and the priors have been sent home!"

Mother shut the door behind them and broke into their excited babble. "Where's Giovanni?"

"He got too close to the horses—you know how he is—and one of them kicked him in the eye," Jacopo said. "But he's coming."

"Blessed Virgin, in the eye?" Mother crossed herself.

"He's fine," Pietro said. "Mother, why did they let the prisoners out of jail? What about the law?"

Mother gave a bitter laugh. "You sound like your father. There is no law at times like these."

Someone pounded on the door, and Mother opened it

quickly. Giovanni staggered through the opening and then leaned back against the door while Mother bolted it. He was gasping for breath, his shirt was torn, and a gash welled blood over one eye. He looked like one of the monsters that sometimes visited my dreams, and I burst into tears.

"Hush, Bice," Mamma said. She started to call for Smerelda, then remembered she was out. "Does it hurt?" she asked Gian, pressing the bone around the eye.

"No, it's just a scratch," he said, wincing.

"Jacopo," my mother ordered, "go get me some water and an old towel."

"Where's Smerelda?" Jacopo asked.

"I sent her to look for you, but she's probably gone home to her people."

"Smerelda wouldn't leave us like that," said Jacopo.

"Oh, wouldn't she?" said Mother. "Go and fetch the water as I asked you, or you'll be the one with the bloody eye." Her roughness to Jacopo scared me, and I cried louder. "Bice, that's enough," she said through her teeth. "I mean it."

I stopped.

"Pietro, have they closed the gates?"

"How would I know?" Pietro said. "Mother, how can they just break the law like that?"

"Oh, for the love of the Madonna, will you stop going on about the law," Mother said. "Jacopo! Drat the boy, where is he?"

Giovanni interrupted impatiently. "The Blacks are keeping the gates open for their exiles. Mother, I tell you, I'm fine. Let me go."

But Jacopo arrived with the bandaging supplies and Mother tore the towel in strips and began to dress the cut. "No, stand still. How many times have I told you this would happen, Gian? What were you thinking? No—don't tell me," she said as he began to make his excuses. "There's no time. Just tell me, do you know the way to the Fiesole farm?"

"Of course," Pietro and Giovanni said together.

Mother took a deep breath. "All right. This is what I need you to do, Giovanni. Take your brothers and sister there. No, no, there isn't time to argue," she said as he began to protest. "You must take them. No one should bother you—even if they recognize you, you are only children." She finished bandaging him. "Bice, come here."

I went, wiping my tears away as best I could to save myself the beating I expected, but instead she drew my gown and *camicia* up to my waist. I wore no other undergarments and waited for Giovanni to comment, but he didn't—a measure, I suppose, of the urgency of the situation. Mother began wrapping the leftover bandaging around my middle.

"But I'm not hurt," I said.

"Hush. Just listen." She knotted the bandages and began stripping off the jewels she wore on her fingers and wrists and tucking them into the bandaging. "All right. So. You will go to the farm in Fiesole. That's far enough outside the gates for you to be safe. I will stay here. Perhaps I will be able to persuade Corso to spare the house, but I doubt it. That *figlio di putata* Bocaccino has had his eye on this property for a long time, and his cousin Argenti is a powerful man." Finished with me, she began climbing the stairs. "Well, come on," she said impatiently.

We followed her into her room. She opened her chest and took out a length of silk, unceremoniously yanked Jacopo's breeches down, and began to wind it around his waist. "Pietro, take the icon. Giovanni, get the silver inkwell from your father's studio. Pour out the ink first."

"Shall I get his papers?" Pietro asked, stuffing the icon inside his tunic.

She hesitated, then said firmly, "No. We haven't time or a way to smuggle them out. Leave them." She pulled Jacopo's shirt down over the silk. "Good," she said, and sat on the bed and lifted me on her lap. "All right. I want you all to listen to me. I am going to stay here and see what I can do to protect the house. I'll be all right, Jacopo. I'm a Donati, and if things get too bad I will go stay at your Nonno Manetto's house. But you are all Alighieris, no matter who your mother is, and you will not be safe here. You will need to walk; they'd take the horse from you before you left the *sesto*. When you get to Fiesole, Giovanni, tell Berto and Marcella what has happened. Have them bury any valuables or cash they have on hand, just in case. And then stay there. I mean it. If I hear that any of you have come anywhere near Florence I will have Berto tan your backsides until the flesh separates from the bone. This is no joke. People are going to die, and I don't want you to be in that number."

Jacopo was crying. "When we will see you again?"

"As soon as things quiet down here. A day or two," Mother said. "Now come and kneel so we can pray."

Before the prayer was half over I heard the same sound of excited voices I had heard on the street. Mother cut the prayer short and hurried us toward the back wall. "Giovanni and Pietro, fetch the water barrel," she commanded.

While they ran to get it, she knelt right down on the cabbages in the garden as if they were nothing and pulled Jacopo and me close to her. "Now listen," she said. "You two are going to have to be very brave. I know this is hard to understand, but you will be safer without me. Do whatever Gian and Pietro tell you to do, even if you don't understand why. Jacopo, do I have your word as an Alighieri?"

He nodded, his eyes enormous black holes in his face. "Bice?"

I nodded, too, at least I think I did, but my body was not behaving normally; I seemed to be watching what was happening instead of living it.

The boys dragged the barrel to the wall, Mother and Jacopo helping them jerk it up over the raised beds of kitchen plants. "Up you go," Mother said. "Take good care of each other. Gian and Pietro, remember that Antonia is younger than you are and her legs are shorter. Don't ask her to do more than she can. Keep the valuables hidden away until I or one of the uncles comes for you. Now, go with God."

One at a time, Gian and Pietro scrambled onto the barrel and vaulted over the wall. Mother helped Jacopo climb onto the barrel, then held his hand while he jumped to the top of the wall. He paused for a moment, then vanished from sight, and it was my turn.

I got to the top of the wall safely, but then Mother hissed, "Stay there!" I froze, terrified. She ran quickly to the stairs and up past her room. Three endless minutes later, she returned, carrying a large, badly wrapped bundle from which a salami protruded. She held it up to me, and I passed it down to Pietro's waiting hands. Then I closed my eyes and walked off the wall.

Gian caught me, but the force knocked him over and I rolled backward against the wall, knocking my head and my left hand hard against the stones. I lay there for a minute, half stunned, and watched my brothers' feet dart away among the weeds and mud of the alley. I didn't know the way to the Fiesole farm. If they left me now, I would be lost amid the fighting.

I pulled myself to my feet and stumbled after them, my head and hand throbbing with every step. I looked at my hand, and had a confused impression of blood and skin torn back until it resembled the curls my father trimmed off his quill pen. My legs failed me, and I sat down hard in the weeds. I couldn't stop starring at the tallow-white curls of skin lying on top of glistening red. I felt the saliva hot in my mouth, but there wasn't time to be sick; I had to go. I knew I had to go, but I couldn't look away from my hand. My brothers were getting farther and farther away and I was going to be left here all alone, but I couldn't stop looking.

Something with hot breath lurched into me. I flinched away, but it was just Pietro. "You have to come," he panted.

I looked at him.

With a cry of impatience, he reached for my arm. His eyes widened when he saw my hand, but he didn't comment, just tugged my sleeve down until my hand was covered, then pulled me to my feet. "Come on!"

We caught up with Gian on the fringes of a large crowd that had gathered outside the Bargello, the residence of the priors of Florence. Babbo had lived there for two months while he was prior, and I saw that his friend, Ser Dino, was on the great wooden balcony with two men whose clipped ears branded them as thieves. The crowd was booing and throwing things at the criminals.

Then my stomach turned over with a sickening lurch and the blood rushed to my face as I saw that it was the criminals who held Ser Dino, and that it was he the crowd was booing.

A man's voice called out beside me, and the boos and catcalls subsided. The voice was familiar, and I looked around to see who it might be. He called again, and I saw him. It was Ser Tomaso, Silvana's father, a man who carried comfits in his pockets for me and whose wit was as famous as his appetite. He was grossly fat, with three chins and hands as plump and round as a woman's, but so charming and urbane that people called him Ciacco, "Hog," out of affection instead of disgust. I sagged against Pietro in relief. He would save my father's friend and make the crowd see reason.

But in this I was mistaken. His normally good-natured face was twisted into a mask of hate and fear as he shouted to the criminals holding Ser Dino, "Which hand did he use to sign the exile order for the Black Baron?"

The thief held up Ser Dino's right hand. The crowd yelled back, "The right! He used the right!"

"You know what to do!" Ciacco screamed, his usually mild eyes almost popping out of his head and spittle spraying from the side of his mouth until he looked more like a wild boar than a man.

"Cut it off! Cut it off!" chanted the crowd.

One of the thieves brandished a dagger, and the two of them held Ser Dino's arm on the windowsill. Ser Dino was crying and pleading with them not to take his hand. It gave me a queer feeling to see one of my father's friends behaving like Jacopo, but the thieves and the crowd were unmoved, and I saw the dagger flash in the sunlight as the thief brought it down onto the sill.

Ser Dino screamed, and was quickly taken away, his arm pumping blood. One of the thieves picked up the hand with the point of the dagger and flipped it into the crowd. A man standing in front of us caught it, and some drops of blood spattered onto my ear and the side of my head. He threw it to Ciacco, and the crowd began to chant again, but I couldn't hear what they were saying. I was trying too hard to scrub the hot blood off my forehead and ear with my good right hand. It didn't matter; no matter how hard I rubbed, I could still feel the corrosive drops burrowing into my skin.

I was dimly aware that Giovanni was yelling something at me, but I couldn't spare attention for anything but cleaning myself until Pietro grabbed my injured hand. The sudden burst of pain cleared my head as though I had been slapped. I dropped my good hand and followed my brothers through the legs and weapons of the crowd, while people chanted, "Eat it! Eat it!" As we rounded the corner and lit off toward Santissima Annunziata and the road to Fiesole, a roar went up, but I didn't look back. I knew what I would see.

We needn't have worried about the guards. They had left their posts and the gates hung crookedly open. We left Florence without a backward glance and started up the long white road toward the farm at Fiesole.

EXILE

Fiesole and Siena, 1301

The long hard march up the hill toward Fiesole was exhausting. We ate the food Mother had packed for us shortly after we left the city limits, crouching beneath a hedge that provided some protection from a cold, soaking rain. We saw no one on the road; the orange glow on the horizon must have warned people that this was not a day to be abroad. And then we walked and walked and walked until my legs ached and my feet were on fire.

We reached the farm at dusk, but the tenants regarded us with suspicion and spoke to us in a dialect so thick that at first I thought Pietro would not be able to make them understand and we would have to spend the night in the fields.

Even when they relented and let us inside, there were no warm baths, no clean, dry clothes, and supper was a scant cup of cabbage soup flavored mostly by smoke. I pressed my nose against the scratchy wet wool of my cloak so I wouldn't have to smell the stench of mildew that clung to everything, and I waited for someone to dress my sore hand and put me to bed. Eventually I realized that no one was going to come.

I sidled up to Jacopo, who was staring into the fire while Gian and Pietro argued about the Black takeover of the city. "Where do we sleep?" I whispered.

Gian, overhearing, snorted. "Wherever you wish, *principessa*."

Abashed, I curled up in my wet cloak as close to the

smoking fire as I could, mumbled a Pater Noster and a Hail Mary into my tangled hair, and quietly cried myself to sleep.

Along with my brothers, I spent as much as possible of the next few days outside. It was dank and cold, but at least the air was fresh. We sat huddled together in a little nest we made on the stone wall that overlooked Florence and watched the city burn, the boys gambling with juniper berries they made me gather for them as we waited for the smoke to clear and for our mother to come to us.

She surprised us while the fires still burned, near dusk on the fourth day. She was on foot, carrying a basket of belongings on her head like a servant, and as she got closer we saw that one of her arms was in a sling.

She said little beyond what had already been made plain by her appearance: the house was gone, and Smerelda had not returned. Then she gave Marcella her bedcurtains to hang around the farm's only bed and disappeared behind them for two days, so that Marcella and Berto joined us on the floor. On the third morning she pulled the curtains back and emerged, pale and rumpled with new lines around her mouth, but still recognizably Mother. She scolded Marcella for the damp, dirty sheets, sent Berto to hitch up the farm's donkey cart and borrow another one from the neighbors, and sat us down to tell us of her plans.

"We don't know when your father will return, and the house and its contents are gone," she said without preliminaries. "Bocaccino has taken it over, as he has wanted to for years. He will try to take the farms, too, but they are outside the city walls and we'll probably be able to hold on to them. The question is what to do with you. As you can see, there's really not room here and the farm in Prato is only slightly better. I have spoken to your Tio Francesco, and we believe that it is best for me to stay in Florence with your *nonno* and try to do what I can to protect the family's interests here. If I am to safeguard your patrimony, I cannot occupy myself with children." She paused. "Take your thumb out of your mouth, Bice. You're not a baby anymore."

I was so overwhelmed by her matter-of-fact cataloguing of these catastrophic losses—Smerelda, our house, our family unit—that I didn't even feel the sting of her reproof. I just waited until her gaze moved on and then slipped my thumb in again, shaking my uncombed hair over my face so that she couldn't see.

"I know your father would want you boys to continue with your education, but education is expensive and we are paupers now. I've talked with your Tio Francesco, and he has agreed to take Giovanni as an apprentice for his office in Lucca."

Gian looked relieved and pleased. He and Tio Francesco got on well together.

"As for Pietro and Jacopo, the only thing I can think of is to leave you as oblates with the Dominicans at Santa Maria. Your father studied there and your Tio Duccio painted the altarpiece for the Laudesi chapel, so they may feel some obligation to the family—I don't know. At any rate, they'll feed you and protect you, and that is the most important thing. We'll have to think of something else by the time you are fourteen and adults, but for now it will serve."

Pietro and Jacopo also received the news without comment or complaint. I guess none of us felt much like talking.

"As for you, Bice," Mother continued, her eyes noticing the dirty dishes on the table, "I have decided to send you to your godmother and Tio Duccio." Tia Taviana was my father's sister. She was married to the painter Duccio, but I didn't remember meeting either of them. They lived in Siena, two days' journey south by oxcart along the pilgrimage route to Rome. "I have heard that your uncle has just landed himself a fine commission," Mother went on, "and they should have no trouble feeding and clothing you until your father returns and other arrangements can be made. Any questions?"

She looked around at us, and I quickly removed my thumb.

"When do we go?" Pietro asked.

"Right now," Mother said. "Berto is going to take you boys to Francesco's house, and Francesco will take Pietro and Jacopo to the Dominicans at Santa Maria Novella. I will take Bice to Siena myself."

An hour later Mother and I were jouncing toward Siena in the farm's donkey cart.

I have only a few disconnected images left to me of our two-day journey to Siena. The endless cold rain, and how much the cart bounced. The way Mother winced and shrank away once when I knocked against her shoulder. The clean fleece she had brought for me, and how brown and dirty her hands were when she wrapped me in it. Pausing once at a roadside well that had a tin cup attached to it for pilgrims, and roasting fallen chestnuts we gathered off the ground for our meal.

We arrived at the huge Porta Camollia late the second afternoon, an hour or so before the city gates were closed for the night. I was tired, and my sore hand sent a shiver of pain through my arm with every jounce of that dratted cart, and I remember how glad I was that I could climb out at the gates and walk the rest of the way.

Even today, I can close my eyes and see Siena as I saw it that first November evening. The iron-gray clouds that had hovered menacingly for a week seemed finally to have rained themselves dry, and their lacy husks drifted lavender and blue far above the city reclining against the Tuscan hills. Siena is a smaller, more elegant city than Florence, with curving streets and buildings of dusky apricot-colored brick, and seemed to me as bright and perfect as a well-set jewel in the sweet, clear-washed air.

Because I had borne the journey without complaint, Mother allowed me to hold her good hand as we made our slow way down the nearly empty streets, accompanied by the reassuringly familiar clink of crockery and an occasional whiff of someone's supper from behind stone walls. We heard no shouting, saw no crowds, smelled no smoke.

Mother let go of my hand in front of a church whose steps were being swept by a brother in the black-and-white habit of the Dominican order, and I looked around expectantly. But it was only because we were turning down a side street so steep we both had to forget our injuries and pull as hard as we could on the back of the cart so that it wouldn't overrun the donkey. And then we were in a small piazza opening onto a fountain dug into the hill that supported the church, and I was looking at a woman who was unmistakably my father's sister, slight and stooped with the same thick, curling hair, the same dark complexion, the same hooded, eager eyes.

She was standing in her door and calling for some boys who were late for supper when she caught sight of us. Her glance was touched with the curiosity with which you greet a stranger in the *vicino*, but it lit only briefly on us before moving on. Almost at once, however, her eyes returned to my mother's face. They widened and, beaming, she crossed herself quickly and came toward us with her arms outstretched.

"Gemma, I would have known you anywhere! What are you doing here, turning up without a word to anyone? Is this one of your jokes? And this must be my pretty little goddaughter. Welcome, Bice!" Then, as she took in my mother's arm, still in a sling, and her bedraggled and road-stained appearance, she checked. "Gemma? Is everything all right? Is it the boys?"

My mother shook her head, and said, "No, we're all fine. It's just that ..." Then, to my horror, her face crumpled and she started to weep.

I had never seen my mother cry before. To have it happen now, just when we seemed to be safe, was as startling as one of Gian's pounces late at night when I visited the necessary. The confusion and fear of the future that had jostled me since Tio Teruccio's arrival a week before came flooding back, and I felt my bottom lip push forward and my eyes begin to prickle. Desperate not to break into the noisy wails that would proclaim me a baby, I pressed my face into the donkey's warm, scratchy neck.

I heard someone descending the wooden stairs behind me. A deep voice rumbled impatiently, "Well, if they're not here, they can just go without dinner."

Fragile control established, I pushed myself away from the donkey and turned to see a large man with a broad red face and lank black hair hanging down his neck. My Tio Duccio, I guessed. He stopped short when he saw his wife hugging a strange woman in tears. "What in God's name is all this?" he blustered. "Can't a man have his supper in peace?"

"Hush, Duccio, it's Gemma and Bice," Tia Taviana said.

"Who?"

"My brother Dante's wife."

"Are you sure?" Tio Duccio said doubtfully. "She doesn't look like Dante's wife. Always dressed to the teeth, that one is."

"Of course it is," his wife said impatiently. "And here's little Bice, my goddaughter."

Duccio looked at us, comprehension dawning. He was a big man, with huge hands, a belly that swelled out over his belt, and small eyes set well back in his red, rough-featured face. "Trouble in Florence, is there?" he said. "They were saying something about that today at the *campo*. Where're the rest of them? You all get out all right?"

To my relief, Mother was behaving like herself again, drying her eyes and smoothing back her hair. "Yes. Dante, as it happens, is in Rome on business for the commune, and I left my sons with his half-brother Francesco. But we have lost the house."

"It's a bad business," Duccio said. He moved out of the way. "Come in, come in, have a glass of wine. We're just about to sit down to dinner, and you're more than welcome to join us."

Tia Taviana put her hand on his arm. "I think they've come for more than supper, Duccio."

He looked down at her, then at us. His mouth opened, then closed. "Well, come in," he said at last, gruffly. "No reason to stand in the street when the food is on the table."

Their dwelling was smaller than ours, a tradesman's house rather than a merchant's residence. The rooms seemed cramped and dark, with low ceilings and no courtyard. The families— Duccio and his brother Buoninsegna shared the house—were gathered in the *sala* on the second floor. There seemed to be hundreds of them gathered around the single large table, some on benches and others perched on boxes, most of them older even than Pietro and Gian. Aside from three chairs for Duccio, his assistant, and his brother, the room was furnished with nothing else except a couple of wrought-iron hooks for lanterns, but the walls were brightly frescoed to resemble silk hangings and ceremonial swags. I forgot my sore hand and my fatigue and made a beeline for the closest painted corner, but my mother cleared her throat and I returned to her side.

"But who is seen!" my Tio Duccio announced to the room. "Your Tia Gemma and our goddaughter Bice!"

A chorus of welcomes rose while Tia Taviana introduced us to Tio Buoninsegna, a younger and more cheerful version of his brother, and a miscellaneous mass of children and apprentices of assorted shapes and sizes. I didn't even try to keep them straight, just bobbed my head so they would think I was listening. Buoninsegna's wife, Lucrezia, assisted by one of the big girls, came down from the kitchens carrying bowls and platters just as the two missing apprentices burst into the room, apologizing and explaining their tardiness. Everyone squashed together to make room, and then Tio Duccio bent his head to offer the prayer.

Without comment, everyone around the table joined hands. One of the cousins, a tall, solemn boy named Segno after his father, reached for my hand, and without thinking, I gave it to him. But it was my sore hand, and when he gripped it I let out a surprised yelp of pain, which Mother immediately hushed. I bit my lip and bowed my head, but I couldn't help the gush of hot tears that spilled down my cheeks during the prayers.

Segno began to apologize as soon as the prayer was over, which only increased my confusion and agitation. Under her breath Mother was telling me to be quiet, and then Tia Taviana took me by the shoulders and turned me around so she could examine my hand.

Mother and I had kept it wrapped tightly to protect it from any evil vapors we might encounter on our journey. Tia Taviana began to unwrap the bandage slowly and gently, but she hurt me. Or maybe it was the strange look of my unwrapped hand, angry and red and oozing green and yellow slime. But the hot spit was back in my mouth and then my eyes began to blur and not even Mother's sternest voice could stop the sickness in the back of my throat and the darkness in front of my eyes from pulsing bigger and bigger until I knew no more.

DUCCIO'S HOUSE

Siena, 1301

When I woke, it was broad day, and Tia Taviana was standing by my bed smiling at me. "How is it with you?" she asked.

I looked around the room. The shutters were open and sun flooded the room, which seemed to serve as a pantry as well as a bedroom. I was alone in the room's only bed, although I seemed to remember snuggling up against my mother during the night and had probably had at least a couple of other sleeping companions as well. "Good," I said, thoughtlessly starting to rub the sleep from my eyes. "Ow!" I held out my hand to inspect it. It was much better. The puffiness was gone and it looked like my own hand again, badly scraped, but no more than that. It was also clean.

I stretched like one of my *nonno's* kittens. That was why I felt so good. Someone had bathed me and put me in an old, soft linen *camicia*, and I smelled as good as the sheets.

"Your hand looks much better," Tia Taviana said. "It just needed some time to air out. Here—I brought you some bread and milk."

I sat up. "Where is my mother?" I asked as I reached for the bread, which was smeared with butter and honey. I was ravenous, and it tasted wonderful.

Tia Taviana sat on the edge of the bed and held out the cup of milk. I took a big swallow and then tore into the bread again. I don't think anything has ever tasted as good as the first few bites of that breakfast.

Tia Taviana put her hand on my forehead. "No fever, good appetite, clear eyes—Gemma said you were just overtired, and she was right. Have some more milk."

She held out the cup again and I drank, then took another bite. With my mouth full, I asked again, "Where is she?"

Tia Taviana hesitated, then said in a matter-of-fact voice, "She left several hours ago. She felt it was important for her to get back to Florence as quickly as possible."

I put my bread down.

Tia Taviana held out the mug again, and I drank dutifully.

"She came in to kiss you goodbye before she left," Tia Taviana said. "But she didn't want to wake you. She said you had had a hard time of it, and needed the sleep."

I nodded, my eyes on the wall. There was no fresco in this room.

"She said to tell you that she will come to see you as soon as things have sorted themselves out."

I nodded again. The plaster was cracked and stained. Maybe they were planning to paint it later. If I were going to paint it, I would use lots of blue. The expensive blue that was the color of the sky.

"Are you finished eating?" she asked after a moment.

I nodded, then belatedly remembered my manners as I handed her what was left of the bread. "Thank you for the fine breakfast."

Tia Taviana started to say something, then stopped and wrapped the bread in its napkin.

I looked around the room. "Where are my clothes?" I asked.

"Your cousin Andrea has taken them to be washed." Tia Taviana knelt in front of one of the chests that surrounded my bed and opened it with one of the keys she wore around her waist. "But there should be—aha! These were your cousin Margherita's. We thought they might do for now." She held out a gown of coarse romagnol, almost identical to my own, and a pair of stockings.

I thanked her for her kindness and started to get up, but she stopped me.

"We are so glad to have you here with us, Bice," she said. "I know everything will be strange at first, but we hope that this soon feels like home to you."

The door crashed open, and a little boy still not quite steady on his legs came toddling in. "Mama, Mama, Mama!" he said excitedly, and then began to babble.

Tia Taviana scooped him up and put her cheek against his while she introduced us. "This young monster is your cousin Francesco, whom we call Feo," she said. He suffered the embrace for a minute, then struggled to get down. She put him on the floor, and he immediately toddled over and held up his arms for me to pick him up. I did, with difficulty, and he carefully touched my hand.

"Owie?" he inquired.

"Yes, it's an owie," his mother told him. "Be very gentle."

He leaned forward and blew some bubbles on it.

His mother laughed. "He's kissing it better for you."

"Thank you," I said, pulling my hand away before he could hurt it. He was a chubby, round-faced little boy who looked just like his father, and he smelled of milk. Impulsively I leaned forward and kissed his round, soft cheek. He wriggled backward off the bed, then toddled as fast as he could out of the room, calling something that sounded like "Mada! Mada!"

"Feo is our youngest," Tia Taviana explained. "He's a year and a half. And here's Margherita. She is almost seven."

Feo had reappeared, tugging at the hand of a girl who looked older than her age. Like her little brother, Margherita had her father's large build and soft, round features, but my *babbo's* big black eyes sparkled at me from beneath strongly marked brows. I looked away almost at once, but I liked her red cheeks and wide, crooked smile.

Margherita was evidently not as shy as I was. "Do you have a doll?" she wanted to know.

I was embarrassed for her, for not knowing what had happened in Florence. I turned to Tia Taviana for help, but she was straightening the linens in the chest and didn't seem to have noticed her daughter's mistake. "No," I said as I sat up a little straighter against the pillows.

Margherita paused only briefly, then brightened. "I bet Tia Lucrezia will make you one if you ask her," she said.

"I'm sure she will," Tia Taviana agreed. She turned to me and added, "My sister-in-law and Margherita both claim we have too many boys in this house."

"Nasty, stinky things," Margherita, said, sniffing.

"And we're all very pleased another girl has come to help even things out." Tia Taviana picked up the dishes and got to her feet, her motions precise and decisive. "Do you need help dressing?" she asked me.

I shook my head no.

"Margherita will show you around the house and the *vicino* after you have washed and dressed. Better show her the studio first, Margherita. A client is coming in later and your father won't want you girls underfoot. And be back in good time to help with supper."

"*Va bene,*" Margherita said.

After I was dressed, we went next door to the kitchen to beg some apples and cheese from Tia Lucrezia, a small, round woman balanced on tiny feet with thick, pale skin the color of suet and a fluty voice as high as a girl's. The cheese she gave us was different from the kind we made at home, salty and elastic instead of smooth and buttery, but my appetite had returned and I gulped it down almost without tasting it. Lucrezia, pleased by the compliment my appetite paid to her good cooking, pressed some honey cakes with raisins on us as well, after making us promise we wouldn't tell Taviana.

"Not that Mama would care two figs," Margherita confided as we licked the last crumbs from our fingers and descended the stairs to the ground floor. "But I think Tia Lucrezia is a little afraid of her."

I don't remember much from the weeks that followed. My hand healed quickly, the only permanent sign of the injury a slight discoloration that itched in the cold. I spent a good part of each day sitting at a place on the city wall that Margherita had shown me, watching the road from Florence. I was not sleeping well. Terrible demons from the baptistery swooped through my dreams, first snatching away my companions— Babbo, Jacopo, my mother, sometimes even Smerelda—in their horrible, sharp talons and then coming back for me. I would lie paralyzed by the cold, sick terror, watching their plucking talons come closer and closer until Margherita or her older sister Andrea shook me awake. They would talk softly to me until the *fantasmi* were gone, then patiently accompany me around the house, waiting outside the locked doors of each sleeping room until I was sure I could hear the safe, steady breathing of its inhabitants on the other side.

Gradually, however, the contours of my new life began to fill in the gaps left by the end of my old. I liked my relatives. Tio Duccio was quick to anger and liked his wine, but he loved his family and was gentle, in his loud and careless way, with children. He complemented my Tia Taviana, a spare, energetic woman who cared for her household with the same passionate intensity with which my father approached poetry. I saw less of Lucrezia, who was happiest out of her sister-in-law's way in the kitchens (a fact that would have startled and distressed Tia Taviana, had she known), and of Lucrezia's husband, Buoninsegna, a smaller and more even-tempered version of his older brother Duccio, who traveled about the region selling the small devotional images that were the workshop's bread and butter. But they were good to me with the undifferentiated, abstracted kindness they bestowed on the whole noisy, untidy lot of children and cousins and apprentices that constituted the household.

There were no frigid silences here, no calculated slights or carefully nurtured disappointments. When people were angry they yelled or slammed doors or threw things. And when they were happy, they touched you and hugged you and called you *carissima* and *tesoruccio* and their sweet little dumpling. Best of all, when the noise and the emotion got to be too much, you could just disappear. No one, not even Tia Taviana, had enough time or energy to keep track of everyone all the time.

Margherita was a good friend to me. Although her body was large and slow like her father's, she was a sociable girl who knew everything that was going on in the *vicino*. When the days were warm enough for Tia Lucrezia, Tia Taviana, and my cousin Andrea to sit on the roof and spin, Margherita and I tended the babies while she caught the rest of us up on neighborhood gossip. "Donna Paula's son has gambled away their goat," she would tell us, or "They say Ser Niccolò has found silver in his mine in Massa Marittima."

On rainy or cold days, we would be sent out of the house

so Tia Taviana could have some peace. Sometimes she had an errand for us to do, and sometimes Tio Duccio could use us in the shop sweeping or holding one of the apprentices' tools while they prepared a leaf of parchment or a wooden panel for painting. Although Margherita thought the studio stank of animal skin and glue and was exasperated by the slovenly personal habits of the apprentices, those things never bothered me. From the beginning, the studio seemed to me a haven of warmth and color and silence. I loved the glow of gold leaf, the smells of wood and chalk and varnish, the soft, springy texture of the parchment, and the crisp order of the horn jars with their brushes and pens and knives. When Feo wouldn't leave me alone or Duccio was launched on one of his rages, I would retreat to under one of the worktables near the fire and play with the scraps of parchment too big to sweep up for glue and too small for any other use. Pietro, Duccio's assistant, noticed my interest and found me some old brushes, a battered tin inkwell with a cork, and a rough pen he kept sharpened for me when he remembered, and I spent hours drawing pictures for my *babbo's* poems. In the evenings, Tia Taviana taught the apprentices their letters and I studied with them so that I would be able to read the letters my mother would send and maybe even write her one in return.

At the beginning of December, two casks of olive oil and a barrel of wine arrived from the farms with a message that the boys were well and that my father was still in Rome with the pope. There was no letter for me, and in the weeks that followed I gradually stopped watching the road from Florence. It was winter, after all, and cold on the stones.

THE ARRANGEMENT

Siena, 1302

My *babbo* arrived one rainy March afternoon just as we were lighting the lamps. Margherita was the first to the door, of course, but I was not far behind her, and Babbo was thunder-struck when he saw me. "What in God's name are you doing here?" he asked, his face rigid with shock.

I had never seen my father shaken out of his habitual detached calm before, and it frightened me. I burst into tears and, embarrassed and confused, started to run away. But he reached out and grabbed me. *"Diamine,"* he swore under his breath—I had never heard him swear before, either—and I could feel him deliberately forcing his hands to loosen on my arms. "It's all right," he said after a minute, sounding more like his usual self. "I was just surprised to see you. *Dimmi*. What's happened? Why are you here? Is your mother with you?"

But I couldn't get control of my emotions as quickly as he could his. I stood there dumb and helpless until, to my relief, I heard Tia Taviana's quick, clipped voice behind me. "Welcome, Dante. Didn't they tell you? Florence fell to the Blacks shortly after you left, and Bocaccino and the Argentis took your house. Everyone is fine. Francesco took Gian as an apprentice and Gemma sent the younger boys to Santa Maria as oblates. She brought Bice to us while she stays with her father and manages the farms."

Babbo looked back and forth from Tia Taviana to me as

though he couldn't quite grasp what she was telling him. "Bocaccino took the house?"

"Yes," said Tia Taviana.

"Gemma's still in the city?"

"Yes."

"But she's all right," my father said.

"Yes. Everyone is fine."

"I didn't know." Babbo dropped my arms and let the bag he was carrying slide onto the floor as though his strength had failed him. "I didn't see anyone. Boniface said it was to give me the peace I needed for my writing. I wondered—but I knew none of this." He drew a hand across his face. "Have they passed a judgment against me?"

"Yes," Tia Taviana answered. "Exile." She darted a quick look at me, then took a breath. "When you weren't here to answer their charges, they changed the sentence to death."

That last piece of news must have come recently, or I would have heard the gossip.

He looked at her. "The boys?"

"They were not mentioned," she said.

"Of course not, or Gemma wouldn't have left them at Santa Maria," he said. "I wasn't thinking."

"Gemma said she would come as soon as she had word you were here," Tia Taviana said. "I'll send one of the apprentices right away."

But Babbo didn't respond. He stared off into space, his face as white as the smeared wax left on the candle stand after a mass and his mouth working like an old man's. I started to cry again, but silently, and backed away. This stranger with the cold, dead face was not my *babbo*. My *babbo* made up poems and held me on his arm on the way to church even when I was too big to be carried.

I trod on Margherita's foot, and she yelped. My father started, then turned his head and smiled at me, and some color came back into his face. He was still pale and a little fierce, but now he was my *babbo* again. "Well," he said. "Well. This is all very new to me, Antonia. I think that for once I am looking forward to hearing all of Smerelda's gossip."

"Smerelda isn't here," I said.

"She's not? Where is she?"

I shrugged. "She left during the riots and didn't come back."

He nodded, then regarded me seriously for a moment. "So now I must be your nursemaid, I suppose," he said. "I hope you are not in the habit of beating your servants, *madonna*, and that your bed stays dry."

"Most of the time," I said, truthfully.

Babbo looked taken aback. I heard Margherita smother a nervous giggle behind me, and then Tia Taviana started to laugh, and it was all right.

The messenger was sent to my mother, and we settled in to pass the three or four days before she would arrive. To my surprise, Babbo seemed to have an even harder time waiting than I did. In the whole house, there was no quiet corner in which he could pursue his customary studies, and at any rate I stuck to him like a burr, so he eventually gave in more or less gracefully and took Margherita and me with him on rapid walks around the Siena hills.

The walks were exhausting, not only because his legs were longer and stronger than ours, but also because he fired questions at us almost without a pause. I hadn't been exposed to the blinding light of my father's restless mind before. He reminded me a little bit of Gian, barely in control of curiosity that burned so powerfully it seemed to strip away the very walls of the buildings we passed.

"That's Cenzo's inn," Margherita would say. "You don't want to stay there. He waters the wine and his wife never airs out the bedding."

Then Babbo would ask her about their children, and his people, and his wife's people, and how much it cost to stay at a poor inn in Siena, and how much at a good one, and how often a proper housewife aired her linens, and what linens a young woman was expected to provide on the occasion of her marriage. When Margherita ran out of breath, he would tell us in his turn what he had learned of Rome.

"The ruins are tremendous," he said. "The whole population of Rome could fit inside the Colosseum alone, with plenty of room to spare. When you stand in a place like that, you feel the grandeur of the stars or the sea and are humbled by God's power—and then you remember that it wasn't God who made the ruin you are standing in, but ordinary men. It's a very odd feeling."

I thought about what he said. "It doesn't seem that strange to me," I told him. "People make special things all the time. That's why I like to go to the studio. It feels like church to be around all those beautiful things."

"Man-made things shouldn't inspire awe, Antonia."

"They do in me," I said.

He laughed at me. "That is just because you are a very little girl. When you are older, you'll see the difference between the things God makes and the things people make. God's creations grow and become more beautiful, while the things men make get old and break and lose their beauty."

"God made people, and they get old and break."

"I think Tio Dante is right," Margherita put in unexpectedly. "My father is always sad when he finishes a painting, because it's never as good as he wants it to be. But the Bible says that when God looked at the world he created, he thought it was very good."

"Sometimes my drawings are very good," I said while Margherita showed my father one of the city's new fountains. But I said it very softly, so God wouldn't hear me and be angry.

The afternoon of the third day was cold and windy. We had already seen most of the city, so Margherita took us out to the *contada* to show Babbo the way they farmed in Siena. On the way back to the city, Babbo told us about Saint Peter's, where the powers of God and man come together in Holy Mother Church. He said a huge bronze fountain in the shape of a pinecone stood outside the basilica, symbolizing eternal life, but that the pilgrims couldn't get to it because of all the vendors' stalls clustered around it, just like the money-lenders in front of Solomon's temple. He said you could buy anything you wanted there: meat pies, wine, commemorative medals and badges, cloth, books, even animals, and no one seemed to notice or care that they were desecrating holy ground. They just went about their business, the tooth-pullers and cobblers, apothecaries and fishmongers, goldsmiths and blacksmiths and bakers calling out to the crowds that passed. He said he'd never seen so much energy and activity in one place before, and it had made him sad that so many people were spending time on things that didn't really matter.

"It would matter to me," I said, "if I had a sore tooth or a hole in my shoe."

Babbo gave one of his sudden, sharp barks of laughter, and Margherita, who was a little scared of him, jumped. "You're absolutely right," he said. "Trust a woman to think of those things. You're all so practical."

"What's wrong with being practical?" I wanted to know. I

was cold, and my words were slightly slurred. I hugged myself and jumped around a little bit while I waited for him to answer.

"There's nothing really wrong with it," he said. "But it's not very noble. Don't you think people should think great thoughts and build great things, instead of thinking of their stomachs or how hot or cold they are?"

"But I *am* cold," I said.

He drew back his fur-trimmed hood so he could see me better.

"Your lips are blue," he said. "Why didn't you tell me you were cold?"

"I just did," I reminded him.

"How about you?" he asked Margherita. "Are you cold?"

"A little," she said unwillingly. It was easier for Margherita to talk about other people than to talk about herself.

"A little," he repeated. "Which, translated, means that the frostbite hasn't quite reached your knees."

She flushed.

When he saw he had offended her, he was instantly contrite. "I'm sorry," he said. "I'm afraid that when I have done something foolish, I often cover my embarrassment by letting my mouth run away from me, and it was foolish of me not to notice that you girls were getting cold. Let's get you two home before you both turn so blue that you become my two luscious ladies of the blueberries and Taviana decides to serve Roast Dante for supper as punishment."

We giggled at his foolishness and turned our steps toward home.

After supper, my little cousin Feo came to sit in Tio Duccio's lap, as he did every night while Margherita helped Andrea and Tia Lucrezia with the dishes and Tia Taviana taught the apprentices. But tonight there were no lessons, and I wouldn't have cared if there were—I had a lap of my own to climb into. While Duccio sent Pietro to fetch some Venetian playing cards he wanted to show my father, I snuggled against Babbo's narrow chest and listened to the strong beat of his heart. From long habit, he handed me the medallion he wore round his neck. It was a beautiful piece of cloisonné that my great-great-great-grandfather had brought back from the Crusades that showed the Virgin with the Christ child on her lap, and I liked to rub my fingers across the smooth pink of her cheeks and the brilliant enamel blue of her headdress.

"Didn't I hear something about you being in Rome during the Jubilee, Duccio?" Babbo asked my uncle. Two years ago, in 1300, Boniface VIII had declared a Jubilee Year. Anyone who went to Rome and said enough masses at the important churches had their sins forgiven.

Tio Duccio nodded as he picked a piece of bone from between his teeth. "I was supposed to do a mosaic at the Lateran, but that young Giotto fellow stole it away from me. Did a couple of small pieces, one for Santa Cecilia in Trastavere, another for the sacristy at Santa Maria Maggiore." He sucked on his teeth. "Couldn't pay me enough to go back there again. Nasty, dirty place, Rome is, and crowded with all those pilgrims! I was glad to get home, tell you that much."

"Did you go to Saint Peter's?"

"Of course. Plenty of times."

"I was telling the girls today how much it bothered me to see all the buying and selling that was going on around its steps. It reminded me of Christ expelling the moneylenders from the temple."

"Didn't bother me," Duccio admitted. "I thought it was

kind of handy to have everything you needed right there."

Tia Taviana had re-entered the room and was kneeling to build up the fire. "You can't mean there's a market on the steps of Saint Peter's?"

"One of the biggest I've ever seen," Babbo said.

"What a shame," she said, putting another log on. "You'd think they'd have enough room in that whole big city to make their money somewhere else."

"At last!" said my father. "Someone with sense! Antonia here was telling me earlier that the most important church in Christendom was nothing more than a good excuse for a market."

I sat up, affronted. "I did not! I said that if I were a pilgrim with a hole in my shoe, I would be glad to have someone there to fix it for me, and then you said wasn't that just like a woman to be practical, and it wasn't very noble to think about practical things like food or staying warm ..."

Tia Taviana looked at him, one eyebrow cocked. "All the practical things that you've never had to worry about because ignoble women worry about them for you."

"Unjust! Unjust!" said my father. "I was talking about a very specific circumstance—"

"I am beginning to feel some sympathy for Gemma," Tia Taviana said distinctly, her eyes very bright.

There was dead silence. I could feel everyone's eyes on me and looked up at my father, puzzled. "Babbo?" I asked.

He looked angry, but not, I saw, at me. "It's nothing, Antonia. Isn't it time for you to go to bed?"

"Feo is still up!" I protested.

But he wasn't listening. "What I wanted to say, Taviana, is that yes, it was upsetting for me to see the desecration of Holy Mother Church. You know that I find merchants and their like

... distasteful. I make no apology for that, besides to note that the merchants there—and the priests who overlooked their presence—were men, not women."

"That's not what I—" she started, but he went right on over the top of whatever it was she was going to say.

"Please allow me the courtesy of finishing my remarks before you tell me what an impractical, self-absorbed cad I am, Taviana. None of your accusations is unfamiliar to me, I assure you. The point I'm trying to make is, in fact, that I was struck by the energy I saw there, and it occurred to me that the Church has overlooked an important truth, which is that most men—and women—find it easier to think in terms of this world, rather than the next. If it were possible to teach them about the next world by making reference to their ordinary experiences—to bring heaven down to earth, as it were, so that they could touch it and taste it and smell it—I believe the world would quickly become a better and more joyful place."

There was another pause, but this one was not an angry one. "Now you're sounding like Saint Francis," said Taviana. "Better that than—what was it?—a self-absorbed cad any day. No, I didn't mean it, Dante, I'm not trying to start a fight, just trying to be clever the way a noble man might be. Feo is asleep, Duccio, and Bice looks like she will be soon, so if you'll pardon me, I will do my humble and ignoble duty and put them to bed."

I looked at my aunt to see if it was any use fussing, but her eyes were still very bright. "Good night, Babbo," I said.

He bent his head so I could slip the medallion back around his neck. Then I kissed his narrow, bristly cheek.

"Good night, my lady of the raspberries," he said. "Dream of paradise."

When I came down to breakfast the next morning, he was waiting for me. "What beautiful thing do you have to tell me this morning?" he asked me in greeting.

"Margherita has a cold," I announced. "She was tossing and turning all night. I don't think she'll be able to take us about this morning."

"That's too bad," said Babbo. "Is she feverish?"

"I don't think so," I said. "Just grumpy." It was true; she had thrown her shoe at Feo this morning when he jumped on the bed to wake us up. I licked some honey that had dripped on my arm. "What should we do without her? Do you want to go to the studio?"

Before he could answer, the door opened and Tio Duccio came in the room. "But look who is seen!" he said, and stood aside for a smaller, caped figure to enter.

"Mama!" I cried, and hopped down from my chair.

But the face that emerged from the pushed-back hood was not my mother's, but that of Ser Giobatta, one of my father's political friends. I stopped short.

"Giobatta!" my father cried. "What a wonderful surprise! Come in, come in—have some breakfast."

Unnoticed amid the commotion of the greetings, I returned to the table. But I pushed away my breakfast. I wasn't hungry anymore.

"I fear that all of my news is bad, and I will not trouble you with it now," Ser Giobatta said once the formalities were concluded. "I will be brief, as my business is pressing. We heard you had been released, and I came to leave a message with Ser Duccio on the off chance you stopped here before returning home. The governing council of the Whites has called a meeting at San Godenzo, and we are hoping you can join us."

Babbo pushed back his chair as the door opened again behind him. "I am ready to leave this moment," he said.

"Not quite this moment, I hope," said a familiar voice. "Or is half an hour too long for his wife to beg from the illustrious Dante Alighieri, poet to popes and counselor to princes?"

My mother had arrived, and she was in a blazing temper.

My father got quickly to his feet. "Gemma! At last!"

"At last, my ass," she flung at him, ripping off her cloak with a splendid gesture of fury so that it billowed in the air behind her. "If I'd been ten minutes later, you would have been gone."

I closed my eyes so I could see the magnificent swirl of the cape again. I heard Ser Giobatta murmuring something about returning later when it was more convenient, and opened my eyes as the door clicked shut behind him. I don't think my mother even noticed that he had gone.

"Do you have any idea what I have been through?" she demanded. "Why didn't you answer any of my messages?"

"What messages?" my father said, speaking in the colorless voice with which he always answered my mother's anger. "I received none. I suppose Boniface kept them from me. I had no idea what had happened until I arrived here."

"That is a lie," my mother snapped. "If you were ignorant of our plight, it was because you did not wish to know."

My father spread his hands. "You may believe me or not, but it is the truth."

My mother stripped off her gloves and threw them on the floor. "Do you see my hands?" she asked him. They were red and cracked, with broken, dirty fingernails. "Do these look like the hands of a Donati woman? What were you thinking of, to come out so openly against the pope? What did you think would happen—he'd congratulate you for the fine points you'd brought to his attention, and give you a gold chain? My children had to run for their lives. *Our* children had to run for their lives. That pig Bocaccino has our house, and I sleep with the animals at the farm, working harder than three servants. And for what? Can you tell me for what? Because my husband values his own words so much he cannot keep them to himself?"

She was sobbing now, and my father went to her.

"Don't touch me," she said, flinching. "You are not my husband. No husband would abandon his family like this."

"Of course I am your husband," said Babbo coldly. "Stop this hysteria at once. It is most unbecoming."

"How dare you!" my mother gasped, and slapped him hard across the cheek.

My father stood still until the red mark of her hand was fully visible on his cheek. "I did not ask to be quarantined," he said at last. "I assumed, in fact, that it was the work of your precious cousin Corso. How is he, by the way? Have you received him in my absence?"

My mother's eyes fell. "He called on my father," she said. "It was not my place to refuse him."

"Refuse him what?" my father asked, each quiet word as sharp-edged as a diamond.

Her head came up, her eyes blazing, and she raised her hand as if to strike him again, but he caught her wrist.

"I am not a violent man," he said. "But you are trying my patience, by God you are. I am sorry that I was not there with you, although if I had been I daresay I would now be dead and of even less use to you than usual. But I am here now, and so, I would remind you, is your daughter."

She dropped her arm and stepped away, and he let her go. She peered around the room and caught sight of me, and, shockingly, her face crumpled. She came and knelt by my chair.

"Bice, *mia*," she gulped. "This is not the homecoming I

had envisioned for you." She put her head down on her knees and began to sob.

I sat frozen, not knowing what I was supposed to do or feel.

"Don't you have a hug for your mother?" Babbo prodded.

I climbed down from my chair, feeling slow and stupid, and awkwardly put my arms around her. She took a deep, shuddering breath, sat back on her heels, and composed herself as best she could. Then she blessed me, and I remembered her scent, and the cool, dry feel of her lips on my forehead.

"I would not have recognized you, *bella*, you are so big," she said. She started patting at my hair and gown, just as she had when Smerelda brought me back from the river. "The boys send you their love. Pietro and Jacopo are becoming very clever at Santa Maria Novella, just like your *babbo*." I slanted a quick look up at her face, but she didn't appear to notice. "They can rattle off pages and pages of scripture, almost like real priests. And Tio Francesco says that Gian has a very good head for numbers." She bit her lip and folded her hands tightly in her lap. "So how is it with you? Are you a big help to Tia Taviana and Tio Duccio?"

"No," I said. "But I try to stay out of the way."

She made a sudden loud sound and clapped her hands over her mouth. For a moment I thought she was beginning to cry again, but then I realized she was laughing in a wild, uncontrolled way that was even more frightening than her tears. "That is a very clever answer, nearly as clever as one of your father's poems," she said, gasping.

"Gemma," Babbo said.

But she ignored him. "I suppose now I am the only dull one in the family. But I should have known that already, shouldn't I, since I am the only one who is doing any actual, physical work that brings in any of that distasteful money that the really clever people eschew. A really clever person doesn't have to work, you know, Bice. A really clever person finds other people to do his work for him and then has the special added treat of despising them for being too coarse to understand the refined, spiritual, intellectual truths that only men of leisure can properly appreciate."

My father came up behind her, looking very tired and very old. "Gemma," he said. "I know I've hurt you, and I'm sorry."

She laughed bitterly. "No, you're not. You're sorry that you are stuck here having to listen to this—let's see, how will you phrase it to your fine friends?—vituperative invective from your coarse and insensitive wife."

"You know I would never say anything of the sort."

She looked away. "I know no such thing."

"I can assure you, I would not. I have not, and I will not."

"Never? Not even as you drift off to sleep, in the midst of explaining that your wife doesn't understand you?" I saw that she was blinking back tears, and I think my father must have seen, too, because his face softened and he wiped one away with his thumb.

"Never," he said.

She shook him away, but she quieted herself, stood up, and went to hang her cloak by the fire. When she was done she sat at the table and Babbo asked me to fetch Tia Taviana and Tio Duccio, and then find Tia Lucrezia and tell her that my mother had come, and could she warm up some of her delicious spiced wine?

So I ran up to the kitchens, and then had to wait while Tia Lucrezia found the proper spices and ground them and stirred them into a firkin of wine and then heated it carefully over the fire until it was hot. Then she sliced some of the bread that had just come out of the oven and had me fetch her some cheese and then remembered she had some figs to go with it.

By the time everything was arranged to her satisfaction and I had carefully carried the tray down to the *sala*, Tio Duccio and Tia Taviana had come and my parents were looking more like themselves.

"Come and sit with me, Bice," my mother said, patting her lap. "I have missed my little girl."

I put the tray down carefully, then gingerly perched on her skirts, my back very straight like a lady's.

"Antonia," my father said. "Your mother and I have been talking with your aunt and uncle, and we have decided it would be best if you stayed here with them for a while."

"Two years at the most," said my mother.

Two years was a long time. In two years I would be eight— old enough to go into service as a servant. I felt stupid that it had not previously occurred to me that, with the loss of our house, that would probably be my fate.

"That must seem like a long time to a little girl," said Tia Taviana. "But it will pass quickly."

I didn't mind that it was a long time. I liked Siena. I felt safe there—much safer than I had in Florence. I liked the combination of warmth and anonymity I'd found in my uncle's noisy household. And I loved the studio.

"Are you going to the farm with Mama?" I asked Babbo.

"I am going with her as far as the farm, but then I am going on to San Godenzo," he said. "We are going to make plans to get the Blacks out of Florence so we can go home and be as we used to be."

I looked back and forth between them. "What will the boys do?"

"Stay as they are," Babbo said. "Your mother's plan was a

good one. They are safe and getting the education they will need to make their way in the world."

I looked up at my mother. "Won't Mama be lonely without any of us?"

She returned my gaze and I saw that, as I suspected, her eyes were bright with tears. "Perhaps a little," she said. "But it is the best we can do. And I can always stay with your grandfather Manetto when I am too homesick for you." She gave me a careful hug so she wouldn't mess my clothes.

Duccio cleared his throat noisily. "All this talk is making me thirsty," he said. "Let's have some more wine."

THE APPRENTICE

Siena, 1307

And so I settled into life in Siena. I soon came to understand that, despite our poverty, my parents had no intention of sending me out to work as a servant, which was a relief to me. My mother worked the farms and kept the family's claim to our property in Florence alive while my father plotted with his friends to win back political power. Mother came to see me every winter solstice on the Feast of Santa Lucia, which is my birthday, bringing oil, wine, and a barrel of apples from the farm, and wrote me not at all. It occurred to me only much later that she probably did not know how.

I didn't see my father, although he sent letters from time to time. At first he hoped to work with the White Guelfs, but when they proved foolish and contentious, he abandoned them and went on to Assisi, then Forlì, Padua, and finally the university at Bologna. He would come for me when he could, he always promised. In the meantime, I would need to be patient just a little longer.

At first I hung on every word, reading and rereading the letters that came and pestering Tio Duccio for scraps of news he might have heard in the marketplace. But as the months stretched to years, my life in Florence seemed more and more like a dream that colored but did not replace my experience in Siena. I still wondered about my brothers and sometimes missed them, but more and more Margherita and Feo seemed my real family, Pietro and the other apprentices my real friends, and the activities that centered around Tio Duccio's studio my real life.

So I was unprepared for the letter when it finally arrived at Easter five years after my arrival in Siena. I was in the studio, as usual, scraping the wool off a parchment skin that was pegged out to dry. It's a tricky business to scrape the hair without poking a hole in the softened skin, and I had only recently been allowed to help with this part of the procedure, so it took Feo some time to capture my attention. Finally Pietro grabbed my arm, pried the lunellum out of my hand, and waved the letter in front of my eyes.

"Oh, *grazie*," I said, drying my hands on my apron and reaching for the letter.

"What does it say?" Feo wanted to know.

I glanced around the busy studio and hesitated.

"Why don't you take it up on the roof," Pietro suggested. "I'll finish here."

"Thank you," I said gratefully, and made my escape to the roof, where Margherita was hanging out the wash to dry. I did not mind sharing my news with her, however, and broke open the letter's seal.

My dear Antonia, my father wrote:

Since I am a failure as a politician, I had thought to become the scholar I once intended to be. But my studies were interrupted when Bologna decided that she has no use for Florentine exiles. I have taken temporary refuge at the Malaspina court here in the Lunigiana, but it is a rough place, ill suited to pursuits of the mind, so I have decided to go and study at the University of Paris. It is a long and lonely journey to France, my Antonia, and I would welcome your company. Your mother won't leave the farms, and the boys tell me they are fine as they are, so it would just be the two of us. Discuss this proposal with your godmother. She is a sensible woman and will give you good advice. My business here is almost done, and when it is I will come south to you to hear your decision.

If I'd had any sense at all, I would have told him that I, like my brothers, was happily established where I was. But I was young and foolish, and the possibility did not even cross my mind.

"What will you do?" Margherita asked.

"Go with my *babbo*, of course. He'd be very disappointed if I didn't," I said, feeling pleasantly bossy as I tucked the letter in the pocket I wore around my neck and began to help her with her work. "I'll miss all of you, of course, but he needs me more."

Margherita was jealous. "First Mama decides that it's time for Tia Lucrezia to teach me housewifery, then you take off for France. It's not fair."

I heard a familiar whoop and instinctively braced myself as Feo launched himself at me. I staggered and almost fell. "Get off," I said. "You're going to tear my letter."

"I can't."

"Why not?"

"Because you're standing in the fires of hell, and if I do, my legs will burn up."

Every Easter, the bankers' guild paid for a miracle play to be performed in the square outside San Dominico, and Feo had been completely insufferable for the week since we had seen it. If he wasn't a demon jumping on you to carry you off to hell, he was a soul being tortured or a saint perishing for want of food who could be revived only by being hand-fed bite-sized pieces of his dinner.

"Get off, Feo," I said again.

"Bless me first so I don't burn up," he said.

I sketched a cross over my shoulder, and he finally got down.

"You have to be nice to Bice," Margherita scolded him. "She's going away."

Feo stopped poking at the laundry and looked at me with his mouth open. "Is that what the letter said?"

"My *babbo* is coming to get me," I said. "He's going to take me to live in France."

"What's France?" Feo said, his bottom lip starting to push out so he looked like the baby he had been when I first came to live with them.

"It's the place on the other side of the Alps where the pigments come from," Margherita told him.

"So you won't sleep here at night?"

"No," I said. I took a breath to better prepare myself for inflicting what was sure to be a bitter blow. "It takes weeks and weeks to get to where I am going. And it is a dangerous journey. Who knows if we will ever see each other again?" I looked beyond Feo to the pot of geraniums and the birdcage that hung outside the window of old Pietro, the comb seller, and thought they had never looked so beautiful. And there they would hang for years and years without me to see them and appreciate their beauty in a way probably no one else did. It was heartbreaking. I felt my eyes fill up with tears, and added, "Nothing will ever be the same between us."

Margherita looked at me, and I knew she felt the solemnity of the moment as I did. She put down the sheet she was hanging out, weighted it with some bits of broken tile so it wouldn't blow away, and came to me. We embraced.

"I will never forget you," I said. I remembered the scripture from last Sunday's mass. "You are written on the fleshy tables of my heart."

"Nor I you," she gulped.

Feo looked back and forth between us, then burst into tears and flung himself at our knees. "Don't leave," he sobbed.

"What in the name of all that is holy is this?" came Tia Taviana's voice from the door.

We broke apart, and Feo ran to her. "I don't want Bice to go!" he sobbed.

"Go? Why should Bice go anywhere?"

"Tio Dante sent her a letter," Margherita wept. "He's taking her to France, and things will never be the same again!"

"Pull yourself together, child. Bice, I want to see that letter."

I handed it to her, and she read it slowly, her lips forming the words while she held the paper at arm's length. She finished it and stood for a moment, staring into space, before carefully folding the letter and holding out to me. "Isn't that just like a man," she said. "Not a word about when we can expect him. That's enough, Feo. Bice is not going to disappear off the face of the earth. She's just going on a trip with her father, the way your brothers sometimes go away with your father to work on a commission. She'll be back." And she brushed her hard hand across my hair and caressed my cheek briefly.

Although I was exasperated that Tia Taviana had managed to dissipate the romance of the moment, her words were still comforting.

"Stop pestering the girls, Feo. The laundry is going to have to be done again if it doesn't get hung out soon. No, you may not stay up here. Next thing I know you'll be throwing yourself off the roof so the saint can come and heal you. Come help me choose the clothes for the new apprentice. Get to work, you two, and no more of your nonsense."

Ambrogio Lorenzetti, the younger brother of my uncle's assistant Pietro, was joining the household as a new apprentice. He was a year older than Margherita, and, from the glimpse we'd had of him when he and his father came to sign the papers, very handsome.

"Do you think he'll fall in love with one of us?" Margherita asked in a low voice as her mother and little brother disappeared into the house.

I looked at her big, homely face. "You know men never marry women their own age," I hedged. "They're always at least ten or fifteen years older than their wives. Maybe Pietro."

She made a face. "Not in a hundred years."

I knew what she meant. Pietro, though a good-hearted person, had the slouched posture, lank hair, and poor complexion of a peasant, and his small, close-set eyes noticed nothing that was not directly connected to the painting in front of him.

Just then a gust of wind seized the nightgown I was hanging and whisked it out of my hands. I was so surprised that I stood and watched like a ninny while it sailed over the edge of the roof nearly to the neighbors' geraniums, then suddenly collapsed on itself and fell. I heard a crash and a cry in the street below.

Margherita ran to peer over the edge of the roof, but I didn't wait. I clattered down the two flights of stairs as fast as I could and burst through the door onto the street.

I saw the nightgown at once. It had blown over a boy and his donkey, who were fighting to be free of it. Beside them, a large jug of wine that the donkey had evidently been carrying lay smashed on the pavement next to a bundle of something that had been white but was now liberally streaked with crimson.

The boy wrestled the nightgown off his head and then his donkey's, threw it in the street so that it, too, began to soak up the wine, and then caught sight of his spoiled bundle. He froze.

My first impulse was to run away before I was discovered. But I forced myself to step forward out of the shadow of the doorway and then stood, shifting back and forth from one foot to the other and trying to think of something to do or say. "Are you all right?" I finally blurted out.

The boy spun around. It was Ambrogio, the new apprentice.

When he saw I was only a girl, he turned away again and mopped at his face. "I'm fine," he said in a muffled voice. He went around the donkey, picked up the dripping bundle, laid it on the donkey's back, and began to undo it.

I saw that it was made up of three fine linen shirts, new, by the look of them. He tried to brush off the rivulets of wine and shards of broken pottery that spattered them, but it was a hopeless task.

"I was hanging up the nightgown on the roof and the wind just tore it out of my hands ..." I reached out tentatively to brush some of the wine and pottery off the donkey's rump, but the donkey shied and the boy pushed my hand away.

"Leave her alone," he said sharply. "*Che tu porti iella.*"

It's a terrible insult to be told you bring bad luck. I retreated, my face hot, miserably aware of my clumsiness. "I'm sorry," I apologized. "It was an accident."

"As if that makes any difference," he snapped. "My shirts are ruined because of you."

He wasn't being very nice about the whole thing. I tried again. "I really didn't mean to—"

"Whether you meant to or not, the damage is done," he practically snarled.

Anger began to overcome my embarrassment. "I told you, it was the wind."

He glowered at me. "All I know is that I was walking along, minding my own business, and now my father's gift to Duccio is smashed and my only clothes are ruined."

"Your clothes aren't ruined."

"Yes, they are! And my mother spent all winter making them for me."

"I'm really sorry," I repeated, "but I'm sure my Tia Lucrezia will be able to make them good as new. She can get the stains out of anything. And if she can't," I promised rashly, "I'll make you new ones."

He looked me up and down as though I were a rabbit he was thinking of buying for his supper. "Does a child like you know how to sew?"

I scowled at him. In point of fact, I didn't, but he was only two or three years older than I was and he had no business treating me like a little girl.

"I will learn," I said with as much dignity as I could muster.

"And what should I wear between now and then?"

I heard quick footsteps behind me—it was Tia Taviana with Margherita and Feo in her wake.

"Oh, my dears," said Tia Taviana, apparently sizing up the situation in a glance. "What a shame. Are those your shirts, Ambrogio? Margherita, take them to Lucrezia right away. Don't worry," she assured him. "My sister-in-law can get the stains out of anything."

"That's just what your daughter was telling me," Ambrogio said politely.

"She's not Taviana's daughter, she's mine," said a familiar voice behind me. "Although from the look of things, I'm not sure I want to claim her."

I spun around, and there was my father, leading two horses.

"Babbo!" I cried, and then flushed, suddenly conscious that I was too old to be using a baby name like that. "I mean Papa," I said.

He hugged me, but did not pick me up and swing me around the way he had when I was a little girl. "My lady of the raspberries!" he said. "You are looking much too big and beautiful to be my Antonia, but I am remembering certain complaints from Smerelda, and I know you by your handiwork."

I felt my flush deepen and was grateful I could press my face against his travel-stained tunic. The smell was familiar, wine and spices and the faint scent of ink, and I could hear his heart beating as steadily as ever.

"Dante," said Tia Taviana. "We weren't expecting you so soon; your letter arrived just this morning. This is Ambrogio Lorenzetti, our new apprentice."

My father stepped back from my embrace and inclined his head toward Ambrogio.

"Ambrogio, this is my brother, Dante Alighieri, and his daughter, Bice. You are fortunate to have crossed their paths; Bice and her father are leaving for France in a few days."

Ambrogio bobbed his head in acknowledgment, but I knew he was thinking that this was one piece of fortune he could have done without.

"So, Antonia, you are coming with me?" my father said, turning to me. "I am glad to hear it. How quickly can you be ready?"

"In no time at all," I said. "There's not much to pack." That was true; everything I wore had come from one of Tia Taviana's chests. There was another gown, another chemise, and a cloak that I used, but nothing more.

"Excellent," Babbo said. "Run along and get your things. I want to get to Monteriggioni by nightfall."

"You can't be serious, Dante," Tia Taviana said briskly. "She received your letter just this morning. We can't possibly let her go with so little notice. Just let me get the new apprentice settled and then I'll get you something to eat and we can talk about this like reasonable people."

"The Blacks have agents all over the place and I want to get through Florentine territory before they've heard that I'm in Tuscany," my father said. "Antonia, do as you're told."

I ran off obediently, but I had hardly gotten to my room before my aunt was with me. "No, don't take that," she said crisply as I reached for my other dress. "It's practically worn through, and you'll outgrow it in no time."

"Where's Ambrogio?" I asked, startled.

"I sent him to Duccio. Margherita took him, and Feo is taking your father to the kitchens for a bite to eat." All the time she was talking, my aunt was opening one *cassone* after another with the keys she wore at her waist and rifling through their contents.

"Tia Taviana?" I said. "What are you doing?"

"If I'd only had a little more time—but men are just so thoughtless—and there are things I should tell you, to prepare you—well, you're only eleven. Still, how can he just descend like that and carry you off, as if he were a pirate? I could string him up."

I had never seen her so agitated before and stood watching like a half-wit while she tossed clothes everywhere. She finally got to the bottom of the last trunk and slammed it shut. "Here. This is all we have," she announced, and pushed an untidy pile of clothing toward me.

There was a pair of brown leather boots, as soft as velvet. A good thick woolen cloak, dyed dark blue, the color of midnight. A woolen dress in a soft green. Three yellowed linen shifts. Two everyday gowns, one gray and warm and another for summer the color of chestnuts. A pair of slippers. Two sets of hose.

But almost before I had time to take in the bounty, she was folding the clothes up and putting them in a small trunk she usually kept by her pillow. "I'd use the gray gown for travel," she said. "It's still a little cool for the brown linen, although it won't show the dirt as much."

Obediently I slipped out of my coarse romagnol gown and reached for the gray.

"It's not enough," she fretted. "And what's more, your father won't notice when you need more."

"What do you mean it's not enough?" I gasped. "I've never had so many things in my life!"

"France will be different," she said. She locked the trunk and set it on the floor with a decided thump, then sat on the bed and patted the place next to her. "Bice, come here."

I came and she took my hands in her thin, hard ones and looked me straight in the eye, as though I were Feo and she was telling me how much it was going to hurt when she took a splinter from my hand.

"First of all, I want you to know that you are as dear to me as a daughter, and that I will pray for you every morning and every night. When you are alone, remember that God is with you, and that if you ask for comfort, he will send it. It may not be what you expect, but it will be enough. This I promise you."

I nodded dumbly, registering the urgency and sincerity of her instructions if nothing more.

"Second, remember that your father has had no mother, no father, no wife or child, no home for more than five years. If he does anything that—confuses you, remember that much can be forgiven a man who has suffered the kind of loneliness

78

your father bears. Third, I want you to remember that things will be better for him because you are there. He will not always remember the things you need. If he forgets, you must remind him. I know that will be difficult for you, but it must be done. So if you are tired, or cold, or hungry, you need to tell him until he hears you. Do you understand me?"

I remembered the long, cold walks of five years before. "Yes," I said. "I do understand, and I will remember. I promise."

Tia Taviana reached out and folded me into one of her quick, hard embraces. "You have been a good girl here, Bice, and we will miss you. Promise me you will come back to us when you can."

I looked up at her tired, worried face and promised, then hugged her back.

"Taviana!" Tio Duccio roared from downstairs. "Dante's here and he says he's taking Bice!"

She let me go and passed her sleeve over her eyes. "See if you can carry the trunk yourself."

I could.

Duccio was waiting for us at the bottom of the stairs. He had left the studio so hastily that he was still wearing his apron. "So you're leaving us, Bice?"

I was trying to carry the trunk and watch my feet on the stairs at the same time, and only nodded at him. With a quick *tsk* of impatience, Tia Taviana took the trunk from me, gave her husband a look that told him not to take too long to say whatever it was he had to say, and brushed past us.

"I wish I could send Pietro with you," Duccio said. "I went to France when I was about his age. Best thing I ever did. It's good to travel a bit when you're young. It puts different colors and shapes in your mind."

My uncle did not usually talk to me, and I stood shifting a little uncomfortably on the bottom step. I muttered something noncommittal and darted a look at his face to see if he was done. But he wasn't.

"I've got something for you," he finally said.

"You do?"

He thrust a small leather-bound book at me. "You've got a sure hand."

I didn't understand.

"For drawing," he said impatiently. "I asked Pietro to keep an eye on you. He says you have a sure hand. So there's some parchment. To help you remember the new things you see."

I didn't know what to say. Neither, apparently, did he. After a moment he patted my head so roughly that he nearly knocked me over. "You're a good girl. We'll miss you," he said.

My father appeared. "Are you ready, Antonia?"

I nodded.

"You don't need all that, surely?" my father asked, catching sight of the trunk.

I started to agree with him, and then remembered Tia Taviana's advice. "If we are going to France," I said, "I will need to be properly dressed."

"That's so," my father agreed. "Duccio, do you have a boy to spare who can load this onto her palfrey for me?"

Duccio looked at my father for a moment, his mouth open. No one in his household called an apprentice to do something they could do for themselves. He found his voice, and with a graciousness I would not have expected, said, "Of course. That will just give us time to offer prayer for safe journey. Let me call the family."

GIAN

Lucca, 1307

Once outside the city, my father led the horses to a group of stones that served as rough seats for people waiting for the gates to open. "Can you ride?" he asked me.

I gulped. The horses suddenly looked much bigger. I had assumed we would be walking, as most of the pilgrims did who passed through Siena on the Via Francigena, the pilgrim road to France. "I used to ride the ponies at the farm," I said.

"The trick," my father said, "is to relax. I got you an astride saddle; I think they are safer than the aside saddles that your mother prefers. Come here, Antonia." He tossed me up on the palfrey's back before I realized what he was going to do.

On closer inspection, I saw that it wasn't a horse at all, but a finely bred mule. The saddle was surprisingly comfortable, with a high fork in front and cantle behind me, but I did not care for the uneasy sensation of the mule's muscles moving beneath me, and I seemed to be very far above the ground.

"Take the reins in both hands," my father instructed. "That's right; just hold them loosely. We'll take it nice and easy for the first few days until you get the rhythm of it. It's not difficult."

"All right, Papa," I said, a bit breathlessly.

He swung himself into his saddle with the ease of the soldier he had been before my birth. "Kick your mule gently, slap her with the reins, and click your teeth."

I did, and she started to move.

"Relax a bit, daughter. Pretend ... pretend you are sitting in Smerelda's lap while she sings you a lullaby."

I hadn't seen and had barely thought about Smerelda for many years, and she had never been the kind to sing lullabies. A cold finger of fear touched gently inside my chest as I realized how many things my father didn't know about me. Well, there were a lot of things I didn't know about him, and we'd just have to learn them together.

"Your Tio Forese's groom used to tell me to soften my hands," Papa said. "He said that if my hands were soft, the rest of me would loosen up as well."

I tried to soften my hands.

We rode for a few minutes, our mounts pulling their hooves from the sticky spring mud with loud sucking sounds that sounded like the boys farting at the table. I started to giggle, then stopped myself. Papa would not be amused. We rode some more. I was beginning to get the hang of it. It was just sitting, after all. I risked a quick glance at the soft green of the spring countryside. It didn't look anything like the barren waste I remembered from the journey south five years earlier.

"Your palfrey's name is Jennet," Papa said. "It's the English name for a lady's mule. But you can call her anything you like."

"Jennet," I said, trying the unusual name on my tongue. "I like it." I leaned forward and cautiously patted her neck. "Good mule," I said. "Good Jennet." I risked another quick look, this time over my shoulder at my father. "And what is your horse's name?"

"Pilgrim."

The road was wider here, and Papa brought his horse up next to mine. We rode some more, both of us trying to think of something to say.

"You see how much I like your name," he finally said.

I had no idea what he was talking about. "What?"

"Your name. I named the horse Pilgrim."

I was puzzled. Bice is a common nickname for the youngest girl in a family, and I knew it meant gift of God or bringer of joy. "My name is Bice," I said.

"Not your nickname. Your birth name."

"Antonia?"

He nodded. "Do you know why you were given that name?"

I shook my head. In fact, I had often wondered, especially since my father was the only one who ever used it. The boys had been named John, Peter, and James after the Savior's disciples, so it was reasonable to think that I might have been named after the Virgin Mary or her mother Saint Anne, or maybe even Saint Lucy, my patron saint, or a female relative. But Antonia fit none of those categories.

"We thought you were going to be another boy," my father said. "We had decided we would name you Paul. But when Tia Taviana came out carrying you and told me that I had a daughter, I was overcome with joy. I had loved your brothers, of course, but there was something special about having a daughter. I looked down at you in my arms, and you fretted a little bit and then found your thumb and opened your eyes and looked calmly around the room. All three of your brothers had been difficult, fussy babies, but from the beginning you had a gentle spirit. I carried you in to your mother, and thought to myself, Poor little pilgrim, to be born into such a rough and contentious world. Your mother was not in charity with me at the time, but when she reached up for you she said, 'Poor little pilgrim. She has no idea what lies ahead for her.' So we asked your godparents to call you Antonia for Saint Anthony, the pilgrims' guide."

"And now we're going on a pilgrimage!" I said.

He smiled down at me, the clear April light touching his thinner hair and the deep creases around his mouth and eyes. "So we are."

My father and I have shared so many journeys that it is difficult now to remember how we established the rhythm of our days together. Tia Taviana had been right to warn me that he would not always remember the things I needed. Despite his promise to take things slowly for the first few days, by the time we arrived in Monteriggioni the first night, I was sick and breathless with pain, the muscles in my back and knees and thighs pushed far beyond their limits. After we had reined in the horses in the courtyard of the small inn, I found to my embarrassment that I could not make my leg swing over to Jennet's back. My father finally had to lift me down after he came back outside to see why I was taking so long. When I could not help crying out, he sent me off to bed and took care of the horses himself. The next night, in San Gimignano, I had no such luxury, however, and from then on it became my nightly chore to rub down the horses and feed and water them when there was no servant to do it for us.

My father preferred silence in the morning, so we did not speak at breakfast or for the first few hours of our journey. He was planning to write an encyclopedia he called the *Convivio*, or *Banquet*. It was to be the first scholarly book written in Italian, the language of the ordinary people, instead of the Latin that priests and scholars used. He thought that there were a lot of merchants and artisans—people like those of Duccio's household—who wished to become learned. Remembering how hard everyone worked and how tired they were at night, I was skeptical that the book would be as popular as my father thought it would be, but I said nothing. Whenever Papa thought of something he wanted to add to the *Banquet*, he reined in his charger and stopped to write it down. If the notes were lengthy, I'd get out my notebook and scribble notes to myself as well, but my notes were in pictures, not words— sketches of the landscape or a clump of flowers or sometimes even my father's thin, absorbed face. When we were on our way again, I'd go back to memorizing the color of the light until my eyes had stored up as much as they could. Then I'd pass the time counting porcupines, boar, and deer, or pick out the bird- calls I knew. Sometimes I composed letters to Margherita and Tia Taviana, although I never wrote them down.

Early afternoon was the worst. We were no longer fresh, but neither were we close enough to our day's destination to look forward to the end. My father took to reciting poetry— Vergil or Ovid or Statius—and quoting ancient philosophers and doctors of the church. "The memory is the poor man's library," he repeated often, and soon I could chant snippets of his sources along with him. I'd never studied Latin, but I'd heard it at church my whole life and it was not so different from the Florentine dialect, and soon enough I grew to under- stand it almost as readily as Italian. It is a tidy and compact language, and I enjoyed unknotting it.

All in all, it was a lonely life for a girl, and I began to turn in on myself in the way I imagined nuns and monks must in their cloistered cells, living more in my mind than in my body. I lost the habit of easy speech, and when the monotony was occasionally broken by a chance encounter with a mounted party of pilgrims or merchants, I listened to the news and smiled at the jokes but was relieved when they moved on after an hour or so. Most travelers who were wealthy enough for horses had little interest in the company of a poor scholar and his wordless daughter. My father never spoke to the foot travelers we passed.

Most of that was still ahead of us, however, when we drew up our tired mounts at the gates of Lucca four days after we left Siena. Apparently Papa had come into some money on the death of his patron, Bartolomeo della Scala, a few years earlier, which had recently been paid to him. He was using the money to finance our journey, and he wanted to settle accounts with his half-brother Francesco, who managed his affairs. It was also an opportunity to visit my brother Gian, who still worked as a clerk for Tio Francesco.

I was breathless and my hands tingled as we led the animals through the city streets toward my uncle's workshop near the church of San Michele. I was excited about seeing Gian, of course, but also a little scared. What would he look like? He'd be fourteen now. I wondered if his face was spotty. He'd probably grown into one of those coarse, nasty apprentices who caused trouble at feast time and whom the servant girls whispered about.

Papa had stopped and was rapping on a wooden door. It was answered by a stocky young man who exclaimed and then clapped my father on the back. Was that Gian? Apparently it was, because a moment later he had me in a bear hug and I was breathing in the familiar smell of parchment and ink.

"Bice! They didn't tell me you were coming!" he said, holding me away from him. He was not particularly tall—perhaps a head taller than me—but he had the powerful physique of my grandfather Manetto. Underneath the thick hair and the beginnings of a beard, however, were the bright, curious, slightly tilted eyes of the little boy I remembered.

"I'd have recognized you anywhere," I said, surprised into speech.

"I can't say the same for you," he said, grinning. "I remember a whiny, pule-faced little brat who flinched every time you looked at her. You've improved."

Then my Tio Francesco, a portlier version of my father, was there, looking very much as I remembered him except that gray was beginning to grizzle his beard and hair. He offered us some luncheon and told Gian to see to the horses. Gian paused, his hand on Pilgrim's bridle, and I remembered how he was about horses.

"Ser Francesco," he said formally, as all apprentices speak to their masters whether they are kin or no, "will you have need of me while my father is here?"

Francesco, who was already halfway into the house with his arm around my father, turned and came back into the street. "No," he said. "I had thought you might want to spend some time with your sister."

"We will only be in the way," Gian pointed out.

"So what do you propose?" Tio asked, as if he already had a pretty good idea of what the answer would be.

Gian grinned at him, the formality suddenly pretense. "Perhaps Bice would enjoy a ride in the country?"

"Not nearly as much as you would, I'd wager," Tio Francesco said. "Well, I have no objection." He flipped Gian a coin, which he caught easily. "Buy her something to eat in the market, then, and be back in good time for Vespers."

I had about as much interest in getting back on Jennet as she did in carrying me, but the decision had been made, and no matter how much Gian thought I had changed, I was not brave enough to contradict a grown man. I sighed, and reached for her bridle.

On our way to the *mercato*, Gian caught me up on Pietro and Jacopo. He saw them every year in Florence during the

Feast of John the Baptist, Florence's patron saint, when apprentices and students were allowed freer rein than usual. He said they were doing well, although neither one was a gifted scholar, and that both were taller than he was. "Even Jacopo," he said. Then, with a flash of the Gian I remembered, he added, "But I'm still the strongest and the smartest."

He bought us a handful of dried dates at one stall, a skin of wine at another, and fried pork ravioli at a third that were so hot you could hear them sizzle when they were wrapped in big green leaves for us to carry. He tucked it all in my father's saddlebag, and we went out the nearest gate and mounted our horses.

We hadn't gotten very far before I realized that Jennet's gait was off. "Hold up!" I shouted.

He cantered back and helped me lead her to a rough hitching post near a roadside shrine. After I tied her up, he took the hoof in one big, callused hand and, more gently than I would have thought possible, scraped at the mud with a twig of acacia until we could see a stone wedged into the soft frog of Jennet's hoof. He worked gingerly at it for a moment and then suddenly the small, sharp-edged piece of quartz was lying in the palm of his hand. But even with the stone removed, Jennet still refused to put her weight on her hoof. Papa would be furious with me.

I was so hungry and tired and sore that this small difficulty overwhelmed me. To my horror, I felt tears beginning to well up, and because I was old enough to be ashamed by my over-reaction but too young to know how to stop it, I turned away and shook my hair over my face and wished I could disappear into the mud.

Instead of teasing or scolding me for my foolishness, however, Gian cleared his throat and said heartily, "I don't know about you, but I'm starving. Why don't we sit here and eat our lunch? Then we'll go for a good, stiff gallop and shake the cobwebs out."

"But my mule—"

"We'll tie her in that grove of chestnuts over there. And by the time we get back, her foot will be better and we'll lead her home. She'll be right as rain tomorrow, you wait and see."

"Sure?"

"Sure."

Comforted, I revived enough to remember the rest of my breakfast loaf and a couple of soft apples in my saddlebag and added them to our feast. While we ate, Gian asked me about our travel plans.

I shrugged. "Papa hasn't said much."

"You're probably continuing on the Via Francigena over the Cisa Pass—"

I shook my head, my mouth full of savory ravioli. "No, Papa said there's too much danger of avalanche this early in the year. He said something about taking passage on a boat."

"Probably in Genoa," he said gloomily, then swore loudly, which startled me so much that I spilled some of my wine (but fortunately not on my dress). Perhaps he had not changed as much as I had thought.

"What?" I asked apprehensively.

"It's not fair! I would give my eyeteeth to go, but instead it's you—a little girl who shrinks at her shadow. *Non vale!*"

I didn't know what to say. "He said he asked you first," I finally ventured.

"He did ask me." Gian threw the end of the loaf into a copse of trees so viciously that even my unflappable little Jennet shied and showed the whites of her eyes. "But I can't go. Working for Tio Francesco is my only hope of getting a decent start in life." He scowled at the trees. "I'm a gentleman's son. But how am I to learn a gentleman's ways when I have no horse, no servant, no standing?" He swung around and caught my worried expression. His scowl softened. "You needn't look so worried, *principessa*. It's different for girls. Manners and a pretty face make anything possible. And fortunately for you, you take after our mother." He chucked my chin. "You'll be a sweet little armful in a year or two."

I looked away, both pleased and mortified.

He laughed at me with a touch of his old malice. "Bashful, are we? There's no need. It's important to know what resources you have at your disposal."

I kept my head down. There was an awkward pause, which I did nothing to break.

"Look, Bice, I'm sorry," he finally said. "I don't spend much time with girls and—oh, hell. Are you done eating? What about that ride?"

I stood up and brushed off my skirt. The hem was heavy with mud, but my fingers still liked to touch the unaccustomed tight, smooth weave of my beautiful new clothes. "You go," I said. "I'll stay here and keep Jennet company."

"Not on your life," he said as he swung up into his saddle. "You're not getting away that easy. Give me your arm."

Five minutes later I was wedged between my brother's square back and the cantle of the saddle and cantering along the old Roman road. The stallion was at least twice as tall and could go at least twice as fast as my poor stiff-kneed mule. I spared a glance for my gown, and said a fervent prayer that I would keep my seat and not spoil it. I tightened my grip around my brother's body.

"Are you ready?" Gian yelled back at me.

"Ready for what?" I said breathlessly into his ear.

He gave a wild whoop of laughter and yelled, "The trick is to throw yourself into whatever it is that scares you, and then you're through it and out the other side. Like this!" Then he kicked the stallion into a gallop.

At first I was sure that my heart had stopped and I would fall and die and my gown would be ruined. But then at last I took a breath and then another and the blood slammed through my body. I unscrewed my eyes and began to feel the rhythm of the horse's strides in my seat and my chest and the waves of hair streaming back from my face. And then nothing mattered but my brother's strong, square body cutting the wind and keeping me safe and the wild joy of his laughter as he called "Faster, Pilgrim, faster!" until we were flying, I swear we were flying, along the hills green and tender with spring.

That night we sat up late and lit candles. Papa and Tio Francesco played chess and Gian tried to teach me its rules, although I was too tired to listen very hard. While Tio Francesco was studying a move, Papa leaned back against the wall, took a sip of wine, and said, "Your uncle tells me you have a real head for business, Giovanni. You must get that from your mother—I know money slips through my fingers like water."

"It's because you have no patience," said Tio Francesco in his growly voice. "Before one thing is done you are on to something else. You've always been that way. But once Giovanni begins a project, it's a fixed nail for him; he can't think about anything else."

Gian didn't look up, but even so I thought I glimpsed the smug expression I had seen on his face a hundred times as a child.

"So, that's the secret of your success?" my father teased Gian. "A one-track mind?"

"The secret of business is to think of it like a game." Gian answered so promptly that I knew he had considered this before.

"Like a game?"

"Yes—like a very complicated game with rules and risks and rewards, just like chess."

I was shocked. "God said that man is supposed to work by the sweat of his brow," I said. "You're not supposed to *play*."

Tio Francesco was still bent over the board. "That's what your father does," he observed.

Papa raised an eyebrow in a gesture I tried and failed to duplicate every time I polished Tia Taviana's looking glass. "I never play," he protested mildly. "I live a very serious life."

My uncle snorted. "Sincere, perhaps, but not serious. A serious man is a practical man, and you are not practical. You dabble with poetry. Then you play at being a soldier. Then you trifle with philosophy. Then you toy at politics, and when you lose you behave like a sulky child and claim that the game was rigged."

My father looked miffed, but he spoke in reasonable tones. "I fail to see how being exiled from all I care most about is behaving like a sulky child."

Tio Francesco sat back and adjusted the fur collar on his robe. "My dear Dante, let us speak frankly. Politicians are exiled all the time. But most of them return within a few months. Why? Because they are willing to compromise, to say what must be said. They understand that words are nothing but little puffs of air, and they use them to achieve what is essential—a good meal, good wine, good company, and, if they are lucky, a night spent between clean sheets with an agreeable woman who will bear them children and manage their household. The reason that you, my dear brother, are still an exile is that you refuse to accept the fact that life is a practical matter. You cherish your pride, your little puffs of air, above your responsibilities. And this is why your wife lives alone and must support herself, your children have no home, and you will be an exile for the rest of your life." He leaned forward and did something with his rook and his king that I didn't understand. "Check," he announced.

Then he looked my father in the eye and said softly, "Not all those who are learned are wise. And what are brothers for, if not to tell us the truths we would rather not hear?"

"I had hoped," my father answered, his face so white and rigid it could have been carved from marble except for the vein pulsing in his temple, "that brothers were for listening with the heart and the spirit, instead of with the pocketbook." And then, instead of finishing the game, he knocked his king on its side with a final little click and rose. "Antonia, it grows late," he said, and left the room, his back as straight as my mother's.

We left Lucca the next morning before the sun was fully risen. I was glad few people were about; I had been unable to comb through all the wind knots in my hair from the day before, and I was sure I looked a sight. But in my saddlebag I carried a beautiful length of blue silk the color of midnight with a woven gold border and gold stars embroidered on it. "For your dowry," Gian had said, not looking at me as he thrust it in my arms.

I was speechless.

"God be with you," he prompted with his old malicious smile.

I ducked my head. "God be with you," I whispered.

He suddenly hugged me hard and spoke in my ear for only me to hear. "When the adventure gets too strong, lean into it."

"What?"

"Lean into it and let it carry you along, just like our gallop yesterday. That's how people become brave—by risking only a little more than they want to."

"I'll remember," I promised, then hugged him back before thrusting the silk in my bag and hurrying after my father, already a block ahead of me and almost swallowed by the early-morning mist.

THE CITY OF THE DEAD

Arles, 1307

Papa said virtually nothing for the next two days. As the miles wore on, I began to admit to myself how homesick I was for Siena. I missed Margherita's gossip and Feo's foolishness and Tia Lucrezia's cooking. I missed Tia Taviana's quick sense and the peaceful rhythm of keeping house. But more than anything, I missed the studio. I would have given almost anything to be sitting in a corner painting while I half listened to the apprentices bicker and Duccio gossip with the clients. I was grateful for the sketchbook—I couldn't bring myself to imagine what the trip would be like without it—but I was beginning to ache for the heft, the sweep, the movement of color.

So I gathered bits of earth and dried leaves and flowers whenever we stopped by the side of the road, and tried to bind them into paint at night while my father drank wine and stared at the wall. But nothing worked—not wine, not water, not milk. I needed an egg white, but there were none to be found.

By the second afternoon I was so thoroughly dispirited that I had to fight back tears when the good Roman road trailed off into a steep, difficult coastal path overlooking the sea. Thunderheads had been massing all morning on the horizon, emblazoned from time to time by a silent fork of lightning, and the bright Mediterranean colors had dropped from the air, leaving a bleak landscape of dull grays and duns that blurred into a featureless nightmare when the rain began.

The path, already difficult, was almost immediately transformed into sticky, slippery, smelly mud. I leaned over Jennet's neck and tried to open myself to the wildness as Gian had suggested, but it was no good. I couldn't stop thinking that in a matter of hours I would be in an unprotected boat in the iron-gray water that alternately beat against and pulled at the cliff on which I rode. The wind howled harder, the rain pelted down more fiercely, and the waves roughened until the dark sea was frosted with foam. When Jennet slipped and I nearly lost my seat, I began to wail, my cries as thin and high as those of a frightened toddler.

My father, riding thirty paces ahead, heard me. He turned in his saddle and shouted something, gesturing with his arm, but the wind blew his words away. I imagined that it would blow me next—I could see myself, a small gray wisp, slipping off my mule, bouncing off the cliff, and falling, falling, into the sea. By the time I caught up to him, tears as salty as the sea were running down my face.

"Francesco said there's a hostel along here somewhere right off the path," he shouted. "I think that must be it."

I looked to where he pointed and thought I could make out a small hut where the road curved a few hundred yards ahead. Lightning struck above us to the right, and our mounts startled, my father's charger rearing and almost unseating him. I began to dismount, thinking it would be safer to lead my mule, but my father gestured at me impatiently to stay where I was, and I sat back in the saddle. Lightning struck again, and Pilgrim broke and ran. Terrified at the prospect of being left alone, I kicked hard at the mule and followed, my eyes focused tightly on my father's shadowy figure so I wouldn't see the narrowness of the track or the steepness of the cliff.

He loomed larger in front of me. He had stopped. We must

be there. But when the lightning flashed I saw that it was nothing but a crumbling shepherd's hut without door or roof. My father, his form wavering and indistinct through the drenching rain, pointed ahead, and I saw what was unmistakably the glow of fire spilling out of what must surely be the hostel a quarter of a mile ahead. But again, it was not. Neither was it the third hut. Or the fourth.

I don't remember arriving at the inn. The cold, wet, fear, and exhaustion had disoriented me, and it took me some time to realize that there were torches, and a wall, and the smell of horses. Someone had my bridle and was telling me to dismount. I half fell from the saddle and stood there stupidly until my father finished giving the stableboys instructions. He turned to go inside and his cape swirled the way Mother's had when she came to see us in Siena. I followed him, more because I wanted to see his cape swirl again than anything else, and then he was handing me a bowl of something warm. I almost dropped it and spilled some of the hot, greasy stew it contained on my hands. That woke me up enough to eat a few bites, and then I must have fallen asleep at the table.

The next thing I knew, I was riding once again along the track by Vernazza. I was trying to catch up with a traveling companion that I could see only indistinctly in the fog. Rain started to fall, plucking at my headdress and my cloak until they slipped from my body as though I were a snake shedding its skin. Then the rain began on me, licking and pulling until I washed off the mule like paint being rinsed from a brush, slithering down the side of the cliff until I dissolved into the sea.

I forced myself awake, choking and shaking, groping for the texture of blanket, mattress, pillow—anything that could bring me back to the real world and shake the cold fear of the dream away.

I was alone in the bed. There was my trunk, but no father. I sat up and peered around the room. I could make out two other beds, full by the sound of the rustles and snores. But my father wasn't there, and I wanted him.

I threw back the covers and jumped out of bed. I hadn't gone three steps before I stubbed my toe hard on something that tipped over with a crash and a spray of liquid. I had tripped over the chamber pot, and someone's piss had splashed my feet and gown. I tore off the dress with clumsy, trembling hands and, clad only in my shift, leaned over the pot and retched until all that was left of the dream was the cold sweat that bathed my body. I scrubbed my feet with the shift, then wadded the shift and my gown together and threw them in the corner. I wrenched open the trunk, my hands fumbling for the thin comfort of well-washed linen. There. I pulled out a clean shift, tugged it down over my head, and burrowed under the covers, shaking with cold and disgust. After what seemed hours, the tears finally came, warm and reassuring, and I cried myself back to sleep.

By the time the nightmare woke me again, my father's back was between me and whatever else was out there. I slid my hand over until it clutched a corner of his shirt and, reassured that he couldn't leave without my knowing, slipped back into sleep.

We took the old Roman "Golden Road" from Genoa to southern France, since it was still too early in the season for passenger ferries to brave the winter surf and my father preferred not to travel on a freighter. Although sailing would have been faster, I was relieved not to have to get too close to the water after all. My father was still silent, responding to my overtures with an absent smile that communicated nothing except that he wasn't listening, but I was becoming more accustomed to the silent rhythms of the journey. It helped when I gave up trying to find the *babbo* of my memories in the silent, preoccupied man riding twenty paces ahead of me and turned my attention to God's handiwork.

The Provençal spring was bursting through the long terraces of gray olives, green vines, and white-blossomed orange trees that stretched down to the sea. Migrating birds and butterflies were everywhere, and clumps of violet and lily-of-the-valley and wild rosemary lined the road. Occasionally one of our mounts would step on a stray tuft of flowers, and then the dust tasted of my mother's perfume.

I stared into the intense blue of the Mediterranean below us and pretended it was an alchemist's glass through which I could see home to Siena. I imagined Margherita and Tia Taviana at work on the spring cleaning, talking about how much they missed me and trying to comfort Feo, who had given up eating and spent as much time as he could watching the road to Florence for a glimpse of me. I thought of Pietro coming upon some of my sketches and showing them to his little brother Ambrogio as pieces to which he could aspire. They would all talk about me at dinner until it seemed to Ambrogio that he had taken the place of a saint, and he would feel sorry and inadequate. Maybe they were composing a letter right now that was begging me to return. I laughed at myself, but it was the silent, mysterious laugh of a wise and knowing woman.

And so we plodded west to Arles and the Rhone River.

The last day was the hardest. We had thought to make Arles well before dinner, but Pilgrim threw a shoe while we were crossing the Crau, a desolate plain of sharp-edged rocks the size of my fist that people say Jupiter threw from Mount Olympus. My father dismounted to lead his horse as best he could, and I did the same for Jennet until my feet were bruised and sore inside their soft boots. Then I remounted. But I had only exchanged one discomfort for another; as the sun moved lower in the sky, the cruel carpet beneath me grew in glittering brilliance until my head ached.

We arrived in Arles, an old Roman city overlooking the marshes where the Rhone River meets the sea, with the blue and purple shadows of the evening. The road ended at the Alyscamps, the city of the dead.

The Alyscamps is the largest graveyard in Christendom. It is planted with beeches and cypress and oak, a cool and welcoming canopy after the bareness of the Crau. My father had warned me, of course, what we would find, but it was still unnerving at first to wander in that garden of the dead. They were stacked three deep along the paths in carved stone sarcophagi, some more than a thousand years old. The only sounds were the wind playing through the leaves and the distant thrum of the sea, faint and rhythmic as a lullaby. The solitude of our journey had already weakened my sense of the ordinary; now as the molten gold of the setting sun spangled my sight, I felt the living quiet of the centuries settle into my bones. We seemed to be outside time.

I said none of this to my father, who had tied up Pilgrim, pulled pen, ink, and parchment from his saddlebag, settled on a large stump, and begun to take rapid notes. And although my feet were still sore and my mouth tasted of dust, I didn't mind; the dramatic scenes cut into the sides of the stone coffins were so animated that I wondered that the bodies sleeping within were not jostled back to life, and I wanted to see if I could capture that quality in a drawing. But by the time I had assembled pen, ink, and parchment from their places in my saddlebag, dusk had drawn her shadowy veil over the carvings.

"I almost expect one of the bodies to sit up and start talking," came my father's voice from over my shoulder.

"I was just thinking that these carvings seem more alive than the bodies inside," I said. It was easier to talk to him when I didn't have to see him.

"Were you?" he said, and laughed softly. "I keep forgetting that you are no longer five years old, and then you say something clever, and I am undone." He had the horses by their bridles and passed in front of me. I could see his eyes and teeth glinting as he spoke.

"Where did they all come from?" I asked.

"In ancient times, the Romans put their dead in barrels and sent them floating down the Rhone with coins on their eyes to pay for burial here."

"Ugh," I said, revolted.

"They still do it. We'll probably see some on our way up the Rhone. Christians want to be buried here because Christ appeared to Saint Trophime in a vision in the Alyscamps."

I was surprised. The sarcophagi at my eye level, which is to say the bottom, oldest layer, showed pagan scenes. "Why would Christ want to visit a bunch of dead Romans? None of them believed in him."

He said nothing, then "As you say," in the preoccupied voice he used when he was interrupted at his studies. Pilgrim nickered at him, and he roused himself. "Well, Antonia, let's go see if we can find a gatekeeper willing to let two suspicious characters like ourselves in the gates after dark."

I started. "Do you think we might have to sleep here?"

"Not for many years, God willing," my father said.

I am embarrassed to admit that it took me a moment to get the joke.

We were able to talk our way through the city gates without

any serious problem, and found the Florentine quarter not long after that. Yes, the innkeeper said, there was a bed, and some bread and cheese if we had not yet eaten. It was a measure of my father's fatigue after the day spent on foot that we were both asleep within half an hour of being shown our room.

We woke early the next morning and went down to the quay to make inquiries about passage up the Rhone. I had looked forward to stopping in Arles, but the boom of the river, the ceaseless rustling of the trees as they pitched back and forth in the wind they call the Mistral, and the press of the smelly, brightly dressed crowd bewildered me. It was all I could do not to press my fingers to my ears.

My father, on the other hand, seemed energized rather than overwhelmed by the stimulation. When we stopped some fishermen unloading their catch of mullet and scorpion fish, and they told us the river was in spate and that it would probably be at least a week and possibly two before barges would be able to take passengers upstream, he shrugged it off. "Well, Antonia, it seems we will see a little more of this city than we had anticipated," he said. "Shall we find ourselves some breakfast?"

We had passed a market near the basilica of Saint Trophime, the city's patron saint, and we retraced our steps. Papa bought us some hot fish pasties and filled our wineskin, and we found a place on a stone bench around a tall stone monument that Papa said was a Roman obelisk. Although the north wind continued to blow, the sun was warm on my shoulders. I ate my pasty slowly, savoring the delicate Provençal flavoring.

We were sitting directly in front of the basilica, which boasts a wonderful doorway covered with brightly painted carved scenes from the Bible. As we ate our breakfast, Papa and I picked out the stories we knew. There at the top was Christ in his glory. Next came the story of man's journey through life, beginning with Adam and Eve and followed by the Last Judgment, with the Just marching off in one line to heaven and the Sinners marching off in another one to hell. Although the sinners were naked and chained together and had flames licking at their feet, the two lines looked remarkable similar to me.

"Isn't it funny that part of the good people's reward is that they *get* to be with each other, and part of the bad people's punishment is that they *have* to be with each other?" I said.

"I wouldn't say that sinners are with each other exactly," Papa said slowly. "Don't you think they're more next to each other?"

Startled and pleased that he had responded to my unthinking overture, I tried to elicit more words. "What do you mean?"

"When the twins were little," Papa said, "they had no idea that they were brothers. Giovanni chewed on Pietro's ear as if he was a rattle, and Pietro crawled over Giovanni as if he was a bump in the road. Both of them were so wrapped up in themselves that they lost the good of having a brother. I think that's what hell is—being so preoccupied with yourself that you lose the good of living in the world."

He gestured with his chin toward the wineskin, and I poured a little more into his leather cup. He took a deep, appreciative swallow. "That's good wine," he said. "I could sit here all day and drink it, and if I let myself I could mourn for the rest of my life that I cannot duplicate how good it tastes to me now. That kind of frustrated craving is hellish. If you love the wrong things, I think your life gets smaller and smaller until you are imprisoned by what you love—money, love, power, wine—and your whole life becomes getting enough of that one thing." He waved at the door with his cup. "They all look the same, those sinners. But the only thing that is the same about them is that each one is stuck so completely within his desire that his body has become a prison."

I thought about how stuck I had felt on those endless, silent hours of the journey, how sometimes I'd wanted to scream and run away from the loneliness and the tedium but I couldn't, because they were inside me. So did that mean that by being lonely I was putting myself in hell?

"How can God do that?" I said.

Now it was my father's turn to look startled. "Do what?"

"How can he draw a line down the middle of the world and say, 'You people there, I'll give you a happy life, and because you love it, you can be saved. But you on the other side, I'm going to give you a sad life, and when you want what you can't have, the wanting will eat you up until there is nothing left. Then I'll send you to hell'?"

My father raised an eyebrow. "It's not sadness and wanting that send people to hell. Wanting and sometimes needing more than you have is the human condition. It's what you do with the wanting that matters. Do you get stuck in the wanting? Or do you use the desire it inspires to create something new?"

He tossed down the last of the wine and stood up before I was finished thinking about what he had just said. "Let's go back to the inn and find out if they have a room for us until the river calms down."

The Florentine quarter was quite close to the wharf. From the street, nothing was visible but a few shops and offices pierced by a large wooden door. But when you opened the door, you were greeted by a courtyard with trees, a fountain, and a large stable and inn to the left, and apartments to the right. On the fourth side, warehouses were built up against a canal calmer and safer than the unpredictable Rhone.

The courtyard had been deserted when we entered the

night before and again when we left early in the morning, but now a half-dozen men sat in the shade of two large oak trees, sharing a small cask of wine and some gossip before starting the day's business. As we entered, they glanced at us curiously and then away. One, a short, balding, heavily built man with eyes like a vulture's, glanced up again. He stiffened, and said something under his breath to the others. They put down their drinks and turned to stare at us.

A tall, gray-haired man with a hooked nose asked, as if he couldn't believe it, "Is that really you, Dante?"

"Whoever doesn't die is seen again," my father said with a broad smile. "Taddeo. Giuseppe. I had not thought to find you here. This is my daughter, Antonia—"

But the fat man interrupted. "What are you doing here?"

My father blinked at his rude tone but answered civilly enough. "We're waiting for the Rhone to subside. We're on our way to Paris, and I've heard that it is dangerous to ride through the Rhone valley unescorted—"

The fat man waved my father's words away impatiently. "You are under interdict."

My father looked startled. "In Florence, perhaps, but not in France."

The men looked at each other, and then the fat man put his drink down, leaned forward, and said, "You are not welcome here."

I moved closer to my father and took his hand, reacting as if one of our friends had insulted Margherita or Feo. "We have as much right to be here as you do," I said loudly.

None of them, not even my father, bothered to look at me. It was as if I hadn't spoken. I was actually relieved by their dismissal; well-bred young girls did not speak to adult men that way, no matter what the provocation. I took a step back until I was half hidden by my father, but I didn't let go of his hand.

"I am a Florentine," my father started, but the fat man interrupted again.

"You are no Florentine," he said, drawing out each word in disgust. "In the eyes of Florence, you are dead. So I suppose that leaves you two choices—either die or disappear."

The others laughed.

My father said nothing, merely wheeled and left the courtyard. Once we had closed the door of our room—fortunately empty of any other guests—he sat heavily on the bed and put his head in his hands. I looked around the bare room for something I could occupy myself with, but before I had found anything, three loud knocks sounded on the door and then it swung open.

It was the innkeeper, looking very uncomfortable. "Excuse me, sir, but they say you are not a Florentine," he said in his heavily accented Tuscan. "If that is so, I must ask you to leave."

My father started to say something, then stopped. Then he sighed and said in a flat voice, "Where do you recommend we go?"

The innkeeper twisted his apron between his fingers. "Most of the city's lodgings are in the arena," he said.

My father gestured with his chin that he understood, and the innkeeper closed the door quietly behind him.

"Well, Antonia, this is unpleasant," he said. "But I don't suppose there's much point in clinging to the furniture until they carry us out." He stared off in space for a moment. He looked at me. "Do you have all your things?"

I nodded.

"Don't look so tragic, daughter. It's not the end of the world—just an inconvenience wrapped in an insult. We'll survive.

Do you suppose they have the horses saddled and waiting?"

They did.

Wordlessly, my father led us through the city's narrow cobblestoned streets toward the ruins of the Roman arena. As we drew closer, it became obvious that the ruins had been scavenged for dressed stone that the neighborhood's inhabitants had used to construct a warren of small, filthy apartments. Not even the strong Provençal light could penetrate into the tiny alleys that honeycombed the place, and it was difficult for us to pass through leading our mounts. My father swore under his breath, then abruptly led us outside the arena's walls. A young Franciscan friar was sitting under a tree reading aloud to a frail brother from his order whose watery eyes were opaque with cataracts.

"Good morrow, friends," my father said to them.

The young brother looked up, startled.

"My daughter and I have business within," my father said. "Would you be good enough to watch our mounts until our return?"

The elderly brother looked suspicious. "What kind of business?"

My father spoke up slightly. "We are looking for lodging."

"And Jesus said unto him, Foxes have holes, and birds of the air nests; but the Son of man hath not where to lay his head," the old man intoned.

The younger brother smiled an apology. "It's all right, Frère Matthieu," he said. "They look quite respectable. Of course we will watch your horses for you."

"God's blessing be upon you," my father said.

"And on you," the brothers returned.

Papa led the way up the winding stone steps inside one of the defensive towers. They were narrow, steep, crumbling, and slippery with moss, and it was all I could do to keep up with him. We climbed for what seemed to be a long time before reaching the top, an enclosed platform with a bell suspended above it to ring in case of alarm. We were not the only ones who had made the climb, however; a very small, very dirty old man who stank of sour wine and unwashed clothes was slumped against one of the walls, singing softly to himself.

We went to a small window cut in the opposite wall and peered out. The sight was not reassuring. Much of the arena's interior was still intact. The rows of stone seats circled the arena as they had for more than a thousand years. But instead of a playing field, they overlooked a cesspool of dilapidated apartments. People were sprawled, drunk or asleep, on many of the flat roofs. They appeared to be dressed mainly in rags, although both bodies and garments were so filthy it was hard to distinguish where one left off and the other began. The smoke from a hundred sullen cooking fires couldn't hide the stench of alleys used as latrines. Although I had seen poverty before, I had never seen it on anything like this scale, and I turned away.

The creature in the corner was watching me. "You're a pretty little thing," it said, feeling for something around its waist. "How much do you want for her?"

Before I had time to make sense of the words, my father was on him. He laid him out cold with a couple of punches to the head that the beggar was too dazed or drunk to dodge, then began kicking his stomach and back. With each blow, the man grunted in his sleep and jerked on the floor like some devil poppet.

This was also part of the nightmare—my cultured father behaving as brutishly as a drunken soldier in a strange city. I tried to say something, but no words would come. I backed away, then tripped on the uneven floor and fell hard.

My father started forward to help me up. But I could not bear to be touched by hands that had touched the filthy old man. I scuttled backward, shaking my head.

"Don't touch me."

"Antonia, I was just trying …"

"Don't touch me." My voice growled like a frightened cat's.

"It's all right, daughter," my father said, approaching cautiously, his hands out. They were bruised and scraped across the knuckles, and they were shaking. I'd never seen my father's hands marred by anything but ink stains before, and I couldn't get the idea out of my head that these weren't really his. "He can't hurt you now. I won't let anyone hurt you."

"Your hands," I said, shrinking away. "His head—I could hear the bones."

"It's all right, Antonia. It's all over now."

I shook my head. "No, don't. No, don't."

But he ignored me and took me in his arms as though I were five years old again. "It's all right, Antonia," he repeated. "We're going now. We're not going to stay in this ugly place. We'll go find something beautiful, and soon this will all seem like a bad dream."

THE CITY OF THE MAGUS

Les Baux, 1307

He took me to Les Baux, a fortified hill town a half-day's journey from Arles where the troubadours had sung before my birth. It was a hot and dusty journey, and as the shock of the episode in the tower wore off and I began to notice my surroundings, I told myself that if this was France's idea of beauty, it was little wonder the Romans had retreated back to Italy. The red soil of Provence lightened and then disappeared as our track wound into the Alpilles, a strange bleached landscape of gorges, boulders, and distorted crags. The only vegetation was the small plants of lavender and thyme and broom that managed to grow in the fissures of the twisted limestone, although from time to time I glimpsed the green of cypress or olive half visible behind the stone walls of the canyon.

I was tired and shaken, and the maddening rasp of the cicadas was rubbing away whatever self-control I still possessed after our long trek from Italy, leaving only disappointment and fear. The silent miles were sharpening those into irritation and finally anger. My frayed nerves snapped, and I dug my heels into Jennet's side. She ignored them. I swore and kicked at her viciously. I imagined that she looked at me reproachfully, but she quickened her pace slightly until we had caught up with my father.

"Why did you bring me?" I flung at him.

He looked up from his thoughts. "I told you. I'm taking you to Les Baux. There was a troubadour at the Malaspina court who said …"

"Not where—why." I enunciated each word very clearly, as though I were talking to a not very bright child. "Why did you ask me to come with you?"

"Because I desired your company, of course," he said in the cold, remote tone that he used when my mother was upset.

But I was too angry to be dismissed. I gestured at the twisted rock formations that towered above the bridle path. "Look at this place. You said you were taking me someplace beautiful, but it never comes, it just gets worse and worse." I started to cry. The words that I hadn't allowed myself to speak, hadn't even allowed myself to think, rose in my throat and spilled out like acrid, burning bile. "I'm your daughter. You're supposed to take care of me. But you treat me like a dog that you can ignore for days at a time as long as you keep it fed."

"Antonia, that's enough," he said, in a tone I hadn't heard him use since I was five. "You are hysterical. You've been very well treated and offered an adventure that very few children your age are privileged to experience, and here you are putting on a vulgar and unattractive display as though I beat you."

"I wish you would!" I said passionately. "Then at least I'd know you remembered I was here."

He slapped my face, hard. I gasped and put my hand to my cheek. He had never struck me before.

His eyes were like the glittering rocks of the Crau. "Is that better?" he asked thinly. "I thought not. Don't betray your ignorance of real pain by ranting so foolishly about trifles. Have I broken your bones? Forced you to go to bed hungry while I was out drinking and dicing? Prevented your advancement by my undisciplined and offensive behavior? No? Then I do not want to hear one word from you about what I am not providing. You have no idea how protected you are."

His dismissive tone hurt more than the blow. "I hate you," I said in a cold, flat tone that matched his own.

"You would not be the first," he said, and kicked Pilgrim into a trot, and then a gallop.

I couldn't catch up with him even if I wanted to, and I didn't want to. Jennet and I had made our slow way a few hundred yards farther when she raised her head. We stopped, and I could hear what she smelled—a trickle of water. I dismounted and led her through a tumbled pile of boulders into a cluster of cypress trees that seemed to be growing right out of the sheer rock face of a cliff. But the lovely tinkling was louder here, and the scent fresher. I pushed in among the boulders and found a freshet welling up from a moss-upholstered fissure. I took my leather beaker from my saddlebag and filled and drained it three times before offering some to Jennet. Then I rooted around until I found the only food I had—a strip of dried jerky, a bit of hard biscuit, some withered carrots, and the last of a packet of dried cherries we'd bought three days earlier. I offered the carrots and part of the biscuit to my mule, then sat there in the shade chewing slowly on the jerky, biscuit, and cherries—all of which tasted more like the inside of a dusty saddlebag than anything else—until the hollow feeling in my stomach was gone. When I had consumed my scanty dinner, I sat enjoying the green freshness of my solitude. But I couldn't afford to let my father get too far ahead, so after a few more swallows of water, Jennet and I returned to the main trail and went after my father. What else could we do, after all?

We followed Pilgrim's hoof prints for a time, but then they petered out. It didn't matter—there was only one way to go, so we kept going. I hesitated briefly when we came to a fork, but the downhill branch was little more than a track, so I turned Jennet's head to the left, up the better-traveled path. It soon became considerably steeper. I patted Jennet's neck. "Don't worry," I encouraged her. "It can't be too much farther."

It wasn't. We plodded around a bend, and found ourselves facing a massive stone gate. I reined Jennet in with difficulty (she was eager to get at the oats she was sure awaited) and let my eyes accustom themselves to the smooth edges of the dressed stone. There was a device, a star of some kind, carved into the arch. I could hear the faint murmur of voices beyond the open gate and, closer at hand, the thin melody of a wooden flute. Jennet snorted impatiently, and I gave her her head.

As we passed under the arch, the music stopped and a boy who had been sitting in its shadow got quickly to his feet. He looked to be about my age, small-boned, with dark eyes and hair and a wide mouth as mobile as a girl's. He said something to me, which I ignored. He repeated it, gesturing with his flute, and I realized the words were Italian although the accent was Provençal. "Are you the Lady Antonia?" he asked.

Nonplussed, I stared at him.

He giggled at the expression on my face. "Your father, Ser Dante, bid me wait for you and guide you to your quarters," he said. His speech was curiously formal, and as my eyes became accustomed to the darkness I saw that he wore livery on which the star I had seen carved on the gate had been embroidered in gold thread. When I still said nothing, he introduced himself. "My name is Tristan," he said. "And I am varlet to the Lady Clémence."

"It's nice to meet you," I said politely. "Most people call me—"

"Antonia. Yes, I know. Your father—"

"Bice," I corrected him.

His eyes danced and he swept me an elaborate bow. "Po, po,

po," he said. "So then I ask you, my Lady Bice, to follow me."

I looked past the gate at the busy market square behind. I felt naked, as though the unpleasantness of the day had stripped away the skin that lay between me and the rest of the world, and cast around for something, anything, that would delay my stepping out into the midst of all those curious eyes. "Wait—Tristan, is it?"

He nodded.

"What is that device on the gate?"

He was amused, and struck the pose of a jongleur, a performer, who had told this story a hundred times. "That is the Star of the Magus Balthasar."

I had no idea what he was talking about, and my face must have shown it.

"Balthasar was one of the three kings who came from the east to give gifts to the Christ child. He was a magus, a magician of great power and learning. It was Balthasar who first saw the Star and divined its message. It was Balthasar who saw the treachery that lurked within King Herod's jealous heart. And it was Balthasar who mourned the wickedness of those who would crucify their King, and so he left the Holy Land, taking his knowledge and power with him. He searched for a desolate place with no beauty that man could desire, in order that only those seeking the precious pearl of learning that lay beneath would follow him. And so he settled here, in the Val d'Enfer, and taught the pure in heart the secrets of his power."

"The Valley of the Inferno?" I asked, shocked. "The Valley of Hell?"

Tristan continued calmly. "But yes. Did you not know that was the name of this place?"

"I thought it was Les Baux."

"That is the name of the court of the lords of Les Baux, the lords who follow Balthasar. But the valley around it is called the Valley of Hell."

"It is well named," I said, more to myself than to him.

He looked at me with interest. "So," he said. "You have some stories to tell me."

I looked at his thin, clever face and then away. "My father is the one with the stories," I said.

I could feel his eyes on me. When I said nothing, he shrugged and took Jennet's bridle. "Allow me, mademoiselle," he said in the formal tones of a courtier, and began to lead me to my father.

Like Siena, Les Baux is a city on a hill. But where Siena's hills are graceful, the rock cliff from which Les Baux is hewn is formidable, brooding like a petrified leviathan over the limestone valley below. The town, a settlement of about a thousand hearths, seems to have spilled forth in some mighty eructation of the rock on which it is built. The main thoroughfare leads from the town's single gate at one end to the massive donjon, or castle, at the other and is separated from the sheer drop to the Val d'Enfer hundreds of feet below only by a waist-high stone wall. Tristan made his way quickly along the street, but I lingered. It was late afternoon, and children were cutting lettuces and picking beans in the carefully tended gardens on the hill behind the houses. I looked at them wistfully. It seemed years since I had seen other children.

"Hurry up!" Tristan called back to me. "I have duties before supper." A church bell began to ring, and was answered by another, deeper bell in the direction of the donjon. "Hurry up!" Tristan repeated, and began to run, pulling an unwilling Jennet behind him.

But like Jennet, I had no wish to hurry, and I was not on a

lead. I was tired of being obedient and keeping quiet when I wanted to speak, of being polite to people I didn't care two sticks for, of being a good sport when I was tired and sore and hungry. I doubted that Papa wished to see me at all tonight, after my "vulgar and unattractive display." Well, that was fine with me, because I had no wish to see him. If he was willing to act with so little thought for my feelings and needs, as Tia Taviana had warned me he might, I felt perfectly justified in doing the same. So I loitered and listened to the carillon and tried to pick out words I knew in the Provençal dialect the children chattered to each other.

Despite my dawdling, at length I arrived at the gate of the donjon, which was guarded by two men wearing the same livery embroidered with a gold starburst that Tristan wore. I looked at their hard faces and at the weapons they held so casually, and hesitated. There was no sign of either Tristan or Jennet, who I assumed had passed through some minutes earlier. I thought of the explanations, of the effort required to make myself understood in the Provençal tongue, and became suddenly, bone-crushingly aware of my weariness. I couldn't do it. I just could not make myself do one more hard thing.

I looked around for a place to sit for a moment while I gathered my courage. To my left, a stone staircase led between two houses to the kitchen gardens on the hillside above them. I cast a glance over my shoulder. This end of the street was deserted. I climbed halfway up the staircase until I came to a step broader than the others. Then I wedged myself comfortably against the stone, still warm from the afternoon's heat, and leaned my head against the whitewashed wall of the house.

The Val d'Enfer lay gleaming beyond the parapet on the other side of the road, its twisted limestone licked by tongues of gold, bronze, and crimson flame thrown by the setting sun.

I'd had enough drama for one day, however, and closed my eyes and concentrated on the way the warm evening breeze stroked my hair back from my face. I could smell herbs planted in the garden above me—sage and tarragon and rosemary and lavender—and, more faintly, the city smells of cats and cooking oil. I listened for the children I had passed a few moments before. I thought I could hear the faint echo of their voices as they called to one another. How high their cries were, I thought drowsily. Like hungry baby birds alone in a nest.

The children weren't making the noise; I was. I was running through a thorny thicket, the branches whipping at my face and ripping at my clothes. When I tried to stop, I realized that I was bound to my father at ankle and wrist, and that it was his long, rapid strides that were propelling me along. "Stop! Stop!" I cried, or tried to, but now the twigs were sprouting from my throat and I couldn't talk or even breathe.

Then we had left the wood, and just as suddenly as the twigs had sprouted, they withered and died. I coughed and spat until the last scratchy bit was gone, but when I called to my father to slow down, he laughed out loud with delight, the way Gian had laughed as we galloped through the hills on Pilgrim. In fact, that was what we were doing, galloping through the hills, and there was the farm at Prato, and I could see my mother in the kitchen. She was standing at the window, her hair tied up in a turban, polishing her mother's silver mirror. I called to her, and she looked up. But all she said was "Poor little pilgrim. Poor little pilgrim." Then she turned back to her work.

Tia Taviana was behind me—had been behind me for some time, I realized, repeating the same words over and over again. "You're the one that tied the ropes, Bice. Untie them or learn to dance. Untie them or learn to dance." I turned my head to see her, and she laughed and pulled Gian out from behind her skirts, and they began to dance, faster and faster until they seemed to turn into a ball of flame, as bright as my grandmother's silver mirror.

I closed my eyes, but the light still pulsed red behind my lids. Someone—Smerelda?—called, "This must be her! Get her father!" I heard the hiss and crackle of resin torches and smelled their pungent smoke. Not just smoke—an unpleasantly strong perfume of orris root and musk. I shook my head fretfully, but the odor only grew stronger. I opened my eyes again and saw a child with the head of a man leaning over me, blond bristles furring his heavy cheeks. It wasn't until a drop of pitch from his torch fell sizzling onto the back of my hand that I realized that he was not part of my dream.

"You must be the Lady Antonia," the dwarf said, and bowed. He was dressed in green and scarlet, as Tristan and the guards had been, and his livery reeked of the unpleasant cologne I had smelled in my sleep, which was not quite strong enough to hide the smell of cooking smoke and unwashed body that had reminded me of Smerelda.

I slowly pushed myself away from the stone steps on which I had fallen asleep—they were cold as death itself now that night had fallen—and fumbled through the clinging cobwebs of my dream for something to say.

But before I could frame any kind of response, quick steps sounded on the street below us. The dwarf moved away from me and bowed again, this time to the dark-caped figure who appeared behind him. It was my father, and he was furious.

"My errant daughter. At last."

I gaped at him, still swimming up through the strangeness of my dream.

He spoke to the dwarf without taking his eyes from me. "You may go. Make my apologies to the men who were awakened."

He handed the dwarf something that glinted in the moon-light, and the man's eyes widened. "It was nothing, *m'sieur.* You are too good, too good," he mumbled, and melted away into the darkness.

"Can you walk?" my father asked.

I nodded.

"Then let's get inside."

He walked quickly, and it was as if I were back in my dream, struggling to keep up with him, my sore muscles and bruised feet protesting with every step. We passed through the castle gate, and I had a dim impression of formal gardens and the smell of rose and honeysuckle. Then we were in the palace, hurrying past brilliant tapestries lit by more wax candles than I had ever seen lit at one time. When I slowed down to get a better look, my father tugged impatiently at my arm. After we had climbed what seemed miles of stairs and traversing acres of passageways, he threw a door open and we passed into a large room.

The first thing I noticed was a huge fireplace with a good fire crackling in it. I made a beeline for the welcome warmth, passing a bed and table already covered by my father's books and papers. But my father called to me sharply, and I saw that he was waiting by a curtained doorway I hadn't noticed.

It led to a smaller chamber with another bed, another blazing fire, and, best of all, a round wooden tub lined with a sheet from which rose clouds of steam. My trunk was at the foot of the bed, and my sketchbook and pens had been set out on a small table by the fireplace. My father pulled on a long loop of tapestry, and I heard the faint echo of a bell ringing. Then he removed his gloves and slapped them against his arm. He walked restlessly around the room, not looking at me.

I heard someone climbing a flight of stairs, and spoke hurriedly. "Papa, I—"

"Not tonight, Antonia," he said. "We will speak of this tomorrow." He turned and left me.

A serving woman entered the room from a door set in the wall that I guessed led down to the kitchens. She was carrying a tray with a steaming beaker of milk punch, a jug of wine, a plate of bread and cheese, a casserole of sausage and cabbage, and a dish of the season's first apricots. The posset was sweet and spiced with nutmeg, and I drank it down thirstily, then reached for the food. I was starving, and it tasted wonderful. I ate everything.

The serving woman took away the empty plates, then undressed me and helped me climb into the large bathtub by the fire. The water was hot and soothing, with lavender and lily-of-the-valley strewn on its surface to sweeten it. By this time I couldn't keep my eyes open, and I felt sponges cleaning me, water being poured over my filthy hair, and gentle hands spreading it over the edge of the tub and carefully combing it out. Then someone else had come, because four hands were lifting me, and then soft towels were drying me and I heard the splashing of water being ladled out of the tub, but before they had finished, I was being nestled into the welcome embrace of a down mattress.

Some noise woke me suddenly the next morning. I lay still, my eyes staring at the high ceiling, listening for the sound to come again. But it didn't. I stretched, my limbs still heavy with sleep, then curled back up in the down-stuffed mattress, luxuriating in the feeling of my clean body against the soft linen sheets. The sun was bright and the birds had stopped singing; it must be nearly midday. My stomach growled so loudly that I almost laughed out loud, and I abruptly sat up and looked around for my clothes.

The tub was gone, and someone had unpacked my trunk. My gowns, newly washed and pressed, were draped over a pole hung next to my bed. I threw back the covers and kneeled, reaching to feel the fabric. My *camicias* were already dry, and the gowns nearly so—the two maidservants who had bathed me must have washed them last night before they left. I climbed out of the bed to examine my gray wool gown more closely. It had lain crushed and smelly in the corner of my trunk where I had thrust it after the awful night in Vernazza, but it now both looked and smelled nearly as good as new, and a small tear on the sleeve had been neatly mended.

I told myself that if I'd known last night that all this—a comfortable bed, a warm bath, clean clothes, and servants to attend me—was waiting, no guards, no matter how many colors of livery they were wearing, could have scared me off. I used the chamber pot I found under the bed, dressed in my chestnut linen gown, and combed my hair with a horn comb I found on the table that was so smooth it neither pulled nor snagged. Clean, sweet-smelling hose next, then my boots, which had been brushed and oiled. I pulled down the gray gown to show the mending and careful cleaning to my father, then hesitated, remembering the way we'd left things last night.

I chewed my lip, looking at the door to the kitchens. Maybe I should just slip out that way and avoid my father until later. But then I thought about trying to make myself understood and trying to find my way about the castle. Besides, delaying our meeting would only make it harder. Before I could talk myself out of it again, I pushed aside the striped curtain and stepped into my father's room.

My father had dragged his table to the window, where the light was better—perhaps that was the sound that had wakened me—and was going through his papers, setting them in neat piles. He looked up at the rustle of the curtain, and then immediately down again.

"You are rested?" he asked his papers.

I started to nod, then said, "Yes, sir."

He raised his eyebrows, still looking down at the table. "Yes, sir, is it? Aren't we formal this morning?"

I stood awkwardly, not sure what he wanted from me.

He finally looked up. "You were not so—respectful—yesterday."

I blushed and looked away. "I was upset."

"So I gathered," he said dryly. He tapped the stack of papers he was working with into alignment, then set them down and turned to me. "As was I. I think we both said things we may have regretted...?" He ended on a slight note of inquiry.

I nodded again, and this time he was watching.

"So," he said briskly. "We will not speak of it again."

"Thank you, Papa," I said.

His eyes smiled in a way that I remembered. "And I believe I must thank you as well." He made me a formal little bow.

My stomach growled again, too loudly for him to pretend that he had not noticed.

"The girl who brought the water said to ring when you woke up and they'd bring you something to eat," he said. "And then why don't you explore the castle?"

THE IDYLL

Les Baux, 1307

My tray was actually delivered through the doorway next to the fireplace by a sullen-looking Tristan, who walked stiffly, as if he'd been beaten—probably because he'd lost me the night before, or possibly because my dawdling had made him late. Or maybe both. I didn't know what to say or how to acknowledge the punishments he had borne as a result of my actions, so I avoided his eyes and went to call my father. When we returned, Tristan had gone.

After we had finished our silent meal and my father had returned to his study, I paced uneasily around my room. I was not particularly eager to take his suggestion that I wander around a strange castle filled with people above my rank whose language I didn't speak. After a minute's thought, I cleared the table of its crockery and then tugged it closer to the window, as my father had done with his, and tried to sketch the view. But the walls were thick and the opening small and high so I had to keep getting up to see it clearly, and the plain black lines I traced seemed dead on the page. I wanted color, washes of gold and rose and indigo. I sighed and put down my pen. No use spoiling precious parchment with halfhearted sketches.

A knock came from the door by the fireplace. "Come in," I called, and Tristan re-entered the chamber. Made braver by my full stomach, I blurted out, "Did they beat you?"

"Pardon me?"

"Did you they beat you last night after I went missing?"

He was piling the dishes on the tray. "That's no concern of yours, my lady."

"Look, I didn't mean to get you in trouble ..." I started, but he picked up the tray and went out the door, closing it behind him. I looked back and forth between the closed door and the drawn curtain across the room. I'd had enough of being ignored. I was going to go out and explore the castle grounds, and if a workman or a guard swore at me, at least I'd know they saw me. And who knew—I might even find a scriptorium with some parchment scraps to spare and maybe some pigments and egg white with which to bind them. I took a deep breath and slipped through the curtain into my father's room.

"Papa?"

He grunted at me, not looking up from his notes.

"Do you know if they have a scriptorium here?" I asked.

"No," he said.

I waited, then asked, "No, they don't, or no, you don't know?"

"Yes," he said absently.

"Yes, what?" I ventured.

He put down his pen and rubbed his eyes. "Run and play, child. Run and play."

The forecourt was thronged with people. In addition to the usual mix of courtiers and servants, a group of stonecutters was at work on the donjon to my right, which was only partially completed. I could hear some of them calling to each other in the familiar cadences of the Tuscan dialect. To my left, ladies and courtiers were watching a party of knights who were playing at some sort of contest. The atmosphere reminded me a little bit of Duccio's studio, with the same busy mingling of laborers and courtiers, artisans and clients, public display and the anonymity that belongs to you only when you are part of a crowd.

I was surprised by how little of the grounds had been formally landscaped. Aside from a sunken Lady garden between the palace and the court chapel, furnished with banks of flowers, shade trees, a fountain, and beautifully carved stone benches, the grounds were disordered and utilitarian. Past the chapel, the entire eastern strip of the escarpment was littered with windmills and workshops set at random among cultivated fields and orchards. Compared to their Sienese and Florentine peers, the lords of Les Baux seemed to care little for *la bella figura*.

The knights were playing what looked like a huge game of darts, except that instead of darts they threw javelins so heavy they had to use both hands to hurl them at the target. I attached myself to the edge of the crowd of spectators and watched for a while, but I have never much cared for athletic contests and I soon tired of it. I wandered out into the fields, poking into as many of the outbuildings as I could slip in and out of without attracting too much attention. I wasn't sure what my position was at the castle, and I was not eager to invite a challenge. But I knew that one of the scarlet pigments we used at home in Siena came from Provence, and I thought there might be a scriptorium, or maybe even an artist's studio like my uncle's, where I could beg some paint or colored inks. But the closest thing to an artist's studio I found was a wood-shop that also made and repaired musical instruments for the troubadours and the jongleurs who entertained the court.

My father was waiting for me when I returned about sunset. His thin face had been freshly shaved, and he looked hand-some and a little foreign in a black padded silk doublet trimmed with black velvet ribbons that I had never seen before.

"You look very nice, Papa," I said a little shyly. "Just like a real courtier."

"Don't be deceived, Antonia," he rebuked me. "Finery lent by a patron is a nothing more than expensive livery. The Lady Clémence simply wants to make sure that her court poet looks the part. Hurry and change, child. I expect our summons momentarily."

But as I went, I saw him checking his appearance in the reflection cast by his pewter water pitcher with a pleased expression on his face.

Once in my room, I kicked my boots aside. Finally a reason to wear the slippers and soft green gown Tia Taviana had given me! I washed my hands, feet, and face, then dressed in my finery. A beaker of tiny white roses had been left on my table, and after I had combed out my hair, I tucked some of them into the fresh braid I made. I looked around the room for anything I might have missed, and quickly shook out and hung my discarded clothing. Then I went out to wait for our summons.

But no summons came that night, just Tristan with a tray and the message that the lady sent her respects, but she had been part of a hunting party and was too fatigued to receive guests this evening. I was just as glad; my father had passed the hour or so we waited by drilling me in the etiquette of life at court, and I was now convinced that I would speak before being spoken to or seat myself before being invited to or do something equally horrible. So although my father greeted the news with the air of a child who had been denied a treat, I was grateful for the reprieve. I ate my delicious stew and fine white bread, licked up every crumb of dried pear tart, put away my finery, and took myself off to my cloud-soft bed.

Once again I slept quite late, and at breakfast—another fine meal that included a bowl of oranges and another of walnuts—my father said that I shouldn't leave our chambers in case the Lady Clémence sent a summons. Although it was pleasant at first to lie on my bed and dream, I soon became restless—too restless to draw. I looked around the room for inspiration. There was nothing—only the unglazed window. I examined it more carefully. The castle wall was two feet thick here, considerably thinner than it was on the ground floor, but still plenty wide to hold a young girl. I climbed up on my table and then pulled myself up to the sill.

The courtyard, the garden, and part of the village beyond the gate were visible from my perch. The chapel bells started to ring, startling me so that I grabbed at the stone in a panic, although there was no reason for me to fall. Below me, the courtiers were emerging from morning mass, their bright clothes like so many flowers spilling from the dour stone. They greeted each other, the men throwing their arms around their friends and the women standing a little apart in small groups. Snatches of conversation and laughter floated up toward me.

It was an attractive little scene, and it inspired a wave of homesickness that left me tearful. Not one of those people knew me. Even if I were to jump out of my window and land sprawled and bloody in their midst, I thought dramatically, they would notice me only until my body had been taken away and my blood had been scrubbed from their clothes. But they would never know me. Not the way Tia Taviana and Margherita did. Not even the way Gian did. I was no one to them, no one to everyone.

The day crawled by. I climbed down from my perch long enough to bring the oranges and walnuts up to the ledge, and sat eating nuts and orange segments, seeing how far I could spit the seeds and toss the shells without anyone noticing. A group of ladies came out and walked in the garden, their large, bright headdresses moving among the plants like butterflies. Some time later, the knights emerged, preceded by varlets, Tristan among them, lugging barrels full of more oranges. They lined up as if for battle, and when the horn sounded they fought each other with the oranges. I was both appalled and fascinated by the extravagance. Oranges are as rare as gold and I had tasted one only once before, at my Nonno Manetto's house. Soon the air was thick with the scent of burst oranges, and their sticky juice ran everywhere—down the young men's ruined doublets, in starbursts on the castle walls, and in viscous puddles on the flagstones. The wasps must have smelled it, too, because soon they were there in full force, and the battle ended abruptly. I stared down at the suddenly empty courtyard, and wondered for the first time how I would spend my days while my father was at his lectures. I could think of no friendly answers.

The summons finally came late in the afternoon, after I had ruined two more precious leaves of parchment with half-hearted drawings. The Lady Clémence sent her compliments, and wished to meet the poet Dante about whom she had heard so much.

I was prepared to dislike the woman on sight. After all, I had spent a nervous evening and a tedious day waiting for her invitation. But when the servant bowed us into her solar, I thought I had never seen anyone so—not beautiful, exactly, but brilliant. The Lady Clémence shone.

She sat at her embroidery by the window, where the afternoon sun danced on her wild red-gold hair until it turned to fire. My father had told me that she had been widowed for more than a decade, but her body was tight and rounded as a peach, and her cheeks were the color of blushing apricots. She had painted her lips the color of strawberries and cream—the first cosmetics I had seen on a gentlewoman—and wore a coral necklace and earrings, all of which looked oddly beautiful against the skin that was as dark as a peasant woman's. I thought that she must love the feeling of the sun on her face as much as I did.

After profuse apologies in Latin for keeping us waiting and invitations for us to take our ease, she turned her brilliant emerald eyes on me. She patted a stool next to her knee. "Come here—Bice, is it? My spies tell me that you have walked all the way from Florence with no company but your grumpy old father. You are the bravest young woman I know."

"It wasn't really on foot," I corrected in Tuscan, then looked at my father, panicked, because I had just contradicted our hostess. But she seemed to notice nothing amiss.

She answered in the same tongue. "No? How did you come, then?"

"By mule," I said. "And I'm about the least brave person I know. I had nightmares the whole way."

She laughed and patted my hand, her small fingers heavy with jeweled rings that matched her eyes. "Well, in my mind doing what you are afraid of because it has to be done is the bravest way to live, wouldn't you agree, Ser Dante?"

"I wouldn't dare contradict a lady," my father said gallantly.

She gave him a look as though what he had said displeased her, then turned back to me. "No, Antonia, what you did was very brave. I admire you greatly." She turned to my father. "And you, Ser Dante, why have you dragged your lovely daughter with you to the barren waste of Les Baux?"

"How could it be called a barren waste when so many beautiful flowers bloom from its majestic soil?" my father said, with a bow toward the lady's attendants, who tittered.

I caught his glance as he rose, but I looked away immediately, embarrassed by the servile note in his voice.

"You haven't answered my question, sir," the Lady Clémence observed.

"My pardon, Lady," my father said smoothly. "We travel to Paris, where I hope to polish away some of my provincial ways."

"At the royal court?"

"No," my father said, sounding slightly scornful and more like himself. "At the university."

She looked at him again, reassessing. "I had hoped for poetry this evening, but now I see that you are no jongleur."

My father bowed again. "No, indeed, Lady, for my voice is best heard on a page. But I would be happy to recite for you, if that is your desire."

She hesitated, then said, "A contest. Gislebert, my dwarf, is a musician of a sort. You and he will compete tonight, words against music, and we shall see who comes out the victor." She stripped one of the rings off her hand and held it up for the room to see. "And this shall be the prize."

We dressed even more carefully for dinner the second evening. A sudden storm had blown up, and I was grateful that we were in a castle, not a city, so that our clothes could stay dry. When we made our way down to the great hall, we were seated at the high table and served the kind of meal that gives rise to gluttony: crawfish fritters, eels dressed in plum sauce, asparagus and cheese tarts, tender new green beans baked in almond milk, roast venison with garlic, partridge stewed with lentils and shallots, chicken cooked with pears and brandy, tiny spring lettuces dressed with olive oil and verjuice, junket, strawberry tarts, and a dozen other dishes. I ate and sipped wonderful wine until the room started to fuzz around the edges.

Conversations spun around me just as I loved them to; I understood phrases here and there but had no need to speak myself.

"The pear blossoms are so beautiful this year ..."

"There's to be a tournament in Tarascon ..."

"Not a day under forty ..."

"Well, if she wants to make a fool of herself ..."

Then, far too soon, the Lady Clémence tapped her knife on her goblet for silence and introduced the terms of the contest, and there was the dwarf who had found me the first night—Gislebert, she'd said his name was—with a lute, accompanied by Tristan with his wooden flute. They began to play, and Gislebert to sing in a strong, clear voice:

"I take great pleasure in the joyous season of spring,
Which makes leaves and flowers burst forth ..."

My mind wandered a bit. I have no real ear for poetry, although I can catch its music if I concentrate.

"And I feel great joy
When I see lined up through the fields
Armed knights and horses ..."

I looked at my father, puzzled. That was not what poetry was supposed to be about—wars and battles. It was supposed to be about love. He caught my glance and grimaced very slightly in return.

"And I tell you that I do not find such pleasure
In eating or drinking or sleeping
As I do when I hear people shout 'At them!'

131

> *From both sides, and I hear riderless horses*
> *Neighing in the shade*
> *And I hear people cry out, 'Help! Help!'*
> *And I see falling alongside the moats*
> *The low and mighty in the grass,*
> *And I see the dead who, through their ribs,*
> *Have stumps of lances with silk pennons."*

The knights cheered lustily, but I shuddered, discomfited by the hauntingly brutal images.

My father bowed. "A vivid scene, indeed, as only Bertrand de Born could write, but possibly not the best choice for noble entertainment. Perhaps the great troubadour Peire d'Alvernhe said it best," and here my father, to my astonishment, began to sing in a thin but pleasant voice:

> *"I shall sing of those troubadours*
> *Who sing in many styles,*
> *And the worst of them thinks he recites very well,*
> *But they will have to go sing elsewhere."*

The court burst out laughing, as did the dwarf Gislebert, but Tristan's face was red with anger.

My father held up his hands for quiet, and when the talk and laughter had died away, said, "I will take my text from the words of Arnaut Daniel, truly the master of the language of Occitan:

> *"To this charming and gracious melody*
> *I compose the words and smooth and trim them,*
> *and they will be true and precise*
> *once I have applied the file to them,*

for Love soon smooths and gilds
my song, which emanates from her
whom Merit protects and guides."

Everyone was listening, rapt and attentive. Especially the Lady Clémence, who had the same expression on her face that Margherita had had when she first saw the new apprentice. My father walked toward her, singing and gesturing with exaggerated ardency:

"I am always improving and perfecting myself
because I serve and honor the most beautiful lady
in the world—this I am telling you openly.
Hers I am from top to bottom.
And although the cold wind is blowing,
Love, which rains deep in my heart,
Keeps me warm even in the dead of winter."

He ended with his hand on his heart, looking mournful and comic at the same time. The others laughed and applauded again, but the Lady Clémence chided him. "These are other men's words. What of your own, sirrah?"

My father glanced at me, then away. "I prefer to let others sing my poor words," he said.

There was a short silence, then Tristan spoke up from behind me. "Let me," he said. The dwarf Gislebert immediately tried to shush him, but he was too late.

"What's this?" the Lady Clémence said in surprise.

"I know his words," Tristan said, with a malicious smile in my direction. "I will sing them."

She looked back and forth between Tristan and my father, whose face betrayed no expression. "Very well, Gislebert," she said. "Let us see if your son shares your talents."

Tristan was Gislebert's son? I glanced furtively from one to the other. Now that someone had pointed it out, I could see the resemblance, despite their differences in build and coloring.

"I shall sing a *canzone* from the *Vita Nuova*," Tristan announced, and struck his jongleur pose.

The *Vita Nuova*? The manuscript my mother would not allow mentioned? I leaned forward, eager despite myself to hear the words that had been forbidden in our household since before I was born.

"As it nears
Its goal of longing in the realms above
The pilgrim spirit sees a vision of
A soul in glory whom the host reveres:
Beatrice!"

That was my name. But I knew at the same time that my father was not referring to me. I looked at him uncertainly, and this time he was the one to look away.

The court applauded enthusiastically when Tristan had finished. The Lady Clémence rose again. "Now this is a puzzle," she said. "I think Tristan must win the prize, because the words he sang were the most inspiring," and she tossed him her ring, which he caught. "But what to do now to reward the man who gave birth to them?" she asked rhetorically.

My father said quickly, "Your pleasure is payment enough, Lady."

She was silent, as though what he said had surprised her. "For your daughter, then," she said. "I understand we mislaid her on your arrival. I would like to make it up to her. Bice, come here."

Did I imagine it, or had she placed a small emphasis on the

name? With a look at my father, who quietly waved me forward, I went.

"What is your heart's desire?" the lady asked me, her eyes dancing. She smelled strongly of lilies and musk, a combination that I found distasteful, and I took a discreet step back while I tried to think of an appropriate reply. Finally I said, "To paint as my father writes, Lady."

"A worthy answer," she said, smiling at me as she had that afternoon in her solar. "What do I have that can help you achieve that end?"

I took a deep breath, glanced at my father again, and said, "Some paints, my lady, and instruction in how to use them."

She bowed her head. "Done," she said. "And now, Bice, I imagine you would like to retire." She signaled to one of her ladies, who stepped forward. "The Lady Isabelle will conduct you to your chamber," she said.

I looked at my father again, who nodded. So I curtsied as deeply as I dared without risking a fall, and went to my soft, comfortable bed and thought about all the ways I would use the colors until, sooner than I wished, I fell asleep.

I woke very early, while the stars were still bright in the sky outside my window. My father was standing by my bed, dressed for travel.

"Papa?" I said, sitting up. "What is it?"

He held out a *camicia* and my chestnut linen gown, and I smelled the lilies and musk the Lady Clémence had worn. "We are leaving, Antonia."

"Leaving?" I repeated stupidly. I looked around the room and saw that he had packed all my things. "No, we can't. She hasn't given me my paints yet."

He sat down next to me and held out my shift. The Lady

Clémence's perfume was strong on his hands and neck, and I moved away to avoid it, but he grabbed my arms and tried to push them through the *camicia's* armholes. "I'm sorry about your paints," he said, "but it would not be prudent to stay."

"Not prudent ... What are you talking about?"

"I have—insulted our hostess," he said.

I stared at him, incredulous, and he took the opportunity to slip the *camicia* over my head and unresisting arms. "You insulted her? How? Why?"

"I refused her a boon," he said.

"What boon?"

He wouldn't answer me, or even meet my eyes. This evasiveness did not match the man that I thought I knew, and it frightened me. I took a deep breath, remembering my aunt's advice in the dream. You can untie yourself, or you can learn to dance. "You can leave if you like," I said, starting to lie down again. "But I'm staying here."

"I don't have time for this," my father said through his teeth. "Now sit up and do as you're told."

"Go on without me, then. I have no intention of—Ow! You're hurting me!" I said as he forced my gown over my head and dragged my arms through the sleeves.

"There is no time," he said, turning me around roughly so that he could do up the laces under my arms.

I fought him, but he was too strong, and I started to cry as I twisted and clawed. "I won't go with you! I won't! You can't make me!"

He didn't even bother to respond as he clumsily tugged a pair of hose up my flailing legs.

"Why should I go with you?" I sobbed. "You don't even want me! You just forget me! I want to stay here, where they are nice to me and there are good things to eat and a bed to sleep in and they give people presents."

He began jamming my feet into my boots, swearing under his breath.

"Just leave me!" I spat out. "What do you care? You'll be rid of me then."

"Why on earth would I want to be rid of you?" he asked, exasperated, as he jammed the second boot on.

I went still, then shrugged.

"Antonia," he said, each syllable as deep and round as a bell, "don't you know why I asked you to come with me?"

I didn't, but I wasn't sure I wanted to hear the answer. I shrugged again.

"Antonia?" he prompted.

I was so tired and so disappointed about leaving without the paints the Lady Clémence had promised me that I just said the words. "Because you and Mama promised Duccio and Taviana that it would be two years at the most and it's already been more than five."

He sat me down next to him on the bed so we could look at each other. "You thought they didn't want you anymore? But you saw how upset they were that I had come to take you away."

I nodded politely. It wasn't really Duccio's family that I was worried about, but it was still nice to hear Papa say that.

"So what is the problem then?" said Papa impatiently.

"Mother doesn't want to have to be responsible for me anymore."

"Why would you think that?"

"She never liked coming to visit," I explained. "She always left as soon as she could, without saying goodbye. And I don't think she liked having to send all those things from the farm, but she felt she had to because I was so much trouble to Tia

Taviana, and probably broke a lot of things." I shot a glance at my father and knew he was remembering the smashed jug of wine and the ruined shirts. "So I think she probably wanted you to take care of me so she wouldn't have to." He didn't say anything, just sat there considering my words. "And maybe," I said, feeling my way, "maybe she thought you'd be sure to come back when you were tired of me."

Papa crossed his arms over his chest and ducked his head, the way he did when he was thinking something through. Finally he dropped his arms and looked me straight in the eye, just like Tia Taviana. "I think that last part is probably partially true," he agreed. "I hadn't thought of it quite that way, but perhaps one of the reasons I invited you, without my being aware of it, was to ensure that I would return to Italy and my family responsibilities no matter how congenial I found my studies in Paris. But your mother never asked me to take you. In fact, she was upset when I did."

I was astonished. "She was?"

He nodded. "I know she looks forward to visiting you on your birthday every year, and feels proud that she can bring things she has grown that will make your life more comfortable. As for her leaving without saying goodbye, she always did, and she made me do it, too. Don't you remember the way I always used to leave on trips before anyone was awake? It was because she never wanted to have to say goodbye to the people she loves."

I sat very still so that I could pay attention to the way the warmth of his words was spreading through my stomach and my limbs.

"But the real reason I brought you," he said, "is that you are my daughter and I love you."

The words came too fast, and I hadn't heard them properly.

"What did you say?"

"I brought you with me," he repeated deliberately, "because you are my daughter and I love you."

A quarter of an hour later, we were riding fast along the road to Tarascon.

OUR LADY OF PARIS

Paris, 1307

We'd been riding for an hour or more in the darkness when we
turned in at an imposing stone gate that my father said
belonged to the Abbey of Montmajeur. It was the only place
between Les Baux and Tarascon that he knew would have
food to sell, and he didn't want to chance a day of hard riding
without any kind of refreshment for us or our horses. So we
turned our mounts free to graze and settled ourselves in the
dusty forecourt and waited for dawn, when the monks would
finish singing Lauds and open the gates. We sat, and I waited
for my father to tell me why we had left Les Baux so suddenly.

But when he finally spoke, his words surprised me.

"I owe you an apology, Antonia, and I want you to know
that it is a sincere one," he said. He glanced at my face and
then away. "I didn't know—didn't want to know, I suppose—
that the trip had been so difficult for you. I had thought it
might be exciting, an adventure—God knows I would have
given my eyeteeth for a chance like this one when I was your
age. And you were such good company that week we waited
for your mother in Siena, not always running on at the mouth
like your cousin Margherita. I didn't know I frightened you. I
thought you just liked to keep things to yourself."

I started to say something, but he held up his hand. "No,
let me finish. I just want to explain—" He glanced at my face
and then away, and swore under his breath, "*Madonna*, this is

difficult." He cleared his throat and began. "You know that your mother and I have been estranged since the *Vita Nuova* started circulating."

The open acknowledgment of a state of affairs no one in my family ever mentioned shocked me. It took me a moment to gather my wits and nod that yes, of course I knew.

"Do you know why that book upset your mother so much?"

It had been a long time ago. I scrunched my eyes closed, remembering Gian's excited whispers and Smerelda's digs. "It was about another woman, not her. And she was angry about that, but also angry that you wrote about things that were no one else's business. And she made you promise that you would never do that to her—talk about her or any of the rest of us in your poems."

"That's right," Papa said as calmly as if he were explaining a Latin idiom from the *Aeneid*. "The woman's name was Beatrice. I first met her when I was a little younger than you are now. I don't know if you've ever known anyone like this, Antonia, but the best way I know to describe her is to say that she seemed to have a candle shining inside her."

I remembered the way the mistress of Les Baux had seemed to gather and refract the light around her like a crumpled piece of gold leaf. "Like the Lady Clémence," I said.

He was silent for a moment, then said slowly, "Not at all like the Lady Clémence, actually. The Lady Clémence uses her beauty and charm the way most of us use our strengths—as tools to help her get the things she wants. Beatrice wasn't like that at all, although for a long time I couldn't tell the difference. But after she died, I realized—"

"She died?" I interrupted.

He nodded. "She died the year before your mother and I

were married. In fact, your Tia Taviana and Tio Francesco talked your mother into marrying me several years before we had planned to because I was so distraught and they thought it might help."

I knew my parents had been betrothed since childhood, and that my father had married at an unusually young age for a man. Now I understood why, and so I asked without thinking, "Did it work?"

It was getting lighter, and I could see the lines around his eyes deepen as he smiled down at me. "Yes, it did," he said, "for—" He stopped.

But I knew what he had been about to say. For a while.

Maybe Papa knew what I was thinking, because he added quickly, "One of the most important things that loving your mother taught me was that I hadn't loved Beatrice the way a man loves his wife. Your wife is your partner. She is like you. You learn things together."

He looked down at me and smoothed back my hair. "I think that's what I miss most about your mother. Having someone to talk with about hard things. She was never very interested in my books, and we frequently disagreed, but we were so different from each other that finding ways to agree was always most stimulating." He smiled at me. "You have her eyes, you know. And her straight back. I always loved her straight back. It made her seem so—gallant, so brave."

"Almost as if she were a man," I said.

"I think I can say truthfully that everything that I find most lovable and most infuriating about your mother is that she is most definitely not a man. And what makes you think that men are not afraid? Childhood teaches everyone to be afraid, Antonia. That's what makes the rest of life interesting—learning how not to be afraid, a little at a time."

But I wasn't ready to hear that my father, who was all that stood between me and the confusion and fear of our journey, sometimes felt afraid. So I turned the conversation back to Beatrice. "So if this lady Beatrice was not your partner, what was she?"

He thought for a moment, then said slowly, "She was a window onto a new world. She had the most beautiful eyes. It wasn't really her eyes, I suppose, but the expression in them. She always looked as though she were looking at what she loved best in the world. Imagine that you were able to feel that kind of love for everything you saw, Antonia. At times it would be painful, of course, but imagine the joy." He took my hand and lightly traced the ebb and flow of my blood down the inside of my arm out through my fingertips and back again. "It would always flow through you, under and around the pain, healing and nourishing your spirit." He patted my arm and released it.

"Beatrice inspired me to consider a way of understanding the world that I would never have been able to find by myself. *Dimmi*, Antonia, have you ever met anyone like that? Someone who opened part of the world that you didn't know was there?"

I thought about it. "Not really," I said. "But I think Tio Duccio did. Every time we went to the *duomo*, Duccio would run his hands over the pulpit and talk about watching it get carved when he was a little boy. He used to run away from his chores every morning and spend the rest of the day watching Pisano make people come out of the stone. He said that until then he hadn't known that people's hands could make things like that, that it was like watching God make the universe, and that was when he decided to become an artist."

"That's it," he said. "Beatrice inspired me to live a more

beautiful life the way the sculpture on the pulpit inspired your uncle Duccio to make beautiful objects. We were both betrothed to other people. I didn't understand, at first, that I loved her because of the things she made me think about. I thought I loved her because she was beautiful and a little mysterious. I was reading a lot of troubadour poetry, and I began to write love poems about her. Then, when I was twenty-five, I contracted a terrible fever. They thought I was going to die, and one night I dreamed that Beatrice was dead. I woke up the next morning and they told me that she had died in childbirth, and it was as if every bit of light and goodness had been sucked out of the universe."

I remembered what it had been like to leave Florence, and shivered. "What did you do?"

"Your Tia Taviana had come home to Florence so she could nurse me. One afternoon after I had recovered I was so miserable that I climbed up to San Miniato—do you remember San Miniato?"

"Of course. That big church on the hill above Florence where the bishops used to go for the summer."

He nodded. "So I climbed up there, where I could be away from everyone, and prayed for guidance. I stayed there all afternoon, but there was no answer. I remember going through the woods on the way down, fumbling for the steps as the afternoon turned to dusk, and feeling completely lost and disoriented. For the first time in my life, I wondered if there was any point at all in going on. But as I came around the corner to the house, I saw your Tia Taviana sitting in the window with your cousin Tommè, teaching him to read by the light of a lamp." He trailed off.

I waited for a moment, but I thought I knew where this was going. "And you remembered the psalm about the word of the Lord being a lamp unto your feet and a guide unto your path," I prompted him.

My father looked surprised. "No, I didn't, Antonia, although I probably should have. Actually it made me think about Saint Augustine. Do you remember that part in the *Confessions* where he heard the child?"

I shook my head. "I've never read the *Confessions*." It was light enough now so that I could see his features clearly.

"Of course you haven't. I was forgetting ... Anyway, like me that night, Saint Augustine came to a point in his life when he had lost all hope. And just then he heard a child singing in the street below, 'Take up and read!' So he picked up the Bible and began to read it, and was saved." His eyes laughed at me. "I was not saved quite so quickly, but there in the darkness it was as if someone had said those words aloud. So the next day I went to see my old teacher Brunetto Latini and he lent me some of his books and bit by bit I became a scholar."

The church bells rang above our heads, startling me.

"So. Now that my experiment with politics has ended in failure," my father said lightly, "I am trying to follow the same advice Saint Augustine gave me that night. I am going to the University of Paris, where there are more books and more knowledge than Florence ever dreamed of, and I hope to take them all up and read."

It took us the better part of a month to get to Paris and, on the whole, it was a pleasant journey. Things were considerably easier between my father and me. Now when he had an idea for the *Banquet*, he sometimes discussed it with me before stopping by the side of the road to make notes. He also took greater pains to instruct me in the words of the poets and philosophers who had meant so much to him,—Vergil (of course), Saint

Augustine, Aristotle, Boethius, and so on. There were still times when he would retreat into himself or become so interested in a conversation with a well-read monk that he forgot about me, but I began to trust that he would, eventually, remember, and so he did.

We arrived in Paris one evening in May just as the light was changing from gold to pink. We entered at the Porte de Saint Victor and, following the guard's directions, continued straight on for a few blocks to the Place Maubert. This was where, Papa told me, his face alight with happiness, the University of Paris had begun, where teachers like Albert the Great had taught students like Saint Thomas Aquinas about the new books of Aristotle that were being discovered in Arab libraries in Spain.

I wanted to share my father's excitement, but I was pre-occupied by trying to calm Jennet, who, like me, seemed overwhelmed by the noise and the crowds that pressed us on either side. I was also tired and had to go to the bathroom, and had forgotten how awful cities smelled. No, I corrected myself as I pulled Jennet's head away from a vegetable stand, no other city could possibly smell like this. I would have remembered, surely, the stench of offal, piss, rotting meat, and dung. I was afraid I was going to be sick, and if I was sick, I would wet myself.

Papa reined Pilgrim to one side, uncomfortably close to the open sewer that bordered the quarter. "Listen!" he said, delighted. "That tradesman is speaking Latin to those students! This is so wonderful—we're in a country of scholars!"

I squirmed in my saddle on Jennet's back. If I didn't get to a latrine soon, I would embarrass my father in front of all these Latin-speaking scholars. I tried to catch his eye, but he was surveying the scene with as much pleasure as a miser counting his gold.

"Where are we staying, Papa?" I asked.

"What? Where are we staying?" he said absently, peering in a stationer's shop that had a dozen books chained to the counter. He didn't notice two students crossing the street and Pilgrim nearly trampled them.

"Papa," I said again, more loudly. "Papa—don't you think we had better get the horses to a stable?"

"Yes, you're probably right, Antonia," he said, pantomiming his apologies to the cursing students. "It seems I'm no better than a drunkard let loose in a wine cellar." He grinned at me over his shoulder so that for the first time I saw the resemblance between him and my brother Gian. "Besides, we've been riding a long time. You'll no doubt wish to refresh yourself."

"Antonia. Antonia, wake up."

I opened my eyes and saw a square of bright blue sky. In the street below, I could hear a woman calling that she had candlewicks, strong, clean-burning candlewicks, and a man singing about his fresh fish. Students were chattering in Latin and another half-dozen languages and laughing too loudly, and mothers were scolding their children. There was another rhythmic sound underneath it all, like the bass note of a choir singing mass, and it took me a moment to identify it as the slap of the river against the shore.

"It's noisy," I said, not fully awake. I sat up, rubbing my eyes. "That's because we're in Paris."

My father, dressed in his street clothes and holding some bundles, looked down at me, amused. "It's after noon, sleepy-head. Here, I brought you something to eat." He handed me some bread and cheese and a beaker of wine. "After I sold Pilgrim and Jennet, I went up to the—"

That woke me up. "You what?"

"I sold the horses to the innkeeper," he said mildly. "They're in the stable downstairs, and you can visit them whenever you like. But we can't afford to keep mounts in the city, and I will have expenses at the Sorbonne."

I pushed away my loaf. I knew he was right, but even though I knew I was being unreasonable, I still felt as if he had sold my best friend.

My father pushed the food right back. "You need to eat a little more, Antonia. I'm taking you over to the cathedral to give thanks for our safe journey, and then I thought we'd explore the city a bit."

I wasn't hungry, but I was eager to see the city, so I choked something down and scrambled into my clothes.

Paris is shaped like a circle with the Seine River running through the middle of it. Its center is the small mid-river island called the Île de la Cité, home to both the royal palace and the cathedral complex of Notre Dame. The island is connected to the Left Bank, with its students and monasteries, by a large stone bridge called the Petit Pont. Our lodgings were only a few steps away from this bridge, and soon we were walking between the small houses and apothecary shops that lined its surface. I imagined I could smell the familiar painting smells of resin, alum, and charcoal as we passed the apothecary shops, and I tugged at my father's hand to stop and look at the colors they offered, but he would neither pause nor let me go.

"You'll have plenty of time to come here once you know the city better and I am away studying," he said. "But right now we owe God our gratitude. Look, Antonia, can you see those spires? That's Sainte Chapelle. Saint Louis built it fifty years ago to house the Crown of Thorns and some fragments of the True Cross that he brought back from the Crusades."

I craned my neck and saw some spires that looked very much like thorns piercing the sky. "Do you think we could go see them?"

"Not without a personal invitation from the king," my father said. "It's his private chapel, and Philip the Fair entertains only those who can bring him money and power. Come on, Antonia, the cathedral is this way."

We stepped off the bridge and turned away from the palace into a narrow street. "So you don't like King Philip?" I asked.

"No," my father said. "Philip is the one whose armies harried Boniface VIII to death at Anagni five years ago."

"I thought you didn't like Boniface VIII?"

"I didn't," Papa said. "But wicked or not, he was the pope, and no king has the right to challenge the pope. Philip is also the one who talked Clement V—"

"The pope we have now?"

"Yes. Philip engineered his election, and now Clement and the papal court have moved to Avignon, where Philip can keep an eye on them. And, my little ignoramus, it was Philip's brother, Charles of Valois, who allowed Corso Donati back into Florence and stood by while the city burned and we lost our property."

Now I remembered Silvana telling me that Charles was the brother of the French king. "No wonder you don't like him," I said.

"No wonder, indeed," my father said. "Fortunately his fraudulent ways have not yet infected every part of Paris."

We had stepped out of the dark little street and found ourselves facing the cathedral of Notre Dame, surging heavenward from the city streets like a prayer. It was the tallest building I had ever seen, and looked even taller since the cathedral square in front of it, the parvis, was so small. The basilica of Saint Trophime that my father and I had looked at in Arles would have fit into this cathedral's pocket, and the sculptured doors that I had thought so beautiful there now seemed stiff and primitive compared to the brightly painted rows of sculpted kings, angels, and prophets that swarmed over Notre Dame's western face.

The colorful statues were so full of life and movement that I was half convinced they were stirring in the soft Parisian light. I looked away, breathless and off balance, and began to climb the large stone steps into the cool, familiar darkness that I knew would welcome me inside the cathedral.

But a statue of Christ was waiting for me at the top. He was teaching from a book and trampling monsters beneath his feet. I had seen many devotional statues of Christ, but none with the roundness, the human force of this man gazing down at me as if he knew me. Mary's son, I reminded myself. He was Mary's son. Of course he was a man like us. But I had never thought of him as a person, as someone I could approach. It was both comforting and a little frightening to think that God could be as close to me as this stone man.

I felt Papa's hand on my shoulder. "He's holding a book," he said with satisfaction.

"Pardon me?"

"Christ is holding a book, Antonia. Do you know what that means?"

I shrugged. The longer I looked at the statue and the more real he became, the more uneasy I felt.

"The priests who designed Notre Dame believed that learning leads men to God," Papa said. "That the more we understand about the way the world works, the better prepared we will be to understand his purposes for us. That's what I've come here to study. Come on. Let's go say our prayers."

I followed him in through the door and stopped dead.

A few years earlier, Siena had experienced the coldest winter anyone could remember, culminating in an ice storm after Christmas. The storm had been a disaster for farmers and herdsmen, but for a seven-year-old it had been nothing short of magic. Margherita and I had spent every minute we could outside in the strange, crystalline world, breaking off icicles and looking through them until the dazzling, frozen white light that encased every stone and every tree broke and re-formed into dancing rainbows.

Stepping into Notre Dame, I felt as though I were looking at the world from inside one of those icicles. The walls shimmered with brilliant colored light pouring through windows soaring so high above my sight line that I had to tip my head back to see that the vaulted interior did not extend right up to heaven.

My father pulled on my arm, and I stumbled after him to light a candle to the Virgin and another to Saint Anthony to thank them for our safe journey. Then we knelt in prayer, but with those luminous colors streaming above my head it was hard to keep my head bent and my eyes closed, even for God.

When our prayers were said, we got to our feet and began to walk slowly around the cathedral. My father stopped at the south transept, peering up at the great rose window there with the same expression of wonder with which he'd greeted the red comet nearly six years before.

I gazed at the great wheel of red and blue with God the Father at the center and the circles of his angels and prophets that spun around him and shared his light. "It's like your golden rose of angels at San Giovanni," I said.

My father shook his head, his eyes on the window. "I never thought I would be saying this, but those are poor, dead images compared to these. Look at the way the light quickens these figures and makes them live. The light of the Spirit of God is pouring its illumination through every part of their bodies, just as it illuminates those who study his word."

"I thought it illuminated those who *obeyed* his word," I said absently. After studying the window for several more minutes, I bowed my head and rubbed my tired neck. I started to take my father's hand, then noticed it was splashed with indigo, gold, and crimson light. "Look, you're holding hands with the window, Papa."

He looked down at me and smiled, brushing a strand of hair out of my face. "And it's dressing you in jewels, my lady of the raspberries. You have rubies and emeralds in your hair."

Then he took my hand, and he didn't let it go.

THE BÉGUINAGE

Paris, 1307

We emerged from the cathedral some time later, blinking in the unaccustomed brightness. Our next errand was enrolling my father at the university. Luckily, the chancellor's office was located a few steps away, in the bishop's palace. The palace was a crowded, busy place complete with an outdoor market and uniformed guards but with nary a woman in sight. With me clinging to his hand for dear life, Papa shouldered his way through the vegetable, fuel, and meat stalls and then the throngs of workmen perched with their tools on the palace steps, spitting and joking while they waited to be hired.

The interior of the palace was no quieter. The church court was here, and officials guarded the gates and talked desultorily with one another. Students who had come to pay fees or collect allowances played dice in the hall and blocked the stairs. Clerks, bailiffs, and church archivists recorded transactions and kept records on portable desks that they moved around the chambers and halls of the palace so they could capture whatever light managed to pierce the small windows of the fortress. Despite the tapestries on the wall and the heavy, polished furniture, the palace was a confused and noisy place and I did not like it. We waited for one official after another until the correct documents had been copied, signed, and witnessed and the fees paid, by which time my legs were sore and my stomach empty.

Papa bought us each a pasty from a vendor on the church steps, and we took them to the canons' close on the north side of the cathedral. The close was not open to laymen, of course, but the gardens sloping down to the river made a pleasant sight from our spot beneath an old chestnut tree.

"There's a library in Notre Dame that's open all the time," my father said, his mouth full of pasty. He must have been hungry, too, to forget his manners that way. "Did you see it?"

I shook my head. "I just looked at the windows."

"Me, too," he admitted. "I talked to some students from the Sorbonne, and they said I could borrow some of the texts I needed from the library and rent some of the others. I was thinking that if you aren't too tired we'll go find a stationer after we eat."

I sat up. "Are we going to the street of illuminators?" I asked.

"Not today," my father said. "They said you could rent them more cheaply from the Beguines."

"The what?"

"Don't you know what a Beguine is?"

I shook my head.

"Well, you're about to meet some," he said. He pulled me up, I dusted off my seat, and we started across the muddy planks that served as a footbridge from the cathedral to the Right Bank. "A Beguine is a woman who has taken a vow of chastity but not one of poverty."

"Like a rich nun?"

"Not rich, certainly," my father said. "But they are allowed to earn money from their labor. They live in communities, in houses of their own, and they are free to come and go. They can even give up their vows and decide to leave permanently."

"So, not so much like nuns," I said. Once nuns took their

vows, they were required to stay inside their convents for life, isolated from all contact with the outside world.

"Not so much," my father agreed. "Some Beguines have been married before, and some even live with their children. Mind the mud—I think we go this way." We turned right, away from the center of the city.

"Why don't they have Beguines in Italy?"

"There are a few, but many people think it is unseemly for women to live unsupervised and they dislike the competition of businesswomen whose expenses are small. Look at us, for example. We're going to the *béguinage* because the Beguines can survive on less than a man who has a large family to support, so they can charge less for book rental."

"But what else can a woman without a husband do?" I asked.

"If she doesn't have a dowry to become a nun? Starve or become a prostitute, I suppose," he said without much interest.

I was shocked. "That's it? There aren't any other choices?"

"My dear Antonia, the plight of the destitute is simply a fact of life, and there's not much that one poor man can do to change things."

We walked on in silence, past boats unloading hay and rye on the firm sand in front of the Place de Grève. I was watching a porter trying to navigate a wheelbarrow of paving stones down a narrow gangplank when he spoke again.

"You'll have a dowry, if that's what you're worried about."

Actually, it hadn't even occurred to me that I wouldn't.

"By the time you're ready for marriage, we'll be back in Florence and things will have returned to normal." His voice turned dramatic. "Young men will travel from every corner of the civilized world to beg for your hand, bearing caskets of jewels and royal birthrights, and your mother and I will have to don court robes every time we want to see our grandchildren."

I giggled.

We had come to the corner of a stone wall that was considerably higher than my father's head. One side extended in front of us for what looked like at least a quarter of a mile along the river, and the other leg ran several blocks inland. "This must be it," my father said. He gazed along the length of the two sides for a gate or at least a porter's window, but there was nothing. "They are certainly well protected," my father murmured. "Let's hope they will let us in."

When at length we found the entrance gate, it was open. We passed through and found ourselves on the greenest, softest lawn I had ever known. A rectangle of stone houses of similar design, each shaded by two trees in front with a garden plot behind, surrounded the green, which included flower gardens, public wells, a simple chapel, a large, two-story hospital, a flour mill, and a fuller's mill. It was a fine day, and almost every dooryard was occupied by one or two women dressed in plain gray-brown robes, spinning flax or embroidering brightly dyed fabrics. It was quiet—the quietest village I had ever been in. No children playing, no raised voices, just quiet, sober labor. When we stopped to ask a gentle-faced elderly woman directions to the stationer, she directed us to a small house set at some distance from the others, across the way from the millpond. We thanked her and made our way down the paved, swept street.

As we grew closer, the sweet, fetid smell of skins rotting in quicklime told us why this particular house was set at a bit of a remove. Here, too, a woman sat working in the sun, but she was considerably younger than the others we had seen—more of a girl than a woman—and instead of needlework, she was carefully stretching a small, scraped skin on a frame to dry—rabbit or squirrel, by the size of it.

"Est-elle ta mère ici?" my father asked, each word loud and distinct as though he were talking to a deaf old woman. I glanced at him, startled, then back at the girl, and realized that she had the broad, flat face, tilted eyes, and large tongue of a simpleton.

She stared at us for a moment, saying nothing. But when my father started to repeat his question, she answered in thick, hard-to-understand French, *"Des amis pour ma Tante Matelda. Des amis pour ma Tante Matelda."* Still chanting the words, she ran loose-limbed and flat-footed toward the front of the house, which like many workshops had a window that could be opened out into a counter during business hours. No woman sat at the window, however, and the girl opened the door and ran inside, calling for her Tante Matelda.

As we waited for her to return, I saw that, as well as the smelly vat of skins, the yard was dotted with several drying frames, rinsing barrels, and a shield-shaped wooden beam for finishing the rinsed skins.

The girl reappeared, leading a broad-hipped, fair-haired woman with clear gray eyes. *"Des amis pour ma Tante Matelda,"* the girl repeated, tugging at the woman's hand.

"Est-ce que je peux vous aider?" the woman asked us.

I could feel my father stiffen. "Matelda?" he said in an odd voice.

Her fair skin went red under its dusting of freckles. "Dante? Is that you?" she said uncertainly. Her accent was Florentine, like my father's. "What are you doing here?"

"I've come to study at the Sorbonne." And then, as an afterthought, "This is my daughter, Antonia."

"Bice," I corrected automatically.

The woman smiled at me. "What a pleasure to meet Dante Alighieri's daughter," she said, her face and neck still red.

"Your father and I were great friends once upon a time."

"Matelda was a friend of Beatrice's," my father said. He bowed. "I fancied myself more than half in love with her before your mother and I were married."

"I think the term that I heard used was 'screen lady,'" Matelda said, her eyes dancing. "Your father pretended he was in love with me so that no one would suspect the real object of his de—" She glanced at me and changed what she was going to say. "Affections."

My father looked discomfited.

"But I unwittingly ruined his clever plan by leaving Florence and going to keep house for my brother in San Gimignano."

"So how did you come to be here?" he asked.

"My brother opened an office in Paris," she said. "I accompanied him here, and clerked and kept house for him. But about a year after our arrival he stepped on a long splinter and his foot became infected. He was dead in a week. So I took what money there was and came here."

"You're the stationer?" my father said.

I thought this rather slow of him. "Who did you think she was?" I asked.

He seemed flustered. "I don't know. I hadn't really thought."

Now she was laughing at him openly. "I am the scribe, and my friend Claire is the illuminator. We have a profitable little business here."

"And you manufacture your own parchment?" my father asked.

She nodded. "The hospital is frequently paid in small game animals. They use the meat and then send the skins on to us. Claire's daughter, Sagesse, helps us prepare them."

"Sagesse?" my father said, one eyebrow quirked.

Matelda looked at him as though he had made an embarrassing noise at dinner. "Yes, Sagesse," she said, and then, without turning, added, "Ah, Claire! Come see a pleasant surprise! Here is my old friend Dante Alighieri from Florence, with his daughter, Bice."

Claire, a slight, vivacious woman with dark hair and eyes, came quickly forward and inclined her head. "You are welcome here," she said in slow, thickly accented Italian. "You will excuse me, please. I must help my daughter."

I saw that she was holding a lunellum, a knife with a moon-shaped blade that is used to prepare parchment. I noticed further that her hands were swollen and chapped. Pietro's hands had looked like that when he worked with limewater. That was why he had taught me to scrape the parchment for him. When I left Siena, I was just getting good enough at scraping the wet pelts that I took pleasure in the grace and efficiency of my movements.

"Would you like me to help?" I blurted, then shrank back, alarmed by my effrontery.

She held up her hands, grimacing. "*Tiens*. You see the limewater is not good to my hands. I wish you could help, *chérie*, but it is more difficult than it looks."

"My uncle is a painter. I help him trim parchment all the time."

Claire hesitated. "You have done this before? Used a knife, I mean?"

"A lunellum? Many times."

She hesitated again, then handed me her knife. "Let us see how you do, then."

I rubbed the smooth handle of the knife for a moment, gauging its weight and balance. I hadn't realized how much I'd missed having things to do that I was good at. I took a firm grip on it, took my position behind the beam, and began the long, lovely, loose strokes that pared the hair from the skin. I could feel Claire's eyes on me, but I didn't care. My hand and shoulder remembered the rhythm of the task, scraping just deeply enough to remove the shiny outer membrane underneath the hair, but not so deeply that the blade poked through the delicate, floppy skin.

Sagesse had been watching, and she was not pleased. "*Nous ne touchons jamais le couteau,*" she said loudly. She came over to me, wagging her finger and shaking her head while she repeated, "*Nous ne touchons jamais le couteau, nous ne touchons jamais le couteau.*"

My French wasn't very good, but she spoke slowly and I could hear the common words under the unfamiliar accent. Girls were not supposed to touch the knife.

"*Ne t'inquiétes pas, cherie,*" Claire reassured her. "*Bice peut toucher le couteau.*"

"Bice?"

Claire took Sagesse's hand and touched first her chest, and then mine, then Sagesse's again. "Bice is our new friend. Sagesse, Bice. Bice, Sagesse. Bice can touch the knife. But Sagesse must never touch the knife."

"*Sagesse ne peut pas toucher le couteau,*" the girl repeated, shaking her head sadly.

"But Sagesse can stretch the skins. She is the best one at stretching the skins. *Sagesse est la meilleure à étirer les peaux.*"

"*Oui,*" Sagesse said with a broad grin. "*Je suis la meilleure à étirer les peaux, moi,*" and she mimed stretching out the skins.

The long, smooth strokes of the knife were familiar and soothing. I fell into a contented daze, aware only of the muscles in my shoulders bunching and then relaxing, bunching and relaxing, and the warm weight of the sun on my neck. Matelda and my father were still talking, and they called a question to Claire. She got up and went over to them, and then the three of them went into the house. Some bees buzzed among the poppies. My shoulder was beginning to ache, but not badly. I hadn't used these muscles for too long. There. The first side was done.

A small, broad hand with short fingers tugged on my arm. I jumped and my knife slipped. For one sickening moment I thought I had gouged the precious skin, but there was no mark. "Bice can touch the knife," she said in French, mimicking a scraping motion. Then she shook her head and looked sad. "Sagesse cannot touch the knife. But"—she brightened—"Sagesse can stretch the skins."

I stood back so she could release the skin from the beam and stretch it out, flesh side up. She sang tunelessly while she worked:

"Sagesse stretches the skins,
Sagesse stretches the skins,
Sagesses stretches the skins until they are tight as a drum.
Rat-a-tat-tat. Rat-a-tat-tat.
They are tight as a drum."

I imitated her while I waited for her to finish stretching the skin. *"Sagesse étire les peaux?"*

She stopped, confused, and I repeated the phrase.

"Sagesse étire les peaux?"

"Oui," she said cautiously.

"Sagesse tend les peaux?"

"Oui!" she said, a broad grin stretching across her round face.

"Sagesse tend les peaux sont qu'un tambour?"

"Non, non, non!" she scolded. *"Sagesse tend les peaux*

jusqu'à ce qu'ils soient aussi tendu qu'un tambour."

I repeated obediently. And when I finally had it right, Sagesse beamed and hugged me as though I had done something brilliant. *"Bice est une bonne fille,"* she praised, rubbing her dry but curiously soft cheek against mine. *"Bice est une bonne fille, et elle est mon amie."*

"Bice *is* a *bonne fille,"* Matelda said from behind me. I turned, startled, to see that three adults had emerged from the house, my father with some folded quires of parchment under his arm. Matelda examined the skin. "You do very good work, Bice," she praised me, then winked. "You are almost as good at scraping the skins as Sagesse is at stretching them," she said in French.

I blushed, pleased, and when Sagesse pouted at hearing that I had to leave and the others invited me to come back the next day while my father was at his lectures, I didn't hesitate. And thus my father and I began our French educations at the same time, his at the Sorbonne and mine at the *béguinage.* Of course I returned as often as I could. The inn was lonely and a little frightening without my father, while the *béguinage* offered friendship and, as time wore on, good work to do.

At first I did nothing but prepare skins and keep Sagesse company. She was prone to wandering off and visiting whatever animals she could find—cats, dogs, the chickens and geese that were kept behind the house, the pigs that rooted in the forest, a peddler's broken nag, the sparrows who ate the crusts of our bread from her hands. She stayed closer to the house when I was there, partially because she enjoyed my company but even more because she was teaching me French, and she loved bossing me around. For all her severity with my mistakes, however, she was a patient and diligent teacher, and since I have my father's gift for languages, I learned quickly.

Eventually I began to be useful in other ways. I prepared inks and pens and applied gold leaf. Occasionally I delivered completed copies, or went to the market while Matelda cooked and while Claire, when her shoulder wasn't bothering her, did the cleaning and mending. They began to treat me as a kind of favorite apprentice. They'd had their hands full between Sagesse and the business, and Claire was beginning to suffer from rheumatism in her shoulder. It seemed silly to spend so much time walking the long distance from the Left Bank to the *béguinage*, especially after my father was offered free lodging with the other Italian students at the Sorbonne, so I moved into their tidy little cottage. On Sundays and holidays I met my father at Notre Dame for mass, and then we would spend a few hours exploring the city and sharing whatever food he had brought for us. It was a good life, and I was content.

THE TEMPLARS

Paris, 1307

The first interruption to our pleasant routine was the Feast of the Assumption in the middle of August. It's a happy time of year, when the first wheat has been harvested and bellies are full again. I had promised to take Sagesse with me to see the stained-glass animals at Notre Dame, and when the holiday came we ate a good breakfast and left early, since walking was difficult for Sagesse.

We got as far as La Grève before our first stop. A young boy was napping in a skiff tied up at the docks with his pet monkey on a lead next to him. Sagesse was in transports, and it took a good twenty minutes to pull her away. Then it was a cage of bluebirds hanging out a window above a shuttered shop, and then a pig running through the streets with a small girl pulled along behind him.

By the time we got to the cathedral, I was sweating and worried that my father had come and gone. But he was waiting for us in the shade of the Saint Anne portal as he had promised, and did not seem perturbed when Sagesse sat down in front of a trained bear performing acrobatics in the parvis and refused to budge.

"Won't go," she said, as I tried to pull her to her feet. "I want to watch the bear."

"It's all right," my father told me. "We're really too late for the mass anyway. Let's just let her watch."

When the bear had finished and been led away by his trainer, Sagesse breathed a happy sigh and slowly got to her feet.

"Sagesse, what a wonderful treat to have you with us!" my father said. "And how lucky we got to see the bear."

She giggled. "He was funny."

"He was funny," my father agreed. "Was it a long walk to the cathedral?"

"There was a monkey," she said. "His name was Gérard. He had a green collar."

My father looked impressed. "You saw a monkey named Gérard?"

She nodded enthusiastically. "With a collar. He had a green collar."

"That's splendid," he said. "Come see the Noah window, Sagesse. There are pictures of Noah's ark and his animals."

"And some birds," she said. "And a pig. And a monkey. With a green collar. And a bear who stood on his head, like this." She tried to demonstrate, but my father picked her up and stood her on her feet.

"There are more animals inside, you know."

"More animals?" she said.

"Animals in the glass," he said.

"I know. Bice told me. We came to see the animals in the glass."

"Let's go, then," he said, and led her into the cathedral before she could change her mind.

It was a good thing that we had missed the mass, because Sagesse was so excited by the window she couldn't contain herself. She kept pointing out all the animals she could find, and then worrying about the evil people drowning in the sea, then comparing the ark to the boat we had seen that morning, then looking at the rainbow and back at the animals again. I didn't really pay attention to either the window, which was normally one of my favorites, or Sagesse's pleasure, but let my father carry the burden.

The only way we could get her to leave the window was by promising to buy her a sweetmeat from a vendor outside. Once that was done, however, she wanted to stay and wait for the bear to return. We told her that he wouldn't be back, that he was home taking a nap, but she didn't believe us. Finally we resorted to a guessing game.

"Can you guess who I would want to be if I lived back in Noah's time?" I asked.

Sagesse loved games, and without thinking she got to her feet and began to follow me as I started walking home. "I know!" she said. "I know! You'd be a bear and do tricks."

"No." I shook my head.

"Noah's wife," my father guessed.

"No."

"A monkey!" said Sagesse. "A monkey with a green collar!"

"No."

"A fish in the ocean, so you wouldn't have to live in that filthy, crowded ark," my father said.

"Close," I said. "You guess, Sagesse."

"A pig."

"No."

"A camel."

"No."

"An elephant."

"No."

"A lion."

We were safely across the footbridge and well on our way to the *béguinage*. "I'll give you a hint," I said. "We saw a picture of it in the window."

Sagesse thought hard. "I know!" she said excitedly. "The

dove! The dove that flies away and finds the branch!"

"Good for you, Sagesse!" I said. "How did you know?"

"I am a wise child," she said smugly. "That is what my mother always says."

Then we guessed what my father wanted to be. Sagesse got it on the first guess: Noah. But neither my father nor I could discover what she wanted to be. After ten minutes or so, I gave up, but my father wouldn't. "A panther?" he guessed. "An eagle?"

She shook her head vigorously. "Shall I tell you?" she asked.

"No, no, I will get it," he said. He thought for a moment. "Is it a real creature? Could it be a griffin or a unicorn?"

"It is real," she said, her tilted eyes dancing with fun. "But it is not a creature."

"But we've already guessed Noah and his family," I said.

"But it is the boat!" she crowed. "I mean, the ark! Noah's ark!"

"The ark?" The possibility had not even occurred to me. "Why the ark?"

"Because it is the ark that keeps everyone safe," she explained. "Without the ark, everyone drowns."

My father laughed her. "Your mother was right, Sagesse. You are a wise child. That is the best answer of them all."

Sagesse was so pleased she practically pranced the rest of the way home.

Matelda and Claire were waiting for us, watching a round dance in the square in front of the gate to the *béguinage*. "There you are," said Claire. "We were beginning to get worried. Did you have a good time?"

"We saw the animals," Sagesse said, and yawned. "My feet hurt."

"Let's get you home and have a little rest together," Claire said. "It has been a long day for you, and my shoulder is bothering me again."

The pipes and the dancing began again.

"No, I don't think so," said Sagesse. "I am going to stay for the dancing."

Her mother laughed. "No, you're not, my lamb."

But Sagesse pushed out her bottom lip. "I want to stay for the dancing. Those girls don't look much older than me."

"You want to dance? Yourself?" her mother asked.

Sagesse was already trying to imitate some of the steps. "I am a maiden," she said. "I am going to dance with the others."

"No, Sagesse," her mother said firmly. "You have already had a long day. It is time to go home now."

"But I want to stay," Sagesse said, and began to run toward the dancers.

Matelda was too quick for her, however, and caught her by the arm. "Sagesse, *chérie*," she said urgently. "Listen. I have an idea. Those girls and young men have been practicing for a long time to dance like that. How about if we practice at home before you dance in front of everyone? They will be *étonnés*. 'Look at Sagesse!' they will say. 'She is so graceful, such a natural dancer.'"

"But we have no music," Sagesse said. "How will we dance?"

"I have my brother's lute," Matelda said, with her eyes on my father. "And I know someone who can play it very well."

He looked surprised, then bowed and smiled. "I am at your command, my lady," he said. "I will have you know that I have played and sung at some of the greatest courts in Europe."

"You play the lute?" I said, astonished.

"I do," he said. "I was rather famous for it as a young man. But your mother does not approve, and neither, most of the time, do I. But I think we can make an exception just this once, don't you?"

Sagesse nodded. "Oh, yes, please!" She wasn't jumping up and down—quite. But she looked as if she might soon.

"But now I think you must rest, my lady," my father said, taking her hand and kissing it. "Court entertainments do not take place until the evening."

"And what will you do between now and then?" Claire asked, rubbing at her shoulder absently.

My father shrugged. "I have no business today. You have taken such good care of Antonia, I feel I am in your debt. Are there any little services I could perform for you?"

"Yes," said Matelda, so quickly that I thought she must have been waiting for him to make that offer for quite some time. "Yes, as a matter of fact, there is. I have several volumes I have copied for the Templars, but the Temple is quite a long way from here, too far for Sagesse to walk, and there are too many manuscripts for me to carry by myself."

"Nothing easier," he said promptly. "And we will make Bice trail behind us to ensure that not one precious scrap is allowed to drop to the dust."

"Splendid," Matelda said, looking enormously relieved. "I must confess that this delivery has troubled me. One of the Templars would come eventually, of course, but once a copy is completed I prefer to return it to the owner as quickly as possible. We have no strongbox, you see, and they are just so valuable ..." She heard her voice going on and stopped abruptly, coloring. "If you're sure you can spare the time?"

"Lady," my father said, mimicking his gallantry to Sagesse of a moment ago, "I cannot conceive of a better use for this lovely afternoon than to be of service. That I will do so in your company makes the prospect all but irresistible."

Sagesse giggled loudly. "You are so funny, Ser Dante."

I laughed too, but my laugh was a little forced. This was all reminding me a little bit too much of the Lady Clémence.

We didn't talk much on the way to the Temple. It was a long walk to the Porte du Temple at the northern edge of the city, and then it was twice as far again through a marshy plain and up the long hill that the Temple crowns. By the time we got to the entrance gate, a marvel of chased iron and massive oak set in formidable gray stone walls, I was tired and ready to be overawed.

The Templars were one of Europe's most glamorous and admired religious orders. Huge, bearded men, they combined the knightly virtues of strength and bravery with monastic vows of obedience, chastity, and poverty and had protected Christian pilgrims to the Holy Land for two centuries. Even Saladin, the leader of the infidels, had admired them and feared their great fortresses. The Crusades had ended, of course, and there were fewer pilgrims to the Holy Land for them to protect now that the Muslims controlled Palestine, but the Templars were still brave, romantic figures, and I was a little afraid of meeting one. The closer we got, the smaller and younger I felt.

The Brother who answered our summons looked the part of a Templar. Although he greeted us with the calm self-possession I associated with monks, he was more than six feet tall, with the broad, square chest and full beard of a knight and a voice as deep as my Tio Francesco's. "Ah, we have been waiting for these!" he said in delight. He took the stack of manuscripts and laid them gently on the wide counter that separated us. He examined them one at a time, gently running his big, calloused hands over the bright, springy pages with as much reverence as my father might have shown. I found the sight of a man who looked like a knight hovering over parchment like a scholar disconcerting.

He glanced up and caught me looking at him. "And who are you?" he asked, his candid eyes seeming to see more of me than I wanted him to. People didn't usually notice me, and I didn't know how to react.

"I am the parchment manufacturer," I said, the words sticking to my throat so I could barely dislodge them.

"Your parents must be grateful for your assistance," he said. There was no mask here, as there was on most people in a city. He spoke to me as naturally and intimately as if we were members of the same household, and I didn't like it. I felt exposed.

I wasn't sure how to correct his assumption about my father and Matelda without offending him. Matelda began to explain, and I slipped behind a clump of half-grown trees, from which vantage point I could see without being clearly seen myself. The Templar reminded me of someone. Who was it? When he picked up the books and began to say something, I realized that his face looked very much like that of the teaching Christ at the entrance to Notre Dame.

"It will take me a few minutes to locate the librarian and for him to fetch your payment," he was saying. "You must be tired after your climb. I will send for some refreshments."

He left, and my father and Matelda turned to look at me behind the trees.

"What was that all about, Bice?" Matelda asked. "You scurried away like a little mouse."

"I do not care for strangers," I mumbled.

"That is true," my father said. "Whenever we met someone on the road to Paris, Bice would curl into a little tight shell, like a snail who had been poked with a stick."

"I have never seen it," Matelda said. "I would not have thought you such a timid little miss."

Even if I hadn't already known that the Templars were rich, I would have known by the refreshments that were brought to us. I had expected a dipper of water, and maybe a crust of black bread. But we were given big, round floury rolls and cool watered wine. After we finished consuming every bit of the repast and my feet had been sufficiently soothed by the cold water of an obliging little stream, I was revived enough to look around.

Normally I would have sat and listened to my father and Matelda reminisce, but most of their shared memories seemed to be about Beatrice, which made me feel uncomfortable. There wasn't much to see, though—just the big stone fortress surrounded by meadows and, behind us, the road leading back toward Paris. I thought of Margherita, and wondered what she was doing. Gathering wildflowers for the Virgin, probably, the way we did every Feast of the Assumption. Well, there were flowers here, too, just as in Siena.

"I'm going to make a Lady Bundle," I told the adults.

To my surprise, Matelda said, "What a good idea! I'll come with you."

My father looked a little disappointed, but there wasn't much he could do about it, especially because flowers make him sneeze. So Matelda and I left him there.

The meadow was full of Lady flowers: white Assumption lilies, of course, which bloom every year on the feast, wild roses, Queen of the Meadow, Lady-by-the-Gate, and poppies, sometimes called Our Lady in the Corn. We brought armfuls back to the bench and wove them into garlands and put them in our hair. We made enough for Sagesse and Claire, too, and when the purse finally came my father had to carry it because our arms were so full of sweet-smelling flowers that bees followed us all the way home. And that night, in a meadow just outside the Porte Barbeel, my father played Claire's lute and he and Matelda sang and she taught Sagesse and me how to dance, just as if we were ordinary girls.

I was awakened early one October morning by the tolling of church bells and the sound of a great army of horses galloping by the *béguinage* wall. Next to me in bed, Sagesse began to whimper. "It's all right," I comforted her as I sat up. "Everything's fine." Through the blue shadows of the pre-dawn hour, I saw that we were alone in the living quarters. The fire was made up, but the cauldron that should have been steaming porridge over the fire was still on the hearth, and a loaf of yesterday's bread had been thrown down on the table in front of it, half sliced.

We called for Claire and Matelda, and when there was no answer, pulled on our clothes as quickly as we could. No one was in the front room, either; the rows of inks and paints and the stacks of parchment looked just the same as ever. But the door was ajar, and I could feel the chill of the early morning mist across the room. Abruptly, the bells stopped. "Get your cloak, Sagesse," I said.

But Sagesse didn't budge. "Where is my mother?"

"I don't know, Sagesse. Look, here are your sabots. Put them on."

"Where is Tante Matelda?"

"I don't know," I said, slipping into my own shoes and shrugging on my cloak. "You need your cloak. It's cold outside."

"They were naughty to go away. We always tell each other where we are going."

I had her by the arm now and was pulling her cloak over her. "Yes, they were naughty. Let's go find them."

"We have to tell them that we are going to look for them, or they will be cross."

"All right. Come with me and we will find them."

At length we got out the door. The dooryard was empty and the mill wheels across the way were still, as was the city behind us. But something was happening to the north, out by the Templars' fortress. There was a weird orange glow, and I could smell smoke, not the friendly smell of cooking fires, but the heavy, acrid stuff that I had last smelled the day Florence burned.

Thoroughly frightened now, I pulled Sagesse toward the *béguinage* chapel. That was where everyone would be. And they were, the whole village. I looked for Claire's tiny form and Matelda's broader one, but Sagesse found them first, near the entrance portal where Frère Dominique, the Dominican priest who served as the community's confessor, was standing.

The meeting, whatever it was, had just ended. The Beguines who were our neighbors slipped by, their faces as closed as if we were strangers. They didn't even stop to greet Sagesse, who was usually a great favorite, but she was too intent on reaching her mother to notice.

"What's happened?" I asked Matelda as we reached her.

Her face, usually so transparent, was as closed as everyone else's. "The king is arresting the Templars."

I couldn't believe it. "Philip is arresting the Templars?" I asked, incredulous.

Frère Dominique glanced sharply at us, and Matelda shushed me. "Let's get you girls home," she said. "We'll talk about it there."

I thought about the Brother who had greeted us at their gate, and the way I had felt the same power and kindness from him that I had felt from the statue of the Christ at Notre

Dame. How could anyone be brave enough to arrest people like that? And why would the king arrest them? Weren't they led by the pope?

Matelda closed and locked the front door before joining the rest of us in front of the fire. "Why is the king attacking the Templars?" I asked again.

"They say," began Matelda carefully, "that the Templars have been engaged in unnatural and illegal activities offensive to God and his holy—"

"Nonsense," snapped Claire. "The Templars no more engage in unnatural practices than we do. The king wants their property. It's as simple as that."

Matelda looked uneasy. "But surely Frère Dominique wouldn't—"

"Frère Dominique will say exactly what his superiors tell him to say," Claire said impatiently. "He's a priest, and he's taken vows of obedience."

"Don't worry, girls," said Matelda, her broad face looking pale and tense beneath its cheerful freckles. "It really has nothing to do with us."

"I wouldn't be so sure," Claire said, and stood to put the porridge on the fire.

"What do you mean?" I asked nervously.

"Only that if Philip is strong enough to take on the Templars, he is strong enough to take on anyone. He's already got the pope in his pocket. Clement V must have agreed to this—not even Philip would dare do this without the pope's support. He must have paid him a pretty penny."

"Claire," Matelda rebuked her. "You are speaking of the pope."

"I know, Matelda. That's what's worrying me. Who's left to stand up to him?"

There was a loud banging on the door, and we all jumped guiltily. Claire went to the door and we heard muffled voices. Then she returned, followed by—

"Papa!" I said, running to him and hugging him.

"Antonia, thank God," my father said, his face as pale as Matelda's. "When they said the Temple, I thought perhaps the Beguines might be drawn into it as well."

"What is happening in the city?" Claire asked him.

"Terrible things," my father said. She took his cloak and he nodded his thanks, then sat down on a stool as heavily as if he were Nonno Manetto. "They're arresting everyone who might be connected to the Temple. They burst in on us this morning before it was light. One of the boys who share my quarters has a brother who is a Templar. They took Elias, who can't be much older than your brothers Gian and Pietro, Antonia, and when he said he knew nothing, they tortured him—coated his feet with fat, then held them to the fire until they burst into flame." He pressed a shaking hand to his mouth. "The boy hadn't seen his brother for a decade. It's ghastly. It's obscene."

Papa stood up and began to pace restlessly around the room. "Someone has got to stop Philip. Underneath that smooth, handsome face and all the graces and jewels, he is nothing more than a festering bag of poison and evil. First he has Boniface VIII murdered, then he sells the papacy to Clement, and now he's destroying the Templars, the last incorrupt brotherhood. Philip the Fair? Paugh!" he thundered, as if he were the prophet Jeremiah himself. "He is Philip the Foul, Philip the Vile, Philip the—"

"Hold your tongue," Claire said sharply.

My father had the grace to look shamefaced. "My apologies, ma'am. I forget myself."

"You certainly do, sir," she said. "We've enough trouble with mutterings about witchcraft as it is. We don't need treason on top of it."

I knew she was talking about Sagesse. Like twins, simple children were widely believed to have been begotten by devils in human form.

"I should go," my father said abruptly, looking around for his cloak. "That was foolish of me. I don't want you to be the victims of talk because I am here."

"Oh, sit down, for heaven's sake," Claire said irritably. "I shouldn't have said that. It was cowardly, and I can't abide cowards. We don't get enough visitors, and I'm sure all of your lectures will be canceled. They've probably closed the Petit Pont, come to think of it, until things calm down. Spend the day with us."

My father looked startled. "But you are holy women," he said. "I can't stay in your house."

"I don't think there's anything wrong with a father visiting his daughter from time to time, do you, Matelda?"

Matelda shook her head. "Nothing at all," she said. "Claire is right, Dante. The city will be dangerous today. You should stay here until this evening. Frère Dominique has already left, and he is the only one who could be dangerous to us. Please." She tried to smile. "Else Bice will spend the day worrying about you and not get a brushstroke done, and we have a Book of Hours that is promised for next week."

"Do stay," Claire urged. "It will help pass the time to have a new voice around the table. We have all said everything we have to say to each other, and it would be nice to have the company."

And to my surprise, and I think to his as well, he did.

After breakfast, Claire, Matelda, and I uncorked our inkhorns and began to work on manuscripts while Sagesse fetched a stack of folded parchment gathers and began the laborious process of ruling lines on them. My father borrowed a penknife and set about sharpening every quill the workshop possessed. When that task was done, he took up a stack of raw parchment and began to rub pumice on its surface to absorb its greasiness and improve the surface for writing, as he did for the parchment he bought for his own manuscripts.

"How is it," he asked Claire, "that a Flemish woman like yourself came to be at a *béguinage* in Paris?"

I looked up, interested. Although Claire had a quick tongue, she never talked about herself. She looked as if she'd rather not do it now, either, but answered readily enough. "My husband made stained glass in Bruges. I helped color the cartoons for his windows—that is how I learned to paint. And sometimes there was a banner to decorate, or someone wanted a small decoration on a letter, and soon we made a good living. But we had no children, which was a sorrow to us. One night, we went for a walk along the top of the dikes—there are stone dikes there, as high as a man, to keep out the sea."

My father nodded. "We have the same thing in Italy, along the Brenta," he said.

"It was a beautiful night. The moon was out, and the sea was silver, and there was a mist. But it seemed so sterile and cold, as though the dike were not keeping us safe but walling us in, and I thought, If I stay here, I will be like this, sterile and cold, and I didn't want that to happen. So I turned to Piet and said, 'God can't hear our prayers here. Let's go on a pilgrimage.' And Piet, who was always very good to me, agreed. And so we began our travels. We went to Chartres, and Saint James Compostela, of course, and Rome, and Canterbury—just everywhere. We had no trouble finding work; there's always a need for a good glazier at a cathedral, and for an illuminator as well. We stayed for a year in each place, then moved on. We saved Paris for last—I don't know why. We had talked of going to Jerusalem after Paris, but I said no, I was getting too old for children, and the traveling was hard on Piet. So Paris was our last stop, and then we were going to go home." She took a breath and glanced at Sagesse, who was working away, her tongue between her teeth.

"It was then, after I had given up hope, that I discovered I was pregnant. We were so happy. Piet teased me that I should have been named Sarah and his name should be Abraham, and we decided that if the baby was a boy we would name him Isaac." She glanced again at Sagesse, and spoke more quietly.

"But then, when the baby was born, he was upset. He wanted me to give it up, but I knew it—she—would not live if we left her at the Hôtel Dieu. It was hard for her to suck, and I knew they had no time to help her. We had a little money, and Piet gave it all to me, then he left. I knew about the *béguinage*—there is a large one in Bruges—and so I came here and took the house. And you know the rest." She became very absorbed in a griffin she was drawing.

"But how extraordinary," my father said gently. "What an adventurous and brave life you've lived."

Claire blushed. "It wasn't me," she said. "I'm just ordinary. It was because God put it in my heart to long for Sagesse. He knew what I could do when I did not, and he sent me a wise child who is happy and good to teach me what I needed to become."

I suddenly realized, feeling like a fool, that "Sagesse" meant wisdom. I had never thought of it as a word before, just as a collection of sounds that meant my friend. I looked at her again as she mumbled to herself and ruled the long, even lines. I had never considered, either, that problems could make you wise and strong. Had my journey made me wise? I wondered. Had my secret griefs made me strong?

I felt a cautious warmth spreading across my chest as I loaded my brush with burnt sienna and carefully began to fill in the planks of Noah's ark.

ADIEU

Paris, 1307-1309

After that day, my father accompanied me back to the *béguinage* every Sunday after mass at Notre Dame to share a meal with Claire, Sagesse, and Matelda. It was a cold and rainy autumn. He brought small gifts when he could—an egg or two, or a fine squirrel-tail brush—but the Beguines assured him that my labor more than outweighed any small expense they might incur on my account.

Time rolled on. Matelda taught me a common scribal alphabet, then another. I began to help Claire illuminate initials, then paint drolleries in the margins, then animals and people. Spring came again, and we had been in Paris for a year. Then it was fall, and then, too quickly, winter.

That second winter was particularly difficult. An outspoken Beguine named Marguerite Porete had moved into the community, and both King Philip and the church authorities were watching us carefully, which was nerve-wracking. My father's visits became irregular, so as not to draw undue attention to Claire and Matelda. Sagesse, who was prone to illness, battled one feverish cold after another until she seemed to be wasting away before our eyes. Claire began to concoct nourishing stews and teas, but they did little good. Claire herself was not in good health. Her shoulder had become so painful that she could no longer build a fire and many days could barely hold a brush. I took over most of the illuminating under her supervision, but of course I was much slower than she was and my illuminations were less beautiful, so both the supply and the quality of our manuscripts began to fall off. In a poorer household, this adjustment might have been enough to make us hungry, but Matelda reassured me that they had a little gold put by.

Then one morning in December, shortly after my thirteenth birthday, I woke up early. My feet were cold, so I pushed them behind me, feeling for the warmth of Sagesse's body. But when I would have burrowed my feet under her bottom, her limbs were stiff and unresponsive. And the bed was silent, utterly and completely silent.

I twisted round, horror clawing at my throat. Her eyes were closed as if she were asleep, but I already knew she was dead.

I must have made some noise, because Matelda, who was entering the room with an armful of firewood, said in a tight, high voice that didn't sound like her at all, "Bice? Bice, what is it?" But I had no words to explain.

Claire's quick footsteps approached the bed, and then the blanket was pulled back. I tried to pull it up over Sagesse again—the room was cold and I wanted her to stay warm—but Claire batted my hands away and began to keen, her face as blurred and crumpled as a terrified child's.

I backed away as Matelda took Claire in her arms. Although we had all tried to pretend otherwise, I was not part of this family, and I didn't belong here. The next thing I knew I was half walking, half running along the windy bank of the Seine, moving away from the *béguinage* and the closed circle of Claire and Matelda clutching Sagesse's dead body to their breasts.

I wanted my father. But I suddenly realized I didn't know where he lived, or what lectures he attended, or where they might be. There was no way for me to contact him. I was cut off. Hot tears blurred my vision, then froze on my cheeks in the cutting December wind.

Unaware of having made a decision, I found myself at the feet of the teaching Christ that guarded the entrance to the cathedral. I looked up at him and saw the face of the Templar staring back at me, seeing more of me than I was ready to show. I turned away and ducked into the anonymous darkness of the cathedral.

Once inside and safely away from watching eyes, I went looking for the living light and warmth of the Noah window—Sagesse's favorite story—and first sat, then later lay, on the floor in front of it. Was Sagesse in heaven with Noah? Would he find her and tell her that I was sorry, that if I had just listened more carefully I would have heard the rattle in her throat and boiled some water and sat with her in the steam until the breathing was easier?

But although the window glowed for me when I first arrived, it was an overcast day, and by the time I left the colors had dropped from the air, and all that remained was dark, dead, rough-hewn glass held together by strips of cold, dusty lead.

I have only one clear image of the funeral: Matelda's face as she held a sobbing Claire against her shoulder and watched Sagesse being lowered into the cold winter ground. The patience with which she accepted her suffering lent her features the dignity and timelessness of carved stone. I thought that she had never looked so beautiful, and it is the way I remember her still.

The house was much quieter with Sagesse gone. Too quiet. No more hugs and kisses at unexpected moments. No more indulgent smiles and pats from the other Beguines in the community. No more getting bossed around. Oddly enough, that was what I missed the most. No one told me what to do anymore. I had to figure out what to do when and then discipline myself to achieve it without any outside help. No matter what I did, I found myself worrying that it might have been better if I had done something else. If I made breakfast, I was sure I should have been airing the linens. If I worked on a miniature, I thought I should have been copying text. If I painted a gown brown, it should have been purple. Food began to disagree with me, and I ate less.

If it hadn't been for my father's weekly visits and the odd customer, I think Claire, Matelda, and I would not have spoken at all. A wealthy benefactor had donated a quantity of candles to the *béguinage* in return for our intercessory prayers for her son, a knight who died before he could be shriven. We were grateful for them—it meant we could work later before taking ourselves off to our beds, where the three of us would lie stiff and silent for hours, willing ourselves to sleep. Reverting back to the fears that had visited me when my mother first left me in Siena, I struggled up out of sleep several times every night, sure that someone else had been taken. I'd lie there calming my breath until I could hear two distinct breathers, then drift off to sleep for another hour or so before starting awake again.

Spring eventually arrived. The fields came back to life, especially the bright poppies and sweet-smelling honeysuckle that Sagesse had loved. The supply of pelts from the hospital, which had trickled to a stop during the winter, picked up again now that it was lambing season, and soon I had more scraping and stretching and rinsing than I could easily handle. My arms grew strong, and I began to sleep and eat better. My clothes fit more snugly, and I realized with a pang that although I had felt beautiful in them on our journey, they must have hung on me so that I looked like a little girl playing dress-up.

Matelda, too, seemed to find peace. Her broad face was thinner and somehow stronger and more definite and she was not as quick to laugh as she had been, but neither was she frozen in her grief. We began to speak of Sagesse from time to time, remembering the small kindnesses she had done for us and even laughing at the funny things she had said or done. But while Matelda found composure and I grew stronger, Claire seemed to shrink within herself. Her shoulder was worse. It became difficult for her to sleep, and Matelda moved into my bed with me. Claire had always had a sculpted face, but now her skin seemed stretched across bones so sharp I wondered they did not pierce her flesh. Even my father noticed. He started visiting more regularly again, and brought small delicacies to tempt her appetite—a fistful of greens, a pomegranate, a hatful of cherries. Once he brought a small bottle of brilliant blue ink, although she hardly touched a brush. He'd stay for hours, sitting with her in the dooryard, reading or reciting to help distract her from her pain. At first he read to her from his *Banquet*, but it was too technical to keep her interest, and eventually he went back to reciting Vergil and Ovid as he had for me on our trip, and that seemed to soothe her.

Finally she could stand it no more. She had a lump, she said. It had started the size of a plum, but now was the size of a large orange, and unless we could find someone to cut it out for her she thought she was going to go mad from the pain. So my father found a barber-surgeon and brought him to see us at Whitsuntide, along with a large flagon of very strong wine. The barber warned her that cutting into flesh often ended in putrid infection and death, but she begged him to try it anyway. So she drank down the wine and he sliced into her shoulder, but the mass was white and nearly as tough as bone, and there was nothing he could do.

After the barber had stitched up the wound and she had finished retching up the wine, she spoke to each of us, thanking us for our friendship and love, and then said it was time for her to join her daughter. "I am going home to Sagesse," she said when we wept and pleaded with her not to give up. "I am sure God will have healed her poor mind, and I am looking forward to meeting the woman she has become." Then Claire turned her face to the wall and neither ate nor spoke again.

She died three days later.

Once again I revisited the familiar pattern of grief, this time overlaid with a new kind of guilt. The truth was that I was glad she had finally died. I was glad that I no longer had to bear her suffering and Matelda's worry, glad that we could sleep through the night, glad that I no longer had to be ashamed of my growing body or my appetite or even the pleasure of another spring.

In fact, I was beginning to chafe at the quiet rhythms of life at the *béguinage*. The very rules and routines that I had once cherished as a source of protection and predictability grated. I felt as though I had been infected with Gian's restlessness and could not push it away. I began to take long walks, but they were not enough.

Matelda did not prove as resilient to this second bereavement as she had to the first. She turned inward, and spoke very little. Any kind of interaction with me or anyone else seemed to require an effort from her, as though we were calling her back from another place she preferred to be.

One unseasonably hot day at the end of June my father came for a visit. This was unusual during the week, and I flapped about a bit, concerned that we had already eaten our dinner and had no scrap of refreshment to offer in this hungriest of months. He brushed my apologies away, telling us he'd had a fine supper and for heaven's sake to stop flittering and sit down like rational creatures, that he had something to tell us.

So we sat down with him at the table, our hands folded attentively without the distraction of quill or parchment, and waited.

He didn't seem to know how to begin, however, and sat twirling a quill between his fingers. "I've had a letter from the boys," he said abruptly.

"What boys?" I asked stupidly.

"Your brothers. Pietro and Jacopo. They have finished their education and are ready to take their vows, but they feel they have no vocation."

I tried to think why he might have made a special visit to tell me this. "Are you thinking of bringing them here?"

He ran his fingers through his hair in an abrupt, bothered gesture. "I don't know. I don't know what to do. I have been—disenchanted by the climate at the university."

"You have?" His words surprised me. "I thought you loved it there."

"I loved the promise of it," my father said. "But the reality has been different." He kicked backward from the table and began to walk around the kitchen. "No one seems interested in truth. The most important thing is the art of argument. Lectures are nothing more than a dazzling show of dialectic, of theses and antitheses and puns and rhetorical flourishes. That is not what I came here to discover, but it seems that that is all I am offered—the art of sounding learned, rather than the learning itself."

He paused, but Matelda and I were silent.

"And even the learning—you saw that the best I had to

offer was no comfort to Claire when she was ill." He stretched out his hands and then touched the inkstains on his writing hand one at a time. "I have begun to wonder if all of this was a fool's errand. The learning I took such pains to acquire seems to have been of little benefit to me or anyone else."

He straightened his stooped shoulders. "I was thinking of returning to Italy," he said. "Perhaps I was wrong to allow others to educate my sons, and if I did not take my degree, there would be a little money to support us until I am able to find a patron. Corso Donati, my most important enemy, is dead—killed by mercenaries while trying to avoid arrest," he couldn't help adding with some relish. "Maybe the Florentines will be ready to see reason. And if they aren't, I still have prospects. The pope is no longer as strong as he once was, and he's in Provence instead of Italy. And the emperor talks of returning to Italy—perhaps, in time, I could serve him."

Henry VII of Luxembourg had recently been elected the Holy Roman Emperor, a position that theoretically made him the political leader of both the German and Italian states. "But if I were to return," my father continued, "I don't know what would become of you."

For one horrible moment I thought he was talking to me, but then I saw it was to Matelda that he was directing his gaze. She returned it, looking like her usual calm, unruffled self. "You needn't concern yourself with me," she said.

"I know I needn't," he said testily. "And perhaps you'll say I shouldn't, but despite the rumors that I'm sure surround my every visit, I mean no disrespect. But I am grateful for the many services you have rendered me and my family, and it would be wrong for me ..."

She was laughing. She put a hand on his arm, and said, "If you'll just let me finish, Dante. I was casting no aspersions on

188

your intentions. I know—who better?—that they are entirely honorable." She took a deep breath. "But I too have been thinking. Bice has been like a daughter to me, and I haven't wanted to send her away. But at the same time …" The calm smile that was as much a part of her face as her fair skin or her clear gray eyes dropped away, and I caught a glimpse of the grief Sagesse's death had stamped on her face. "I am tired of this life. I have tried to do my duty to both God and man, but—" She shrugged and opened her hands, palms up. "I'm not sure that I still have it in me to lead an active life, out in the world. There have been too many disappointments. They say nuns serve God by listening to him, and right now nothing sounds sweeter than withdrawing from the world so that I can hear God better."

Practical, sensible, capable Matelda was going to shut herself up as a nun? What kind of nun? If she became a Poor Clare, the Franciscan order that idealized poverty, she'd be dead in a year. I looked at her as though I had never seen her before. "You're not going to be a Poor Clare, are you?"

"Heavens, no," she said with some asperity. "I'm not *that* tired of the world. I like eating and I like staying warm. I think I am better suited to the Dominicans. Even if they don't want me, they'll be glad enough for my books."

My father shook his head, whether in admiration or disagreement I could not say. "You are so good at managing the things of this world that I never thought of you as a nun. But I daresay you'll be a good one, if that's what you really want. As for you, Antonia"—he reached for a packet inside his cloak—"I have a letter I've been asked to deliver. Your Tio Duccio has been given an important commission, and he and your Tia Taviana want you to come back to them and help with the household. Would that suit you?"

Oddly enough, my first reaction was relief. I hadn't realized how completely drained I was from the grief and responsibility of our shrunken household. "Yes," I said, reaching for the letter. But then I couldn't open it. Tears were welling in my eyes, tears too private to share even with Matelda and my father. I looked down and made a business of putting the letter in the pocket I wore around my waist, but I think Matelda must have seen because she slid a little closer to me on the bench and put her arm around me.

"It's not exactly what any of us planned, is it?" my father said. "But I suppose having one's plans disrupted by Providence is the human condition." He stared off into space for a moment while I got myself under control, and then he put his hand down heavily on the table. "So. I think this momentous occasion deserves a toast."

He produced a flask of wine, and I got some cups. He poured out three equal portions and then bowed his head for a moment, thinking. He stood and raised his glass, and we did the same. "To Claire, who loved her daughter and who made not only her manuscripts but her home a work of art that blessed and healed all who tarried here. To Sagesse, truly the wisest of us all, who taught us that the greatest use of human life is in assisting others to become their best selves. And to Matelda, who reminds all those around her in all she says and does of the promise of redemption and new growth. May she experience in her new life the eternal bloom of hope and refreshment with which she has blessed all those lives that have touched hers."

We drank.

A week later, my father and I passed through the city gate for the last time and turned our horses southeast, toward the Alps. Along with the sketchbook Tio Duccio had given me and the blue silk from Gian, I now had a set of brushes, some bags of pigment, and three illuminated manuscripts tucked in my saddlebag.

But after all this time, I couldn't make myself believe that Taviana, Margherita, Feo, Duccio, and all the others were really there in Siena, waiting for me to come home to them. What I did know was that I was once again saying goodbye to the people with whom I had made a family.

HOMECOMING

Tuscany, 1309

This trip was very different from our first. For one thing, we were accompanied by two young clerks who worked for Sers Biche and Mouche, bankers from San Gimignano who kept an office in Paris. They were irritating, callow lads and I would have preferred to be rid of them, but they knew the road well and made us less vulnerable to robbery. For another, although the Alpine landscape we passed through possessed a strange, wild beauty, I did not respond to it with the intensity of our first trip. Most of my attention was devoted to mourning Sagesse and Claire, as well as Matelda, who I felt was as lost to me as if she too were dead.

My father had abandoned the *Banquet* and had begun a new work of political philosophy, which he called *The Book of Monarchy*. It was meant to be a defense of the new Emperor Henry VII, a defense that he hardly seemed to need. Every hostel and inn was abuzz with news of him. King Philip had made no secret of the fact that he had hoped to have his brother, the detestable Charles of Valois, elected Holy Roman Emperor, but Henry was so virtuous and noble that even cowardly Pope Clement V had found the courage to stand up to Philip and support Henry's election. Henry was generous— he had given property away to various noblemen, and reduced taxes. Henry was witty and wise, at his ease with subjects hailing from every corner of the empire, from northern

Germany all the way to Sicily, while Philip was known never to speak in company. Even Henry's wife, Margaret of Brabant, was said to be as intelligent and learned as any of Philip's court scholars, and welcoming and gracious besides.

And now he had left on his coronation journey to Rome and his soldiers with him. No, he was waiting for more men. Clement V had withdrawn his support. No, Clement had sent him twenty thousand gold pieces. He had left Luxembourg. He was at Paris. No, he'd gone to Frankfurt. Or was it Bruges? It didn't matter—wherever he was, men were flocking to his cause. Europe finally had an emperor worthy of the name.

My father hung on every word of this gossip as though he were a kitchen wench being sold a love potion. "It's as it should be," he said again and again. "After the dark night of our trials at the hands of the foolish and the greedy, God has heard our prayers and has sent us an emperor to restore all things."

His fevered anticipation overcame him the afternoon we emerged from the mists of Saint Bernard's Pass to see Italy spread out before us. He began to weep. "It's almost over, God be praised. The hour of redemption is come. We'll be home by Christmas, Antonia. Easter at the latest. Now at last we have an emperor worthy of Vergil's words," and he quoted from the *Aeneid*:

"In Italy he will fight a massive war,
Beat down fierce armies, then for the people there
Establish city walls and a way of life ...
For these I set no limits, world or time,
But make the gift of empire without end."

"I don't know what you're so worked up about," grumbled Luca, the shorter of the two clerks. He pushed his lank, greasy hair off his pimply forehead. "A strong emperor is going to be bad for business. He and the pope will just fight back and forth, with the rest of us caught in the middle. The only thing emperors have ever brought Italy is blood and taxes. They're not worth the trouble."

My father, who I think was as tired of our companions as I was, didn't even turn around. "Men require monarchs to establish justice so that they can live together with civility."

Andreas, Luca's companion, wiped a drip off his enormous nose. "We already have a pope, and he's monarch enough for me."

"Popes rule men's souls, while emperors rule their bodies," my father said.

I had no wish to hear any more of this, so I didn't. With the ease of much practice, I was back at the *béguinage*, copying animals onto a scrap of parchment for Sagesse while Matelda set out dinner and Claire told us what Soeur Marie-France had seen the last time she had taken a length of her fine embroidered wool to sell at the castle. Then I wondered, as I always did, where Sagesse was, and if her mind had been healed and she had animals to keep her company, and if she missed me the way I was missing her. I hoped she and Claire were together. It would be much less lonely that way.

The two days after we left the clerks in San Gimignano were the longest of the trip. It was the wheat harvest, and the roads were hot and dusty. It was more difficult than usual to find accommodations or even bread for sale, since anyone who could be spared was at work in the fields, and I began to worry that perhaps Duccio's household had left the city. He had a small vineyard outside of Siena, but I wasn't sure exactly where it was. I couldn't picture resuming my former life. Too much had changed. And I soon had myself convinced that my uneasiness about the reunion was an indication from God that something would prevent its happening.

So I wasn't surprised when we arrived in Camporeggio to find Duccio's house shut up tight. We banged on the bolted door—it, like everything else in Siena, looked a little smaller and a little shabbier than I remembered—but there was no answer. They were gone. They'd packed up and left Siena forever—or maybe there had been a fever. Ridiculous fears chased themselves around my head for a minute or two until old Pietro the comb seller hobbled into view, out to fetch water in a chipped earthenware basin.

"Good day, Nonno Pietro," I greeted him.

"Good day," he replied, his gums working. He stared at me suspiciously.

"It's me, Bice, Duccio's niece," I said, stepping closer. "Let me take that basin for you."

He peered at me for a moment, our faces close together. I had grown taller, or perhaps he had simply shrunk in the way of the very old. He worked his gums, then finally recognized me.

"Bice! Of course! Duccio's niece!" he said. "Why didn't you say so?"

I lifted the basin from his gnarled fingers as the years slipped away and I remembered Pietro's kindnesses to the small, scared young girl I had been.

"I thought you'd gone. They said you'd gone," he said.

"I was in France," I said. "With my father."

Papa gave the old man an elegant bow, and he looked pleased.

"Where's Duccio?" I asked while Papa took the basin from me and filled it at the fountain.

"Not here, not here," he said.

The fears that were slowly melting away under the flood of memories tightened in my chest again. "Where did they go?"

He pointed up the hill behind us. "They have a fancy new house on Via Stalloreggio," he said. "Said he needed more room. Told the commune that if they truly wanted to honor the Virgin, he needed a larger place with bigger windows, more convenient to the *duomo*." He shrugged. "So. They are gone."

"But not from the city," I repeated, making sure.

"No, no, not from the city. He's working for the city."

"Thank you, Nonno. I was afraid that something terrible had happened."

"*Prego*," he said, the toothless smile splitting his wrinkled face as familiar and reassuring as the smell of baking bread. "You are home now, Bice?"

"Yes. I've come home," I said. And knew that it was true.

THE MAESTÀ

Siena, 1309–1311

They were at dinner. I breathed in the robust scents of Tia
Taviana's good Tuscan cooking and realized just how much
I'd missed it, how pale and unsatisfying French food was after
all. There were benches enough for everyone in this fine new
stone house, a fireplace right in the *sala*, and fancy iron lantern
brackets studding the walls. If the lanterns were all lit, the
room would be light enough for handwork even on a dark
winter's night. The adults looked just the same and the children a little taller, but—was that Margherita? She had a
woman's body, with full breasts pushing out the front of her
gown and her collarbone clearly visible beneath a long, elegant
neck. And who was the handsome boy she was sitting next to?
I felt my breath catch in my throat. Then he smiled at me and
I realized he was Margherita's cousin Segno. The whole table,
it seemed, was surging toward us, hugging me and clapping
my father on the back and exclaiming over how well we
looked, and here we were at last, and how were the roads?

I looked down, overwhelmed by the press of people, noise,
and emotion. But not for long—Feo launched himself at me
and I had to put up both hands to catch him. Then Tia
Taviana had me in a hug so tight I could feel each one of her
ribs, and Duccio was patting me on the shoulder so enthusiastically I thought I would lose my footing. By the time we had
all gotten ourselves sorted out and I was sitting between

Margherita and Feo, it was as if I had never left.

Except for Segno. I kept looking at him out of the corner of my eye. He had always been a skinny little thing, but now he was a head taller than my father and his shoulders were at least twice as broad as they had been. His dark hair was thick and straight and the eyebrows over his black eyes as definite as a man's, but he held his mouth as stiffly as the shy boy he had been two years earlier.

I looked away and caught the glance of another young man seated across the table who looked vaguely familiar. He continued to observe me, unembarrassed to be caught watching. I couldn't place him at first. He was shorter than Segno, and built more powerfully, with lighter hair and eyes and a face that was all planes and angles, with small, well-formed features. Some unpleasant association nibbled at my mind, but it wasn't until I looked away that it came to me. It was Pietro's brother Ambrogio, the one whose shirts I had ruined—or at least spilled wine on, I amended. No doubt Tia Lucrezia had gotten the stains out, and he had been very rude. I had nothing to feel guilty about. But I was careful not to make eye contact again.

"I have missed this good bread," my father was saying as he broke off a hunk and dipped it in a dish of pale green olive oil. "You have no idea."

"How long can you stay?" Tia Taviana asked.

"Just until the morning, I'm afraid. I'm eager to get to Lucca to see the boys."

"Well, we're certainly glad to have Bice," Taviana said. "The Maestà is half killing all of us. Duccio can't keep enough assistants in the workshop, and Lucrezia and I are nearly run off our feet trying to keep them all clean and fed."

My father took a piece of fish. "You should think about

putting Antonia to work in the studio, too, Duccio. She boarded with some illuminators in Paris, and her work is quite good for a girl of her age."

I looked at him, surprised, and he winked at me. He's going to miss me, I realized with a warm spurt of pleasure. Then, before I could stop the words, And I will miss him.

"She always did have a sure hand," Duccio said, beaming at me. But I was suddenly so bereft at the thought of my father's leaving that I took no pleasure in his compliment. "Well, we'll have to see. The Maestà is such an important project that they've had me sign all sorts of documents swearing that no one will touch it but me, blah, blah, blah." He shook his head in disgust. "Why they did that I'll never know. They know as well as I do that no painter can afford to do every stroke of the work himself—it would take ten times as long. But still, I'm having to keep a pretty tight ship."

"Don't you give him any ideas," Tia Taviana scolded, wagging her finger at my father. "He's got plenty of help. It's me that needs the help. There's Andrea married and living in Murlo, and Margherita will be next, and Lucrezia and I will be left alone with all these men and driven to an early grave."

I laughed with the others, but when I tried to catch Margherita's eye I saw that Segno was whispering something to her and she was blushing furiously. I glanced at my father and saw that he had not missed the byplay. He raised an eyebrow at me, and I made a little face in return.

When we were by ourselves in the bedchamber we shared, Margherita and I were shy with each other at first. Once we had blown the candle out and settled in bed, she asked me, "What was France really like?"

I tried to think of an answer, but nothing presented itself. "I don't know, Margherita. Different."

"Different how?" she wanted to know.

"In lots of ways." I was too tired to think that hard. "Could we talk about this in the morning?"

"Of course," she said.

The silence between us grew uncomfortably long. I tried to think of something to say, but my mind was a sleepy blank. Finally I asked one of the questions that had been troubling me at dinner. "I have something to ask you, but you have to promise not to laugh."

"Cross my heart," she said promptly.

"What exactly is the Maestà?"

Margherita sighed dramatically. "The Maestà—oh, the Maestà! I hope I never hear the word again." She crossed herself hastily. "Not that I mean any disrespect to the Virgin. The Maestà is an altarpiece for the *duomo*, the cathedral, with the Virgin in her majesty on one side and scenes from Christ's passion on the back, and more paintings from the life of Christ on the top and sides. The commune is determined to make it bigger and better than anything they have in Florence, as big as that whole wall, and they've given us this house and a lot of money and all the materials we need for free. So naturally my father is worried that it won't be good enough no matter what, and so he's always in his studio, and when he's not, he's shrieking at everybody and making them do everything a hundred times."

"They gave you the whole house?"

She giggled. "He told them it would be too difficult to bring things up and down the hill from Camporeggio. All the other artists are mad with jealousy. Simone Martini—do you remember him?"

"Was he the assistant before Pietro?"

"Yes. Well, he's come back as an assistant after all this time, he's so eager to work on it."

"Where is Pietro? I didn't see him at supper."

There was a long pause. Had she gone to sleep? "Margherita?" I tried again.

"He's in Castiglione d'Orcia. It's his first commission. A Madonna."

"Good for him," I said. "Although I'm surprised Duccio didn't want him for the Maestà."

"Pietro's eager to set up his own workshop," she said.

"Really? Is he courting someone?" I yawned. "He's a nice boy, even if he does look a little bit like a fat lizard."

Dead silence.

"Margherita?"

Still nothing. Then a small, stifled sound. Was she crying? What had I said? And then my sleep-fogged mind finally realized what I should have guessed long ago: Pietro was courting Margherita. "Oh, Margherita, I'm so sorry," I gulped, mortified by my clumsiness. "I didn't mean—"

"Yes, you did," she said in a thin voice. "You always thought he was ugly."

It was true. I always had. Suddenly, horrifyingly, I felt a giggle rising in my throat. "Don't be mad at me, Margherita," I gasped. Then I snorted and was gone. "I'm so sorry," I managed between whoops. "It's not what you think—I'm not laughing at him—it's just I always say the wrong thing ..."

Now her choking sound was louder. I was such a clumsy idiot.

"That's right," she managed. "You always did," and then she whooped.

I sagged with relief, and then we were in each other's arms laughing and crying and gasping for breath, and it was all right.

After breakfast the next morning, Duccio took my father and

me to the studio to see the Maestà. He had Ambrogio, who was polishing some gold leaf, and Segno, who was in charge of the cabinetry, lay the half-finished panels out on the floor so we could get some idea of the total effect.

Once they had stood back, Ambrogio with a little mocking bow, I felt the way I had the first time I'd seen the stained glass in Notre Dame: the altarpiece was more beautiful, more urgent and alive and splendid than anything I had encountered before. Its power did not lie entirely in the colorful brilliance of Duccio's brushstrokes, graceful though they were, but also in the sense Duccio had somehow conveyed that the painting was true, that it was a window onto a way of being and understanding that I dimly recognized and almost remembered.

My father finally spoke. "*Talia per clipeum Volcani, dona parentis, miratur rerumque ignarus imagine gaudet, attollens umero famamque et fata nepotum.*"

"What's that? What's that you say?" Duccio said.

My father said nothing, rapt before the shimmering panels of the altarpiece.

"It's from the *Aeneid*," I explained. "Venus has Vulcan forge armor for her son Aeneas, including a shield that's decorated with images of the great deeds the Romans will do. Even though Aeneas doesn't understand what all the pictures mean, he is awed by the power and beauty of his quest."

Duccio heaved a huge sigh of relief. "So it's a compliment. I was afraid he was swearing in one of his fancy languages."

"No, it's a very great compliment," my father said, coming out of his trance. "Great beauty like this must inspire great love, and I am one who, when Love inspires me, takes note."

Ambrogio raised his polishing rag to hide a grin. That was when I decided to hate him.

An hour later, my father was ready to go. I accompanied him as far as the Porta Camollia, then handed him two tow bags I had woven and sewn. Inside the first was an illuminated Book of Hours I had made to help my mother with her daily devotions. The other held an astronomical almanac I had copied for my father. The almanac had been one of our most popular manuscripts, the work of an Arab Jew from the university at Montpellier. "I remembered how much you liked the comet," I told him. "Remember? The night before you left for Rome? And I thought you might like to know about the stars and seasons and things."

He said nothing for a moment, just stared down at the manuscript in his hands. "I forget how carefully women listen," he finally said. He brushed his hands over the painted linen binding I had sewn the quires into, then replaced it in its bag. "I have received many gifts in my life, Antonia, and this is one of the best. God bless you, child. I will miss my traveling companion." He kissed my forehead, then mounted his horse and rode out the Porta Camollia without looking back.

I was happy to be back in Siena. I loved the anonymity of being one among many again, with no need to live up to any particular standard of excellence or self-discipline. After Margherita had pulled me away from half-done tasks two or three times and Tia Taviana had been publicly exasperated but then let the matter drop, it dawned on me that the adults expected us to seize any opportunities to shirk our work, and I was glad to oblige. Not that the work was particularly distasteful; I enjoyed the familiar routines of cooking and weaving and laundry and gardening. I didn't miss illuminating at all.

In fact, this was one time when I was happy to avoid the studio altogether. As Margherita had told me, the Maestà was taking its toll, and the workshop rang with oaths and tears. Segno and his father were in charge of the carpentry and the finishing of the panels, and walked around looking like ghosts, with bits of plaster sticking to the hair on their arms and legs. Sunny-natured Feo, who had been promoted to apprentice, began to spend his leisure hours at the public stables off the *campo*, as far away from the tension at home as he could be. As for Ambrogio, Duccio fired him at least twice a week. Every once in a while Ambrogio, who had a temper of his own, would take him at his word and strip off his smock and pack his things, and there would be a new round of tears and shouts and imprecations.

The Maestà affected the women's work as well. We had to weave more drop cloths, and the men were constantly interrupting us for egg whites for their paint and bits of cheese for the glue they used for the panels. And there were more bodies to clothe and feed and clean up after. But I didn't really mind. I liked being part of a bustle, and I liked being around people my own age.

We were part of a neighborhood brigade, Segno and Margherita and I, that went on picnics and to performances in the cathedral square and walked to and from church and other public meetings together. When the day's work was done, we would call on Christina, the barber's daughter, and Luigi, the innkeeper's son, and Isabelle and Lorenzo, whose fathers were bankers. I had never been part of a large group of friends, and although I didn't say much, I enjoyed getting to know the families and interests that made up the commune of Siena.

One afternoon in early October, Margherita and Segno and I were sitting on the stone wall from which I used to watch for my mother. The city was quiet; most people, including the rest of our household, were in the country helping with the grape harvest. Margherita and I had been left behind because there wasn't room for everyone in the wagon and we were girls and not as much help as the apprentices, and Segno had stayed to put some finishing touches on one of the panels and to mind the shop. But he'd finished early, so we'd locked up and come along to the wall, from which we would be able to see Duccio returning.

We were eating grapes and having a contest to see who could spit the seeds farthest. Margherita was winning. "Pietro had better watch out," Segno teased her. "He doesn't know what he is getting."

She spit another seed even farther. "Nonsense," she said smugly. "He knows exactly what he is getting, and that is why he is a happy man. Although he won't be if he doesn't hurry up and send me a letter. I haven't heard from him in nearly two months."

"Does he know how to write?" I asked, surprised. I remembered Tia Taviana teaching the apprentices how to read, but not how to write.

"Of course he knows how to write," said a scornful voice over my shoulder. It was Ambrogio, red-faced and sweating, back from his cousin's farm with a basket of cheeses. "Just because he's not some hoity-toity scholar flitting off to France and Germany and leaving all the real work to the people at home doesn't mean he's a complete illiterate."

I flushed angrily. "That's not what I meant."

"You never 'mean' anything," he said. "You are the most insincere person I have ever met. And the clumsiest."

I gaped at him.

"*Zitto!*" said Segno sharply. "What's wrong with you, Ambrogio?"

"I will not *zitto*," Ambrogio said. "I'm sick of the way

everyone is always tiptoeing around her as if she were something special. 'Bice did this' and 'Bice did that' and 'Poor Bice—can you imagine, having parents like that?'"

There was a long silence.

"Like what?" I asked. "Parents like what?"

Margherita and Segno both started to say something, but I ignored them. "I'm asking Ambrogio," I said. "Parents like what, Ambrogio?"

"Parents who care nothing for themselves or their children," he said slowly and distinctly. "Parents who are the laughingstock of their community. Parents who refuse to acknowledge when they are not want—"

The cheese I had seized from his basket hit him full in the face, and he went over like a ton of bricks. His head hit a paving stone with an ominous crack, and his eyes rolled up in his head.

Margherita ran to him while I stood frozen. She put her hand to Ambrogio's neck, then jerked it back again.

"Is he … Is he …" I couldn't finish the sentence, even to myself.

"No, no," she said. "But he's burning up."

Ambrogio groaned, opened his eyes, and started to sit up. I recoiled and started to sob—both of his eyes were bathed in a hot crimson wash of blood. They were open for only a second—the effort was too great and he slumped back to the ground almost immediately—but I will never forget the sight of those sharp, knowing eyes shrouded by that obscene red. I still see them, sometimes, in my dreams.

I thought I was going to be sick; then the ground was tilting toward me. Segno caught me and propped me half sitting against the wall.

"It's all right," he said, patting my shoulder gingerly. "I'm sure he'll be all right. It looks worse than it is."

"Oh, holy Virgin, what have I done?" I moaned. "He's an artist. What will he do? Where will he go?"

"He's not blind, Bice," Margherita said. "He looked right at us and focused and everything."

I clutched at the straw she offered me. "Do you really think so?" I gulped.

"No question," Segno said. He patted my knee and stood up. "Wipe your eyes, Bice. You're going to have to help us get him home."

We somehow got Ambrogio home and in bed, although I'm sure I was no help at all. He came back around as soon as we sponged him with some cool water, but he wasn't rational. He did seem to be able to see—he was raving about the lizards on the wall that had come to eat the Maestà, and why wouldn't anyone help him drive them away?

Segno fetched Giannelli, the barber who lived on the next street whose daughter was in our brigade. They emerged from the bedroom looking serious.

"He's not blind," Segno said. Giannelli, who wasn't very talkative, pursed his lips. "Or not yet, anyway," Segno added. "Giannelli thinks Ambrogio'll probably be all right. He should stay in bed for the next few weeks and keep his eyes covered, but as long as he doesn't move his head too much and it stays protected, it'll probably heal all right."

"What's all this?" Duccio roared from the front door. "Cheeses all over the floor and the shop shut up?" He came storming up the stairs and stopped short at the sight of the barber. "What's happened? What is it? Is this one of your damn-fool tricks, Segno?"

"No," I said. "It's my fault, all of it, and you are going to be very angry."

He was, so angry that Tia Taviana finally took me away while he was still shouting. I don't think I could have moved by myself.

"Don't worry, dear, it was an accident," she said. "These things happen. It's just that Duccio is worried about the Maestà."

"I know," I said shakily. "Oh, Tia Taviana, I am so sorry. And what will I do if …"

"Time to think about that if and when it happens," she said. "Sufficient unto the day is the evil thereof. Now, why don't you go up to your room and I'll have Lucrezia send some supper up and you can just be by yourself for a while."

I climbed the stairs and lay down on my bed, then dreamed all night of eyeballs cooking in a stew of blood.

Ambrogio was not a good patient. He, too, was worried about the Maestà, and kept trying to get out of bed and feel his way down to the workshop, although what he thought he could accomplish there with his eyes bandaged I do not know. I'm not sure he had even thought that far—he was just so desperate to help that he couldn't make himself lie still. I was of little use myself, since every time I heard a step on the stairs I was sure it was Ambrogio knocking his head about and starting up the bleeding so that his eyes would be permanently damaged. After an exhausting day or two, it finally occurred to me that if I were to sit with him, I could both keep him in his bed and perform a penance so painful that it must surely wipe away the sin of my carelessness.

"It's a good idea, Bice," Tia said. "I should have thought of it myself." She gave me an amused look. "And I think you're right about the penance. I don't envy you your duty."

So I took the little chest that held my illuminating supplies and, my stomach churning with nerves, went to sit with

Ambrogio. For greater privacy he'd been moved to a store-room on the ground floor with a small, high window that opened onto the street. It reminded me of the room I had shared with Smerelda back in Florence. It was bare and unpainted, but pleasant with the breeze that came in at the window. I greeted him and began to set out my things on the table by his bed.

"Oh, it's you," he said. "Come to gloat over your handiwork?"

"No. I'm supposed to make sure you stay in your bed."

"Why'd they send you?" he asked. "You're the only one who doesn't have something important to do?"

"No, I'm the only one stupid enough to be willing to put up with your bad manners," I said, losing the temper I'd sworn to control.

He gave a brief, unpleasant laugh. "That's fair enough," he said. He listened for a moment. "What's that you've got there? Smells like parchment."

"I thought I'd bring a manuscript to keep my hands busy."

"Just don't spill the ink all over everything," he said. "You remember those shirts you spilled the wine on? They never did come clean."

I said nothing, just trimmed a quill and dipped it in the horn I'd filled with ink.

"Did you hear me?"

"Yes."

"Well?"

"I'm sorry about the shirts," I said. "Truly. And I'm very sorry about your eyes."

He said nothing for a moment, just drummed his fingers on the blanket. "Now I suppose you want me to apologize for the things I said to you," he finally said.

"Only if you mean it," I said.

"*Porca misera!* You are the most annoying …" He shook his head in frustration.

"Don't do that! You'll start the bleeding up again."

He bit off something he was going to say and drummed his fingers some more. "Do you know any stories?"

I was so surprised I made a blot and had to scrape it off. "Everyone knows stories," I said.

"I was thinking maybe you might know some I didn't. Like that one you were talking about the other day in the studio."

"You mean the *Aeneid*?"

"Yes."

I didn't know how to phrase the next question. "Do you want me to recite it? Or tell it?"

"Which one's longer?" he asked. "If I don't get something new to think about, I'll explode."

"Well, reciting it would take longer," I said. "And it would be better. But—"

"But what?"

"The poem's in Latin," I said.

He shrugged. "I know a little Latin," he said.

"You do?" I said, too surprised to recognize my implied insult of Ambrogio.

"Just because I'm a craftsman doesn't mean I'm stupid."

"There are lots of smart people who don't know Latin," I said. "Even I don't know it all that well." I bit my lip, hearing what I had just said.

"You know, Bice, sometimes you make it too easy," he said wryly, then relented. "I went to the cathedral school before I was apprenticed."

"Then you probably know more Latin than I do." A new worry struck me. "I might make mistakes," I said.

"I won't tease you if you won't tease me if I need something explained," he said, so quickly that I knew he was worried about the same thing.

"All right," I said.

"All right," he said. Then, a few seconds later, "Well? I'm listening."

Two good things came out of the month I spent reading to Ambrogio—well, three if you count that he kept still enough for his eyes to heal properly. The first was that we became friends. Edgy friends; unlike Margherita and the soft-spoken Segno, Ambrogio was prone to pouncing on ideas and worrying and barking at them like an impatient little dog. I never knew when something I said might spark a quick and devastating response.

On the other hand, he was always entertaining. He made a game of the Vergil I taught him. When Duccio was in a rage, Ambrogio would whisper, "What race of men is this? What primitive state could sanction this behavior?" And when Margherita appeared at the door to show off the gown she'd been working on all summer, he intoned, "How shall I address you, girl? Your look's not mortal; neither has your accent a mortal ring. O Goddess, beyond doubt!" We began to try to stump each other with quotations from the *Aeneid*.

And I was painting again. I'd forgotten how much I enjoyed it, especially when the household's livelihood did not hang in the balance. Segno, especially, was impressed and pestered his uncle to come see, and Duccio would occasionally ask me to fill in a block of flat color or do some other minor bit of painting. My hands were smaller than the men's, and more dexterous, and eventually I did most of the workshop's gold leafing as well.

To my surprise, Ambrogio disapproved of my painting and gilding. "You shouldn't do it, Bice. It'll just confuse you when you are a wife and mother," he said one afternoon when I was helping Segno finish his day's work. Ambrogio's eyes were better now, but he painted only a couple of hours every morning so that he wouldn't strain them, which meant he was usually in a grumpy mood.

"That's nonsense," I scoffed. "Plenty of women help with their husband's business. No, look, Segno, you want to make sure the hatching runs parallel to the line, more like this."

"Yes, I see," said Segno. Then, to Ambrogio, "I don't see what the harm is, especially when she's so much better than most of the apprentices. Let her do as she likes."

Ambrogio looked up from the sample book he was examining, into which I had copied patterns, drolleries, and alphabets since I first began with Claire and Matelda. "That's the point," he said, exasperated. "The girl who painted these things will never be happy as an assistant. You're too good at what you do, Bice. And if you keep at it, it will take over your life, until you can't think of anything else—not your babies, not your household, not your husband."

Segno said, "You're describing yourself, Ambrogio, not Bice."

Ambrogio scowled. "So what if I am? It's what all good artists do. Look at Pietro. He says he's in love with Margherita, but how many times now has he put off the wedding to finish just one more job first? People expect that of men. But can you see your mother, Segno, or Monna Taviana telling the rest of us that they're sorry, they won't be able to make dinner tonight, they're too busy? Or bringing their babies by the workshop for the men to watch? The whole way of things would come undone."

"You're taking this too seriously, Ambrogio," said Segno. "She's just helping me with the shading on the skirt. It's not the end of the world."

"All over the city, daughters are helping their mothers get dinner. Margherita is in the kitchen, Giannelli's daughter is no doubt in her kitchen, but Bice is painting in the workshop with the apprentices. What man in his right mind would choose a wife who doesn't do what she's expected to?"

"You sound like a *nonna*, Ambrogio, fretting that I won't be able to catch a husband," I said. "That's a long time away still."

"Not so long as you think," he said.

"And who says I'm going to marry, anyway?" This was something I was beginning to give some thought to, now that Margherita's marriage to Pietro was only a few months away. "As you yourself have been quick to point out, marriage has made neither of my parents happy. Perhaps I'll become a nun. I'll bet there are a dozen convents that would want me in their scriptorium."

But that didn't seem to placate him either. "Don't talk nonsense," he said roughly. And then, changing the subject, "Aren't you finished yet? I can't lock up until you're done."

AMONG GENTLEWOMEN

Florence, 1311–1312

My father quickly forgot his resolution to be my brothers' teacher. Swept up in the excitement of the Emperor Henry VII's descent into Italy, he stayed in Lucca just long enough to assure himself that the boys had a place with his brother Francesco before he moved on to Forlì, where some of his old political friends waited. From time to time I'd hear something of him; he'd been at Asti to welcome Henry into Italy, he'd gone to Milan to see Henry crowned, he was in the Casentino on an imperial mission.

I didn't see my mother, either, and heard from her only indirectly. She had rented out the farms and was caring for my *nonno*, who was not well. But he seemed to be making a good recovery, and she'd try to get away at Christmas. But Christmas passed without a visit, and then the week before Easter my *nonno* had another stroke and could no longer walk. She couldn't possibly leave him now, but perhaps after the harvest, when the servant of one of her friends was free to watch him. But by then he was so weak he could neither feed himself nor speak.

In April of that year we heard that my father had written an intemperate letter to the Florentines, urging them to submit to Henry as their rightful monarch. When they (predictably) ignored him, he wrote to the Emperor Henry instead, urging him to hasten to conquer "this dire plague called Florence," and was promptly exiled from Florence again for his pains. But beyond joking with Ambrogio about just exactly how one went about being exiled from exile, I paid little attention to all the fuss. We were much too busy working on the Maestà to spare much time or energy for anything else.

In the end, I suppose it was worth it. The finished Maestà was a triumph. The city fathers were so pleased with the altarpiece that they called for a day of public thanksgiving and paraded the Maestà, glittering with more gold than some of the Sienese banks had in their vaults, all around the city. Duccio, resplendent in a velvet doublet and a plumed hat, accompanied it every step of the way, and then installed it in the *duomo* with more care than most mothers showed their babes, as Ambrogio said. That night there was a feast for the entire city on the *campo* and the cathedral square, served on trestle tables contributed by individual families and illuminated by torches thrust in iron brackets on the walls above, and followed by a horse race through the city that was sufficiently terrifying to satisfy even Feo. Best of all, Pietro returned for the celebration, so Margherita finally had her wedding.

I woke early on the morning she was to be married and stared at her back. It was the last time we would sleep in the same bed, and I couldn't help remembering how lonely it had been when Sagesse had gone.

"Bice," Margherita breathed without turning over. "Are you awake?"

"Yes."

"Bice, I'm a little afraid."

"Afraid?" I said blankly. "Of Pietro?"

"No, not of Pietro. But of going off by myself. Of being in charge of a household, like my mother. I don't know if I'm smart enough."

I laughed at her. "That's ridiculous. You're one of the best housekeepers I know, easily as good as Tia Lucrezia and your mother."

She flipped over so we could see each other, and I saw she had tears in her eyes. "I'm serious, Bice. I'm not clever like my mother—or like you."

"Like me?" I pushed away her words. "I'm not clever, Margherita. You know I'm not. I'm always tripping and dropping things and saying things I don't mean. You're much better at managing things than I am. You never forget what you've put in the oven, or to start the water boiling for the laundry, or when it's time to make soap again. You're going to make a much better wife than I ever will." Those last words left an unexpectedly bitter taste in my mouth as I recognized their truth.

She didn't contradict me. "I know all that," she said. "But what if he gets tired of me? I'm not interesting and learned like you. What if he finds out it's just me he's married? I'm no one special." She buried her head in her pillow and began to snuffle, as if she were still seven and we were launched on one of our enjoyable melodramas.

I put my arms around her. "Margherita, husbands don't want learned wives. Even Ambrogio, who's half a scholar himself, tells me every chance he gets that I'm ruining my marital prospects by all my reading and painting." I was surprised how hard it was to say, and even more surprised to discover that I myself was on the brink of tears.

"He doesn't mean it," Margherita said stoutly. "He's just scared of you. Everyone is."

There was a short silence.

"No, that's not what I mean," she said hastily. "I mean that they all respect you. Much more than they respect me."

"*Ci sto*," I said, trying to shrug off the painful words. "I know I don't belong, not the way the rest of you do."

"But in a good way," she said, looking anxious.

My affection for her overcame my hurt. "You are a good lady," I said. "And my best friend under the sun's cape. What on earth will I do without you?"

"Lots of splendid things," she said. "Much more splendid than cooking meals and keeping house. And you must write me and tell me all of them, so I can pretend I'm with you, and you must complain about them so that I am not too jealous. And I will write you about how awful the butcher's meat is, and how Pietro never thinks of me, and how if I never cook another meal in my life I will be happy, and all the things that women always say, and then we will both be content with our lots."

"See, I told you that you were more sensible than I," I said.

The wedding mass went off beautifully. Margherita, resplendent in the blue silk that had been my wedding present to her, looked serene and happy. It was Pietro whose hand trembled when he took hers—but, as far as I could tell from the dazed expression on his face, from joy, not fear. What would it be like, I wondered, to have the power to make a man tremble? Especially a man you loved. And when, at the meal that followed, the two of them kept touching each other as if for reassurance, I wondered what it would be like not only to be assured of a companion for the rest of your natural lives, but to be that companion, to know that someone else's happiness would not be complete without you.

The longing that swept over me was both so unexpected and so intense that I almost dropped the little cask of wine I carried. Of course it never worked out that way, I told myself quickly. Look at what happened to my mother. And to my father. But I couldn't stop my eyes from sliding to Pietro's square, powerful hand entwined with Margherita's smaller, smoother one under the table where they thought no one could see.

I tossed my head and stepped forward to fill another goblet. I caught Segno's glance from across the table. He raised his goblet and then, his eyes still on me, drank. I flushed and looked away.

A moment later, he was by my side. "Come dance with me," he invited, his breath sweet and fruity with the wine.

I shook my head. "You know how I am, Segno, I'll just trip all over myself."

"She will, too," Ambrogio said from behind me, startling me so that I almost dropped the cask again. He reached out and caught it in time, then set it carefully on the floor.

"Thanks for the advice, Ambrogio," said Segno, taking my elbow. "I'll keep it in mind. Come on, Bice."

He led me away from the party, out into the garden and behind some honeysuckle bushes. "So you don't like dancing?" he said. He took my hands. "It's not so difficult, you know. It's just moving together," and he stepped closer to me so that our bodies were nearly touching and I had to tilt my head back to see him properly. His shoulders brushed the honeysuckle, which gave off a heavy, languorous scent. He didn't look shy anymore, or like a boy. When had his jaw hardened and his arms filled out? He met my eyes and then dipped his head very slowly so that I would have time to turn away if I wanted to. But I didn't. I leaned forward, wanting to taste the wine on his lips, wanting to get closer to his bright black eyes and to put my hands in his thick black hair. And after our lips had touched and I had tasted the wine, I pulled him closer so that he would hold me hard against his broad chest and I could be cherished.

"Bice!"

I looked behind me on the narrow stone street. It was Segno, of course. I sighed. I had hoped to get to the market and back before he realized I'd gone. That was all right, I comforted myself, he'd probably insist on carrying the basket for me.

He came panting up behind me, his eyes as open and guileless as Sagesse's had always been. "Mama said she had sent you to the market. I thought I could carry the basket for you," he said with a delighted grin.

He loved doing things for me—carrying heavy baskets of wet clothing and vegetables, building fires, chopping wood. The other apprentices all teased him about it, calling him goose-whipped and a nancy-boy, but he just smiled and kept on doing it. I was grateful, of course, not only for the service, but also for the pleasure he took in finding some little thing that he could do to make my life better. But every time he looked at me with his heart in his eyes, as he was doing now as I handed him the basket and we ducked under an arched entryway and entered the *campo*, I became obscurely angry. "Keep something for yourself!" I wanted to tell him.

He took my elbow to guide me through the crowd to the butcher's stall on the other side of the *campo*, touching me as reverently as if I were a piece of fragile crystal. I racked my brain for something to say but could think of no topic we had not already discussed to death a half-dozen times. Segno was an attractive and attentive beau but, like me, no great conversationalist.

"When do you think they'll start work on the Palazzo Pubblico?" I asked him.

"I don't know," he said. "I love the way the sun lies on your hair."

I sighed again. No one had told me that being in love rotted your brain, but I'd seen it with Margherita and Pietro and now with Segno. Maybe I really should be a nun. My heart seemed as fickle as my parents'. As soon as Segno had responded to my blandishments, I had lost interest. It would be a lonely life, but then I always seemed to be lonely. And at least no one would be calling my eyes big purple violets.

"Here's the butcher," I said brightly.

To my surprise, Segno handed me the basket. "I'll be back in a moment," he said.

"All right." I turned again to my friend Volpe, minding the stand for his father. "We need two kids, nice and fresh, and a brace of hare."

Segno was back a moment later, bearing a gift. A bunch of violets. "I couldn't resist," he said. "They reminded me of your big purple eyes."

I wished that I had someone to talk to about the uneasy mix of gratitude, affection, guilt, and irritation that I was feeling toward Segno. I missed Margherita desperately. Tia Lucrezia was no help. "You'll want to remember this way of preparing mutton," she'd say with a wink. "It's Segno's favorite." Or, "I believe Segno prefers the way you wore your hair yesterday."

Ambrogio was no help either. He seemed to have gone into hiding. It was natural to see less of him, of course, since I no longer spent much time in the studio. But as time passed I began to wonder if he was deliberately avoiding me. We no longer played the Vergil game, and after I had decided to ask him if I had done something to offend him, I could not find an opportunity when we were alone together. I tried to comfort myself that it was just because he was realizing that now that I was sixteen, I deserved the same respect accorded any young woman, but I didn't really believe it. Perhaps now that his brother Pietro had established his own household,

Ambrogio was beginning to think more seriously about making his own way. Or maybe, as he had told me before, once an artist reached a certain level of proficiency everything besides his art receded in importance. I knew that had been true of my father. And Ambrogio's paintings were becoming more beautiful and exciting with every month that passed, rivaling those of Duccio himself.

Normally I would have turned to Tia Taviana for comfort and sensible conversation, but she was absent for much of the period. Her daughter Andrea was expecting twins in Murlo, a half-day's journey to the south, and needed her mother.

As I suddenly, agonizingly, felt that I needed mine. So when Tia Taviana returned home, full of news about the babies and gossip from the Florentines who put up at her daughter's inn, and mentioned that one of them had told her that Ser Manetto Donati had had yet another stroke and was not expected to live, I knew what to do.

"I'd like to visit my mother," I told her. "Could you and Lucrezia manage without me?"

"Of course we could, darling," she said instantly. "It's high time you saw her again. Now, let's see. I think someone was saying that the widow Renata is going to visit her daughter in Prato sometime next week. She'll be going right through Florence. Shall we see if she'd like some company?"

And so, almost before I had finished making the decision, I found myself bidding goodbye to the widow Renata at the gates of Florence.

The city still smelled the same. I would have recognized that smell blindfolded—the scent of the Arno and piss and leather and bread. The river was the same, and the light. But the city had shrunk and turned in on itself, so that the streets no longer lined up as I remembered them. But in the end, I found the old neighborhood without much trouble.

My mother answered the door to my grandfather's house, looking exactly the same, her hair in the turban she used when she cleaned and her high forehead still smooth and unlined. She didn't recognize me for a moment, and then quite suddenly she did. She threw her arms around me and burst into tears. "Bice! I am so glad that you came!"

I patted her back gingerly. "How's Nonno Manetto?" I asked.

She drew back, wiping away her tears with her slender fingers, which were no longer work-roughened but white and smooth, with the pink oval fingernails I had admired as a small child. "He left us Saturday," she said.

"I'm sorry I'm too late."

"Don't be," she said. "He hasn't known me for a long time, and the end was quite difficult. I'm glad you were spared that." She took me by the shoulders. "Let me look at you. Yes, same big smoky eyes and crooked mouth—I would have known you anywhere. But you are thin like a breadstick! We shall have to work at fattening you up so you have some curves."

I flushed.

"Here I am gabbing when you are no doubt half dead from the journey. Come in and sit down and I'll get you something to drink." She ushered me up the interior stairway to the *sala*. "I am so glad you have come! I have been longing to see you, but Teruccio is gone so much that I did not dare leave the house unattended, for fear it would be taken."

She led me into the old-fashioned *sala*. It was a dark, cramped room, a testament to the house's beginnings as a defensive tower. It was also nearly bare and smelled of musty smoke, although there was no fireplace. The only furniture that belonged to the room was a rough table covered with a faded and patched tapestry and two benches, and the carved wooden chair and slanting desk that used to be in my *nonno's* study. The desk held the only ornaments in the room—a silver candelabra I recognized as my *nonna's*, polished and gleaming, and the Book of Hours that I had made for my mother.

I glanced at her out of the corner of my eye, my lips twisting into a foolish grin I could not control. "So do you like it?" I asked.

"Someday I hope you have the experience of seeing one of your children do something you cannot," she said. Then, before the moment enlarged itself beyond decorum, she said, "Your uncle Teruccio should be here soon. He will be glad to see you."

That was the second time in as many minutes that she had mentioned her brother the priest, whom I hadn't thought about in years. I answered at random. "He must visit you often."

She tsk'd. "Bice, I could not live here alone, you know that. He now has your *nonno's* room. I am to be his housekeeper."

"Of course," I said. "I should have realized."

She shook her head. "*Santo cielo*, you remind me of your father, Bice. So quick to think and so slow to see."

I would have liked to protest, but I didn't want to disrupt the fragile understanding we appeared to be establishing, so I did not.

When he arrived home a short time later, Tio Teruccio seemed as pleased as my mother that I had come. Straight-backed and slender, like my mother, he was nonetheless begin-ning to show his years. His dark hair was flecked with gray and there were deep lines between his nose and mouth. "So here's the world traveler!" he said heartily, absently accepting the cool watered wine my mother had waiting for him. "Come up to the *sala* and talk to me while your mother gets the meal ready."

"You're taking my daughter away from me on her first night home?" my mother protested. "Why doesn't she come help with the cooking now so we can all talk together sooner?"

My uncle put up his hands defensively. "You see how, even without a wife, I am treated like a child in my own home?" he said. "Do this, do that. All right, all right. We will wait."

That evening and for many that followed, I described the journey to France and my life at the *béguinage*. My mother and uncle made a good audience, hanging on my every word as if they were children being told a bedtime story. I found their attentions at once gratifying and disquieting. My transition from anonymous child to honored guest was too extreme for me to absorb quickly.

Which is not to say that I did not welcome the change. With just one man to care for and two of us to share the labor, my mother began to introduce me to the pursuits of a comfortably situated Florentine matron. The farms were going well enough now that she had been able to hire managers that she trusted, and she was as eager as I to take advantage of the pleasures available to city women at their leisure. We washed our hair with citron water and combed it dry on the roof where the sun could bleach it. We attended mass in different quarters of the city to keep abreast of the doings of the various families, and to gather ideas for the fancy-dress gown my mother planned to make for me. Even my mother's housekeeping was a revelation. Where Taviana's had tended toward the ruthlessly efficient, my mother valued quality. She willingly crossed town half a dozen times in a morning if it meant she could be assured that her roast lamb was the freshest and tenderest it could be, and dressed with the finest spices and vegetables. If linens had to be laundered, they were rinsed in lavender water and well aired before being carefully folded and stored.

I soaked up my mother's attention and approval like a grapevine after a drought. As long as the time was spent in her company, I could happily take an entire morning to decide whether the flavor of a fowl would be better complemented by chestnut or prune sauce, a whole afternoon in search of the sweetest chestnuts, and that evening to ponder the virtues of a length of apple-green silk versus those of the cornflower blue. I began using the fragrant lotions and hair rinses she preferred and tried to modulate my own loose-limbed walk into her graceful glide. That I could choose the way I presented myself to the world was a new and exciting idea.

One afternoon my mother's closest friend, Beatrice Cavalcante, came to the house for gossip over almond biscuits and sweet wine. She lived in a different *sestiere* than we did, on the Via degli Alfani on the other side of the *duomo*, and she and my mother enjoyed keeping each other up to date on the happenings of their neighborhoods. After they had disposed of the usual cast of characters, she turned to me with one eyebrow beautifully arched over her small, close-set eyes.

"This must be very boring for you, Bice," she said. "All this chatter about people you don't know and events you haven't seen."

I murmured something polite, disguising my alarm at being addressed directly by the exquisitely gowned and coifed Monna Beatrice as well as I could.

"Your father and my poor dear husband were the best of friends, my dear, did you know?"

Yes, I did.

"My Guido flattered himself that he had taught your father

some small appreciation for the sonnet form of the troubadours. This was, of course, some time before his premature death, a tragic event that I know your father in particular has always regretted."

I cast a quick glance at my mother for an indication of how I should respond, but she simply looked resigned, so again I murmured something indistinguishable but, I hoped, soothing.

"These have been lonely years, my dear, lonely years."

This time I did not dare meet my mother's gaze, since I knew very well that the marriage between Ser Guido and Monna Beatrice had been stormy. It had been arranged in an effort to stop the warfare between the Ghibelline party Beatrice's father Farinata had led and the Guelf party that Ser Guido's family had supported, but it seemed mostly to have perpetuated ill feeling until Ser Guido's death shortly before my father's exile.

"My son has been a great comfort, of course, but these are not times in which a young scholar is valued as he ought to be, especially in the difficulties since the fire."

The fire she was referring to had happened nine years earlier, when my mother's kinsman Corso Donati, the Black Baron, hired a simpleminded priest to throw firebombs of pitch and tar into the Cavalcante compound. It was completely destroyed, just as the city of Florence itself had destroyed her family's property during her childhood in punishment for her father's betrayal to the Sienese. No wonder Monna Beatrice was so interested in gossip and innuendo, I thought to myself. It was all she had been left with. But it was difficult to remain sympathetic for long.

"You do read and so forth, don't you, Bice?" she said, somehow making these activities sound a doubtful virtue. "So you must understand how difficult it is to find a spirit that is sufficiently refined to support Farinata's endeavors. You do recall Farinata, I suppose?"

I nodded, remembering the way the sun used to dance along the strands of his long, wavy chestnut hair. From her description, it sounded as though he was still something of a prig.

"You're not promised, are you, Bice?" she said casually, just as if this had not been the whole point of our conversation. "So you must have some sense of the difficulties—I've just had the most marvelous idea!" she interrupted herself, actually clapping her hands together like a child who had been promised a treat.

My stomach sank.

"We should really get you two together. I'm sure you would have a sack of things to talk about."

I looked at my mother for help, but she just mouthed "*Corragio!*" to me. "*Va bene,*" I said, trying not to sound sulky. "That sounds delightful."

Farinata looked very much as I remembered him, beautiful hair and all. I had forgotten the way the color of his eyes matched his hair too exactly, almost as if he were a girl who gave herself rinses, but not his pallid complexion or supercilious air. We were standing in the baptistery, underneath the golden circle of angels, and I had a weird sense of déjà vu as his mother cooed, "You remember little Bice, don't you, Dante Alighieri's daughter?"

He muttered something in Latin which instantly revised my opinion of him: "How the man towers over everyone."

Without thinking I said, "Book VI of the *Aeneid*. Well done."

We looked at each other with new interest.

"What age so happy brought you to birth? How splendid were your parents to have conceived a being like yourself!" he quoted.

I dimpled. There is no other word for it. And then responded, truthfully, "I stand in astonishment at the sight of such a captain."

Farinata was the first friend I'd ever had who was smarter and better read than I, and I liked it. I much preferred being an audience to being a performer, and if there is one thing I can say without reservation about Farinata, it is that he always craved an audience. I was his lady fair, lovely but unavailable— the Guinevere to his Lancelot, the Iseult to his Tristan. He paid me elaborate compliments in four languages—Italian, French, Provençal, and Latin—and was especially pleased when there was a line or image that I had to have explained to me. He had read everything and remembered it all—not only Vergil and the Bible, but Ovid, Statius, Augustine, Boethius, the troubadours, and the *canzone* our own fathers had composed. Our conversations were stimulating, witty, and exhausting. I thought that this must be what my father had been like as a young man—so full of cleverness and wit that it spilled out of him in one long stream of talk.

Farinata and I spent lots of time together during the dark months of winter and early spring—probably more than was proper, as his mother was indulgent and mine preoccupied with other family worries. Although Pietro and Jacopo seemed happy and well working for Tio Francesco, Gian and my father were apparently not getting along at all. Gian had met a girl and was anxious to establish a household. He was afraid that my father's outspoken and (to Florentines, at least) unpopular support of the new emperor might hurt his, Gian's, prospects. But his protests seemed only to egg my father on to more intemperate exhortations that all right-thinking men abjure their evil ways and prepare to welcome Henry VII to their bosom, and so on.

Gian's worries found fertile ground in my mother, who had struggled for nearly a decade to repair the family fortunes and had now finally achieved security, only to have it threatened afresh by my father's antics. She and Tio Teruccio were soon spending every minute plotting strategy and composing letters that they hoped would persuade my father to moderate his stand. But all their machinations bore little fruit, and by the summer of 1312, my elegant and engaging sister-mother had reverted to the tight-lipped, brittle woman I had feared as a child.

As for me, I was impatient with the whole lot of them. I was young and having a good time, and I was not interested in being party to anything that might cut my pleasure short. So I spent as much time as I could with Farinata Cavalcante, and if we raised some eyebrows and set some tongues wagging, I did not care. He was a good friend who made the time pass pleasantly, that was all.

His proposal, when it came, was a shock. It was June 24, the Feast of Saint John the Baptist, and Florence was on holiday. We had spent the day with the rest of the city, dancing and eating and watching processions and boat races and athletic contests, but by the late afternoon both of us had had enough. We decided to climb the hill to the bishop's palace at San Miniato and watch the festivities from above. I'd brought some food and he'd brought some wine, and after we'd found a flat place with a good view of the city and eaten, we lay on our elbows and chatted through a haze of contented fatigue. Dusk was falling, bringing with it the heavy scent of roses. Far below us, lanterns began to blink on, one by one.

Suddenly a bat came zooming out of the woods, nearly grazing my cheek. Startled, I knocked over my wine, which puddled beneath me so that my whole front was damp and stained. "*Che jella!*" I said, jumping to my feet. "I hope I haven't ruined it."

Farinata was laughing. "Only you, my little *imbecila*, can so consistently evoke such disasters from such little cause. Hold still," he added impatiently as I brushed at the stain. "You're just making it worse. Come over to the bird bath."

He shook out the napkin that had held our supper and dipped it in the warm water, then began to blot at the front of my dress. Despite myself, I flinched.

"You're not afraid of me, are you, Bice?" he teased.

"Don't be an idiot," I said crisply. "I'm just not used to anyone touching my—"

"Your what?" he said. "Your breasts?"

I flushed.

"But you think of me like a brother," he said, blotting more slowly until his hand was cupping my breast. "I could never arouse inappropriate feelings in the girl who is like my sister."

"Let go," I said, both dismayed and excited by the unexpected feelings that my old friend was suddenly inspiring. "Really, Farinata, it's not funny."

"Do you really want me to?" he whispered, drawing nearer.

"Of course I do," I said, not moving.

"Are you sure?" he breathed, an inch from my ear.

"Yes," I said breathlessly, and then he kissed me.

But Farinata's kiss was not at all like Segno's, a gentle salute between friends. Farinata kissed with an open, seeking mouth that seemed to swallow me up.

I broke away. This was more than I wanted. I remembered the Templar in Paris, and the way the power of his spirit and his body had overwhelmed me. Farinata was overwhelming me too, and I didn't like it. "Stop it," I said, as he reached for me again.

"Don't you like it?"

"Yes—no—it's too much, Farinata. We shouldn't."

"Why shouldn't we?" he asked, his pale brown eyes glinting down at me by the light of the rising moon.

"Because we are friends, not—" I had started to say "lovers," but changed it to "man and wife." I bent over to gather up our things. "It's time we left."

He knelt down so he could look me in the face. "Would it be so bad if we were?"

"If we were what?"

"Man and wife, you goose."

I gaped at him. When I could find my voice, I said, "Don't be ridiculous. You don't think of me that way."

"How do you know?"

"Because you've never—I mean, I've never—we just don't!"

"You mean you haven't," he said.

"No, I haven't," I said, truthfully. I saw him wince. It was a small movement, but unmistakable.

"Could you now?" he asked, his voice a little too casual.

I looked at his face. Never sharply defined, it looked smoother and more innocent than usual in the flattening light of the moon—a child's face. But I knew him too well. He was no child. And I doubted very much that he was innocent. "Why should I?" I asked.

A muscle moved in his cheek. "Because I love you."

"No, you don't," I said. "Not the way a man loves a woman."

He gripped my arm hard. "Why do you say that? Have you heard something?"

"Heard something? Why would I hear something? I just know, that's all."

"I just kissed you, didn't I?" he said belligerently.

I blushed again. "Yes."

"So how can you say I don't feel what a man ought to feel for his wife?"

"It's not the kissing," I said.

"What is it then?"

"I don't know," I said helplessly. "But what's between us hasn't felt like a courtship."

"Maybe it hasn't been," he agreed. "But could it become that?"

I studied his face again. There was something here I didn't understand.

"Come on," he pressed. "Think what fun we'd have. My mother would go into a convent, I know she would, and we'd have the whole house to ourselves. We could do as we liked."

A house of our own. A place unencumbered by my mother's bitterness or my father's absence, where I could do exactly as I liked, as I was doing now, for the rest of my life. The prospect was much more inviting than a nun's cell. I glanced at him. And Farinata would never hover. I would have a place to be myself.

He caught my glance as he caught everything. "It would be fun," he pressed. "We are such good friends, you and I, and we would rub along well together, don't you think?"

He was right. We were comfortable together, and we made each other laugh. But there was something—I wished it were daylight, so I could see his face properly. "Why are you doing this?" I asked him. "The real truth, not what you think I want to hear."

I had the impression that I had taken him aback, but he hesitated only a moment. "Fair enough," he said, and his tone was no longer cajoling, but frank. "My mother—wearies me. She wants me to live in her pocket, but I prefer my freedom. She was so miserable with her own mother-in-law that she has always sworn she would retreat to a convent rather than share a house with another woman again. That would suit me very well, and her too, I suppose, since she would have an audience ready-made for her endless talk. Whereas you—well, marrying you would be almost like marrying another man. No fussing, no hurt feelings, no haunting each other's steps. More like a friendship than a marriage."

I tried to make a joke out of it, but I don't think I succeeded at keeping the hurt out of my voice. "So you want to marry me because I'm not really a woman."

He laughed and chucked me under the chin. "Don't be so thin-skinned, Bice. It was a compliment. I meant that you live your own life, and you seem to like it that way. You're not the kind of girl who's going to demand that everything be just so."

I was still nettled. "In other words, you can neglect me with a clear conscience."

"As you would be free to neglect me," he pointed out. "We'd have the best of both worlds—freedom and friend-ship."

I considered. "I wouldn't have much of a dowry. Maybe one of the farms."

Farinata shrugged. "I'm not exactly wealthy myself. We'll get along all right, and if the emperor takes Florence, your father will be in a position to give us a little more."

Did I really want the passion and complications of a love match like the one Segno had offered? Before I had finished the thought, I felt again the shame and suffocation that that little interlude in the honeysuckle bushes had inspired. And having my eyes compared to violets, and being adored. No, that was not what I wanted. I wanted security, but I also wanted peace.

"You want to," Farinata said, the wheedling note back in his voice. "I can tell."

He was right, I did. By the robe of the Virgin, I did. Companionship and a home of my own, uncorrupted by disappointed hopes or hovering lovers.

"Yes, I think I do," I said.

He wrote a letter to my father that very night, and spoke to my mother and Tio Teruccio the next day. We would be married at Christmas, after the harvest, and my parents would give us the farm at Fiesole for a dowry. And then I would be free.

THE MESSENGER

Florence, 1312

I was awakened by a pounding on the door. I surged up, my heart matching the blows on the door beat for beat. Nothing good could come from visitors in the middle of the night. I heard Tio Teruccio leave his room and start down the stairs. From across the room my mother's voice asked, "Do you know anything about this?"

"No, nothing," I said.

I heard the bolts being drawn and male voices, low and urgent. The door closed again and was locked. The voices sounded again—at least one man was inside the house. Then quick steps were climbing the stairs to the *sala*. Tio Teruccio's voice called, "Gemma? Bice? Come quickly."

Blinking and patting our hair into place, we pulled on some clothing, drew back the big bolt of our bedroom door, and followed my uncle into the *sala*, where a man was drawing the shutters and lighting the lamps. There was something familiar about his compact build. He turned, and I saw it was Ambrogio, his face gray with fatigue and something else.

Warm relief flooded my body. "Oh, it's you," I said stupidly.

He smiled at me, and he looked as he always had. The last wisps of nightmare terror floated away. "Turning up like a bad penny," he agreed.

"Bice, who is this person?" my mother asked, her voice high.

"It's Ambrogio, of course." Then I realized they'd never met. "He's Tio Duccio's assistant, and a very fine painter. Ambrogio, this is my mother, Monna Gemma, and my Tio Teruccio."

"I'm pleased to meet you," Ambrogio said, bowing slightly as we seated ourselves. He took a breath, and I saw the strain in his face again. "I am here with an urgent message from Ser Dante. Henry VII is marching on Florence, and Ser Dante thinks it would be better for all concerned if you withdrew to Lucca until the fighting is over."

"Certainly not!" my mother said instantly. "We'll lose everything."

"With all due respect, Monna Gemma, Ser Dante is of the opinion that there is little to be gained by staying. The farms are rented out, and this house is less likely to be disturbed if you are gone than if you are here."

My mother chewed her lip.

Tio Teruccio said, "He's right, Gemma. They won't go after me. I'm just a priest. But they may well want to hurt Dante Alighieri's wife, especially after the letters Dante wrote last spring."

"What about Bice's wedding?" she said.

"It's not until Christmas," I said. I had no desire to be in Florence during an attack or a siege, and thought it would be fun to see my brothers again. "I'm sure the fighting will be over by then."

"Won't your fiancé have something to say about that?" Ambrogio asked me.

I shook my head, trying to imagine what the boys must look like now that they were practically grown men. "Farinata would want me to do what I thought was best, and I think the wisest course is to go to Lucca until this all blows over."

Ambrogio looked hard at me, then shrugged.

My mother looked back and forth between us. "You must be exhausted," she said in her gracious lady-of-the-manor voice. "Let me make you up a bed, and we can settle all this in the morning."

Ambrogio was polite but definite. "Ser Dante was quite explicit. We are to leave tonight."

"Disappearing in the dead of night will cause talk," Tio Teruccio broke in. "Perhaps we could get word tomorrow that one of the boys has taken sick. A few hours won't make any difference, and this young man looks as if he could use the rest."

Ambrogio and my mother stared at my uncle with identical expressions of indecision.

"*Va bene,*" Ambrogio said, capitulating. "We can wait until morning. But I'd feel better about it if you packed tonight in case anything does happen."

We all looked at my mother. "Oh, very well," she said crossly. "I don't appear to have much choice in the matter. Bice, take Ambrogio to the kitchen and get him something to eat while you put together some provisions. There's a sack of dried pears and another of dried peaches the farm sent to us this week; be sure to bring those, and whatever bread and cheese we have in the house. I'll make up a bed for Ambrogio in the storeroom and pack our things."

"*Va bene,*" I said, but when I would have followed her out the door Tio Teruccio touched my elbow. He waited until the door of the bedroom had closed behind my mother, then said to me, "I have some papers you should take with you." He went into his studio and emerged a moment later with a small casket, which he unlocked with a key he wore around his neck.

He handed me a stack of parchment tied together with a

ribbon. "This is a poem your father started many years ago. He left it behind when he went to Rome. You know how your mother feels about his poetry—when she lost the house she left the manuscript there, thinking it would be lost. But I managed to retrieve it a few years ago, and I promised to send it to your father when I had the means to do so safely. I believe you two"—he nodded at me and Ambrogio—"will be trustworthy messengers. I dare not"—this to me—"ask your mother."

He held the packet out, but I put my hands behind my back, unwilling to do something that would hurt my mother. He looked up, surprised, and saw the expression on my face. He laughed. "It's not that kind of poem, Bice. It's something entirely different that I think your mother, were she in a mood to be reasonable, would encourage."

I looked suspiciously at his thin face, so similar in shape to my mother's but so different in texture. Where her skin was smooth, his was lined; where her eyes were as opaque as two black pebbles, his were lively and penetrating. He was a priest, I told myself, and a good brother to my mother besides. I took the packet.

Tio Teruccio smiled at me, his eyes disappearing in a mass of wrinkles. "Thank you, Bice. I must confess, the manuscript has weighed heavily on me. I will be glad to have it restored to its rightful owner." He closed and locked the casket. "It was generous of you to come all this way to fetch Bice," he said to Ambrogio, making conversation.

"And Monna Gemma," Ambrogio added.

Tio Teruccio smiled. "Of course. And Monna Gemma." There was a small pause, as if he were waiting for something.

"I'm on my way to Arezzo for a commission," Ambrogio said.

"And Florence is right on your way," Tio Teruccio said dryly. "Yes, I see. I see. Indeed I do."

Ambrogio lifted his chin slightly. "Is there anything wrong with my coming to fetch them?"

"Oh, no, quite the contrary," said Tio Teruccio. "We are all quite grateful for your exertions. Well, I will not keep you from your supper any longer."

I went first to indicate the way to the kitchen. When he thought I was out of earshot, Tio Teruccio, who did not approve of Farinata, murmured to Ambrogio, "I would be very interested to hear what you think of the intended. Very interested indeed."

I sniffed as I stepped into the kitchen. As if a rough apprentice like Ambrogio could appreciate Farinata's wit and grace! I pulled some sticks of wood from the stack that stood ready, and paused. What *would* Ambrogio think of him? I glanced at Ambrogio's square, workman's body as I knelt to build the fire, noting the patches on his hose and the paint stains on his hands. And what would Farinata think of Ambrogio?

"There's no need to build a fire, Bice," Ambrogio said. "A piece of bread and a swallow of wine will do nicely."

I said nothing, but cut him a slice of black bread and spread it with artichoke paste and poured out some wine. While he ate (I'd forgotten how good his manners were—Farinata would have no reason to criticize him there), I lit a lantern and began to assemble food for the journey.

Dried fruit and meat in the attic. Wine and oil from one storeroom. Biscuits and cheese from another.

The more I thought about the journey to Lucca, the better pleased I was. Florence was dull just now with all the talk of war, and after months of leisure, time was beginning to hang heavily on me. I enjoyed the stimulation of travel, and Ambrogio was good company. And my brothers would be waiting for us at the other end. I began to sing as I moved from room to room, a song my brothers had teased me with in the nursery:

"If you can answer questions three,
O then, fair maid, I will marry with thee.
O, what is louder than a horn?
And what is sharper than a thorn?
What is heavier than the lead?
And what is better than the bread?
O, what is higher than the tree?
And what is deeper than the sea?

"O, shame is louder than a horn,
And hunger is sharper than a thorn.
And sin is heavier than the lead,
And the blessing's better than the bread.
O, heaven is higher than the tree,
And love is deeper than the sea.

"And now, fair maid, I will marry with thee."

There. That should be enough. I tied a cloth over the basket and set it on the table with a thump. I felt Ambrogio's eyes on me as he drank the last of his wine.

"What?" I said.

"You don't seem very upset."

"I'm not. I love going on journeys."

"What about Farinata?"

I shrugged. "We are good friends, but we will have the rest of our lives together, and I haven't seen my brothers for a very long time."

"Don't you worry about him being caught here during the siege?"

In point of fact, I hadn't stopped to think about it. "Oh, he'll be fine," I said airily, avoiding Ambrogio's eyes. "He's a survivor."

He grunted, and pushed his plate and cup toward me. I rinsed them quickly and put them away, then reached for the lantern.

"Do you need anything else from me?" he asked. "Can I help you pack up your paints, or carry anything?"

It was not like Ambrogio to offer his services without reason, and I looked at him curiously as I led the way out of the kitchen. "I don't think so, but thank you for the offer. I haven't touched my paints since I got here, so they are ready to go. You'll sleep here—oh, good, it looks as if Mother did take care of the bed." I lit the lantern that hung from the storeroom bracket. "The privy is beyond the kitchen, out that little alley. Is there anything I can get for you?"

He sat on the bed with a thump, and I thought again how tired, almost befuddled, he looked. He shook his head.

"Thank you for coming," I said. "I'm sure it was a hard journey, and we are grateful to you. The angels watch over you."

"And you."

This was the second time Mother and I had left Florence in a cart, but this time it was she who nestled in a comfortable little nest in the back and I who was driving, along with a silent Ambrogio.

When he finally spoke, it was not what I expected. "I can't imagine not painting."

"Excuse me?"

"I've been thinking about it all morning, and all night, too,

I suppose. That you haven't used your paints since Siena. I can't imagine not painting for six months."

More criticism. "I've been doing other things," I said defensively. "Like getting to know my mother and finding a fiancé."

"Yes, you certainly have," he said dryly. "I don't believe I congratulated you properly on your ... efficiency. None of us would have believed that you could catch yourself a husband so quickly."

"Well, thank you very much!"

"Segno seemed particularly surprised by your announcement," he observed.

I was silent for a moment. I hadn't let myself think about how Segno would feel about my engagement and was not eager to start now. "I made no promises to Segno."

"Perhaps not in so many words. But you certainly implied—"

"Once," I said. "I implied I cared for him once, for five minutes at Margherita's wedding. But that was the only time I ever gave him any hint—"

"You know that isn't so. You always looked at him as though he were the sweetest peach you'd ever laid eyes on."

Now I wasn't just irritated but angry. "Maybe it's because, unlike every other apprentice in Siena, he is kind and thoughtful. God give me strength, the way you all talk about women, as if I weren't even there! So I kissed him one night when my best friend had just gotten married and I was lonely. So what? You've kissed plenty of women, and you never thought about marrying any of them."

"It's different for girls," Ambrogio started, but I wouldn't stop. It was such a relief to get the whole confusing mess off my chest, even if it was only to a hostile Ambrogio.

"I didn't mean to start anything. It was just that one time. But then suddenly he was always there. It was like he was between me and everything else, like I had to poke a hole in his skin to even breathe. I didn't want to feel that way. But I did, and I didn't know what to say. I didn't know what to do."

"You could have told him how you felt."

I shook my head impatiently. "I couldn't say anything to him. You know how sensitive he is. It would have hurt his feelings."

"That was inevitable," Ambrogio pointed out. "There's no way to tell someone who loves you that you don't love them back without hurting them. But then at least they know. You played Segno for a fool."

The words stung, as I knew he meant them to. "How is any of this your business, anyway?" I snapped. "I don't want to talk about it if you're just going to scold me like I'm some little girl. I'm nearly seventeen, if you hadn't noticed."

"It's my business because Segno is my friend, and I saw what the news of your engagement did to him."

That took the wind out of my sails. "Did he take it hard?" I asked in a small voice.

Ambrogio kept his eyes on the road. "He didn't scream and cry and throw things, if that's what you mean. He just sat there while Margherita read your letter, looking like a little whipped dog."

I could see Segno in my mind's eye. He would have avoided everyone's eyes and pretended to smile, but he wouldn't have fooled anyone.

"I don't think he's said two words to anyone from that time to this. He's stopped eating and, from the looks of him, sleeping."

I was suddenly breathless, my ribs seeming to melt into my

stomach. I had hurt Segno, my gentle friend whose only crime had been thinking me better than I wanted him to. Ambrogio's words kept coming, pelting me like chips of stone.

"When somebody offers you his heart, you have a responsibility to—"

"All right," I said nastily because I thought I might cry. "I've heard you. And how have I survived these six months, I wonder, without the benefit of your constant advice? Did you want to complain next about the way I dress? Or perhaps how much I eat?" I swallowed a sob. I would not cry. I would not.

"Don't cry."

"I'm trying not to." I bit the inside of my cheeks to stop the hot tears from seeping out beneath my eyelids. "I didn't mean to hurt his feelings," I said to my dress. "But I didn't know what to do."

We plodded on in silence for a few minutes, except for my gulps and sniffles. Finally Ambrogio sighed and brought the cart to a creaking stop. I could feel him casting around for something to do that would stop my tears. Finally he swatted my shoulder a couple of times and said, "You didn't do anything that every silly girl in Tuscany doesn't do at least once."

I could withstand an irritable Ambrogio, but not one who was trying, in a clumsy-boy sort of way, to be nice. I started crying in earnest.

"He'll mend," Ambrogio said over my sobbing.

Finally my crying began to taper off again.

"Just don't make the mistake," he said in his bossy way, "of thinking that ignoring an uncomfortable situation will make it better. Sometimes it's kinder to say the hard things up front. That's all I'm saying."

I nodded, unable to trust my voice, and wiped my face on

my sleeve. I felt the cart start up again. I was frozen with embarrassment and kept my attention on my dusty shoes.

Just when the silence between us was getting so oppressive that I was beginning to think seriously about jumping over the side and walking the rest of the way to Lucca by myself, I felt Ambrogio nudging me.

I looked up to see him proffering one of Tia Lucrezia's raisin buns. I reached for it hesitantly.

"Only refrain from other acts of war," he intoned.

I jumped, almost dropping the bun, and answered automatically. "Book IX."

I smiled tentatively at him, and he grinned back at me.

"Now let us 'talk of various things to make the long path easy.'"

"Book VIII," I said, and we were comfortable again.

THE COMEDY

Lucca, 1312–1316

The next few weeks were among the happiest I have ever known. I liked the young men my brothers had become. Pietro was nearly a foot taller than his twin Gian, with the presence of the lawyer and public man he wanted to become. Jacopo was half a head shorter than Gian, and despite a predilection to quote canon law, seemed more at peace with himself than he had been as boy. And Gian was in love.

The girl was named Gentucca. The daughter of his land-lord, she was a lovely young woman with olive skin smoothed over high cheekbones and a wide, generous mouth. It was impossible not to like her, especially because it was so obvious that she calmed and steadied Gian. "Gian," she'd say with a pout, and he'd come down from whatever extreme or reckless pronouncement he was making and smile sheepishly. We all adored her, although each time I saw her look at Gian with her heart in her eyes, I wanted to warn her to hold something back, to protect herself just a little.

We were at dinner one afternoon about a week after our arrival. Everyone was there: my father's brother Tio Francesco, my mother, my three brothers, Gentucca, and even Ambrogio, who it transpired did not have to be in Arezzo until Michaelmas and planned to stay on until my father arrived.

"Have a little more, Mama. I know how much you love terrine of boar," Jacopo said as he passed a platter to my mother.

"Do you remember that time with the bishop and the juniper berries?" Pietro asked, and the three of them roared with laughter while I looked down at my plate and fought an unwelcome spurt of jealousy. I kept being brought up short by reminders of the intimacy that existed between them. I had thought of my brothers as living apart from my mother, as I had, but of course Santa Maria Novella was only a few blocks from Nonno Manetto's house, and they would have seen each other during feasts and other holidays.

I told myself that I had just spent half a year alone with her, and two years before that with my father, but when my mother added something about the bishop's housekeeper that set them off again, I could cheerfully have knocked their silly laughing faces together.

Pietro must have seen something of what I felt—he was the quickest of the three—because he abruptly brought the conversation back around to a subject I could share: the *béguinage*, whose existence seemed to fascinate my brothers.

"I suppose you didn't have housekeepers at the *béguinage*," he said. "I just can't get over all those women living unchaperoned. What could your bishop have been thinking?"

"It wasn't the bishop that established the *béguinage*," I said. "It was the king, Saint Louis. His sister thought that women of a certain age should have a place to go so they could live independently after their husbands died."

"But if it is a religious order, surely the pope should be the one to oversee it."

"Well, it's not really," I said. "It's more like a village than a convent. So really the king should have the final say."

Jacopo shook his head, his forehead creased in a way I remembered. "It's just not orderly," he said. "It just doesn't fit. I think the Church was right to condemn Beguines at the

Council of Vienne. Thank His Holy Name that there are no Beguines in Italy."

"But there are," Ambrogio interrupted unexpectedly.

He had said nothing for the entire meal, and I had almost forgotten he was there. We all stared at him. "How would you know?" I said.

He gave me a look I couldn't read. "My mother," he said. "She was a Beguine in Romagna."

"What? Why didn't you ever tell me?"

"She's dead," he said matter-of-factly. "She died of the coughing sickness just before I was sent to Duccio's."

My eyes widened. No wonder he had been upset when I ruined his shirts. For the thousandth time I cursed my stupidity. "Oh, Ambrogio, I am so sorry."

"It's all right," he said. "It was a long time ago."

"At least she is with her God," Jacopo said piously.

My mother gave me the brief, careful look we always shared when one of her friends said something extremely silly, and I felt better. "Was she a weaver?" my mother asked before Jacopo could go on in that vein.

I winced, and felt Ambrogio notice. He hesitated and picked his words carefully.

"At the end of her life, yes, but before that she had been a painter. Her father was an artist, and he had taught her his trade."

"But how interesting!" my mother said. "And your father? Was he an artist too?"

"No. He's a cabinetmaker for the artists in Arezzo. He's the one that got me the commission."

I had known the Lorenzetti brothers were from Arezzo, but not the rest. There was a short, uncomfortable silence while everyone worked through the implications of his story— Ambrogio's mother had left his father for the *béguinage*.

Women simply did not leave their husbands, no matter what the provocation.

"How very interesting," Jacopo said faintly.

My mother smiled at me then, really smiled, so that you could see the way her two front teeth overlapped slightly and that she had dimples. Not dimples, exactly, but places where the hollows beneath her cheekbones became more pronounced and her skin thinned.

Then the door opened behind me, and she smiled so brilliantly that the lines deepened not only around her mouth but also around her eyes. Puzzled, I turned my head to see who it might be.

"The prodigal has returned," my father announced.

"Papa!" I said, jumping out of my chair and running to him as if I were still a little girl.

He appeared relaxed and fit, with his hunched shoulders straightened and broadened by the cut of his beautifully tailored black tunic with a large gold eagle, emblem of the emperor, worked on his chest. The imperial eagle was also embroidered again around the hem of his black cloak, and his boots were of black leather, polished so that I could catch glimpses of my face beneath the dust of the road. He brought a whiff of fresh air into the stuffy room. He opened his arms to me, but his eyes were watching my mother.

"Gemma," he said. "You are looking as lovely as ever. I see that Ambrogio persuaded you to come. I was not sure that he could, but he was most eager to make the attempt."

She inclined her head, her smooth face schooled once again to its habitual calm.

"Pietro, Jacopo," he went on. "I have your finished tunics in my bags. I think the dark blue was the right choice. And Gian, this must be your fair Gentucca?"

Gian was standing behind her, his hand on her shoulder, bristling with pride. "Yes, this is my Gentucca," he said.

"Enchanting," my father said, and bent to kiss her hand.

The next few weeks floated by like a dream. We did very little—just ate, slept, dreamed, and talked, catching up with each other after a decade apart. Because we were staying at an inn, my mother had little to do with her time and joined in with the rest of us, laughing and talking as freely as if she were one of the children. My parents began to sit together at meals, my father's arm thrown around her shoulders as if in imitation of Gian and Gentucca's happiness, and sometimes when we walked around the city gates they dropped behind and spoke softly to each other, hand in hand.

At the time, I didn't question the speed of their evident rapprochement; our happiness at being together again seemed a solvent powerful enough to disperse any stains of bitterness or regret. My father's exultation at the prospect of Henry's victory was so genuine that it convinced all of us that we were living the miracle of a happy ending. Even Ambrogio, a worry-wart if there ever was one, had been sufficiently reassured that we might be able to survive without him that he had set the date for his departure.

"My mother talked to him three times at dinner," I said the evening before he left. We were walking home from San Martino, where we had been sketching together after my father had said pointedly at dinner that my mother and Gentucca needed some time to become better acquainted.

"She talks to him all the time," Ambrogio said. "Mind the cat, Bice. You never look where you are going."

"There's no harm done. No. I mean she started three conversations instead of just answering questions. And when they came back from getting the wine, her lips were all pink, as if they'd been kissing. And you've seen the way he looks at her."

"It's not right that a daughter should notice these things about her parents," he said.

I looked at him to see if he was serious. The sun was setting, and for just a moment his outline shimmered with the gold of the light behind him, like the brilliant edging of a cloud in front of the sun. Then it was gone.

"With the sun behind you like that, you look like a mosaic picked out in gold," I said.

He looked annoyed. "Don't talk nonsense."

"I wasn't. I was just pointing out an interesting visual phenomenon." I chose that last word on purpose. Ambrogio never tired of reminding me that it was my father who had studied at the Sorbonne, not me, and that if I weren't careful about the way I talked, potential suitors would be frightened away, et cetera, et cetera.

But he refused the bait. "Don't you think you're all getting a little carried away?" he asked. "I hope for your sakes that the Emperor Henry does besiege Florence, and is successful and rewards your father and all his other lieutenants with wealth and power. But what if it doesn't work?"

"What are you talking about?" I said. "Henry is the emperor of Germany and Italy. Florence is one city. And my father wouldn't have brought all of us here unless—"

"Unless he was worried about reprisals if Henry fails," Ambrogio said quietly.

I looked at his face. I knew every line of it, I suddenly realized. I knew the small, squared-off features and bright eyes—not deep-set, like my father's, or pretty, like Farinata's, but alert and honest. Today they looked patient and sad. That was ridiculous. Ambrogio was about the least patient person I knew.

"You don't think the emperor will win, do you?"

"No," he said. "I don't."

It had literally not occurred to me that the emperor might lose. There was a cold, panicked feeling in my stomach, but I pushed it away. Surely my father would have told us ... "My father is a public man," I snapped. "He's been performing diplomatic missions for the emperor for more than two years now. I think he would know better than some nobody like you."

Ambrogio didn't give me the set-down I deserved. That was when I first began to think that perhaps he was right, that maybe we had all been living a silly, dangerous dream.

He just said, "Sometimes people will say and do things in front of a nobody that they would never do in front of an important man like your father."

"What have you heard?" I said quickly.

"Nothing in particular. It's just a feeling."

"Oh, a feeling."

He started to say something else, then stopped.

I stubbed my toe hard on a protruding cobblestone and nearly fell.

"You never watch where you are going," Ambrogio said again as he caught me and set me back on my feet.

I snatched my arm out of his hands and concentrated on not crying. Some part of me welcomed the pain. It gave me something to fight.

But it wasn't enough. Just before we turned into Tio Francesco's street, I heard myself asking, "And my mother? Would he leave her again, just when they are becoming friendly again?"

He said nothing, just shrugged with that same patient, sad expression on his face, and I realized that, like Gentucca and Segno before her, I had forgotten to keep something back for myself.

I didn't see Ambrogio again. He left early the next morning, and although I thought I heard him moving around and saying goodbye to the others, I pretended it was nothing but the wind knocking the shutters against the house and Gentucca's brother in from the milking.

As Ambrogio had warned it would be, the siege was a disaster. Henry had waited too long, and his army had lost its edge, or perhaps it was that his spirit that had been broken by the death of first his brother and then his wife the previous Christmas. At any rate, it was clear from the beginning how things would fall.

My father aged twenty years during the month of pretense that followed. Henry's armies were still winning victories in the Florentine countryside, so I was suppose there was still some hope, but not for me, and I think, despite his unwillingness to acknowledge it publicly, not for my father. The most obvious disappointment was his hope to return to Florence in triumph, as he believed he deserved. But the greater part of his sorrow must have been his growing conviction that God had not willed Henry's victory. Although he tried to tell himself and others that as long as Henry had breath left in his body there was hope for the establishment of the Roman empire he dreamed of, some part of him knew that the failure of the siege was the beginning of the end.

And our family did nothing to ease the blow. Gian, seeing his own chances fading away like morning frost, could not contain the bitter words he heaped upon my father's bowed head. They had planned to use Gentucca's small dowry to establish a business of their own. Now her parents were keeping it as payment against the month's lodging and meals for all of us, since the emperor was no longer in a position to support his diplomats as he had promised.

I think the defection that hurt my father the most, however, was my mother's. Faced with the loss of all she had worked for for over a decade, she withdrew from us all as completely as she had before. But I was no longer five years old, and when a message came from the emperor that my father should retreat to Forlì with his other lieutenants and she made it known she would not accompany him, I could contain myself no longer.

I tried my mother first, but she refused to discuss her decision. "This is a matter between your father and me, Bice. It does not concern you," she said from her seat in the courtyard, where she was finishing the last bit of embroidery for my beautiful gown.

"What do you mean it doesn't concern—"

"You will be married in a few weeks and have a household of your own to manage, as I have mine." She bit off the thread and stood up, shaking out the gown over the sheet she had spread under her stool. "There. This is done."

"It's beautiful," I said, stroking the soft blue silk. "The most beautiful gown I've ever seen."

Her eyes softened, and she put her hand to my cheek. "But not as beautiful as its owner," she said. "Wear it in good health, child," and she blessed me. "Now I will take it in and pack it. We are leaving very early, and everything must be ready tonight."

"But, Mama, I—"

"I have no wish to continue this conversation, Bice. You will obey me in this matter, please." She gathered the gown carefully into her arms and walked into the house, her back as straight as ever.

I looked after her, biting my lip. Then I fetched something from the *cassone* I kept by my bed and went to find my father. He was sitting on the stone bench outside the *duomo*, as

I'd known he would be. It was where he had gone in Florence when my parents had an argument, and it was where he had been since the messenger had come. He was leaning his head back against the cool stone of the cathedral, his eyes closed and his mouth working, and I was struck by how old and frail he looked. I would have guessed him to be a *nonno*, I thought—and then realized with a shock that he was old enough to be one, and I was almost old enough to be a mother. I'd talked about it with Farinata, of course, but the whole thing had seemed remote and far away. Except now, suddenly, I knew that it could happen.

I didn't want to disturb him, but after just a few seconds his eyes opened and he looked calmly at me. "Antonia," he said. "So you've come to say goodbye to your old father?"

"Actually," I said, "I wonder if we could talk about something."

He sighed and stood up stiffly. "Yes, yes, we can talk," he said. "What else have I to do? It's a beautiful afternoon, Antonia, one of the last of the autumn, I have no doubt. Shall we take a promenade around the city walls?"

He offered me his arm, which he had never done before. It was lean and ropy, still strong, and he walked a little more quickly than was comfortable for me through the brilliant fall afternoon to the city gate. Once we were through, my father stopped and breathed in the air.

"*Santa pace*," he said. "I have missed our jaunts, I must say, Antonia. It has not been the same without my little artist at my side, saying the most surprising things when I least expect them." He smiled at me and put his hand to my cheek, then added abruptly, "I am sorry I have not been able to meet your young man. Guido was a good friend—the best—and a very fine poet. Judging by his letter, Farinata is as learned as his father, and that pleases me. You have a quick mind, Antonia, and it would be a tragedy if it were smothered by some well-meaning brute of a peasant. I hope that Farinata also possesses some of his father's kindness?"

I had never thought of Farinata as kind, but upon reflection I decided that he was. "Yes, I think he does."

"I am glad to hear it. His wife was a proud, cold-hearted woman, but Guido was always quick to forgive those who had done him injury. It is a quality I would have done well to imitate, and I am happy that you will be marrying his son."

I found his words discomfiting. Farinata did not seem to me to be the forgiving sort; in fact, there were many who would describe him as both proud and cold-hearted. The qualities that I valued in him were his quickness, his wit, and, I realized now that I had seen Gentucca and Gian together, a certain reserve that I thought would always remain between us, a buffer to urgency and intimacy and dependence.

I looked up to see that my father had been watching me. "So, Antonia, what is so important that it cannot be said where there are other ears to hear?"

I took a deep breath and then just said it. "Why don't you make Mama come with you?"

His face closed. "She has said that she will not be with me until I can offer her a house of her own, as is her right."

I waited, but his silence was a rebuke. Well, two could play at that. So I silently rebuked him right back until we were at the most isolated portion of the walls, where no one was likely to see us. "There's something else," I said, and leaned one hand against the cold, rough wall while I felt under my skirts for the pocket I wore around my waist. "Tio Teruccio gave me a commission to perform on his behalf." With some difficulty, I withdrew the untidy sheaf of parchment, tied up in a piece of chamois. "These are some of your old papers he thought you might want."

"Why didn't he just give them to Gemma?" Papa asked, taking the bundle and starting to untie the leather cords that bound it.

"I think he didn't want to disturb her. It's poetry."

He pulled the covering away, looked at the top sheet of inscribed parchment, and went completely white. I thought he might faint, and hurried to help him to an outcropping of rock that might serve as a rude bench. He came with me, unresisting, his attention entirely given to the untidy, blotted writing, devouring each word with hungry eyes.

"Where did he find this?" he asked hoarsely.

"The papers were in our old house. He didn't tell me how he came by them, though."

I realized my father was weeping, the tears coursing freely down his hollow cheeks.

"Papa?" I said, frightened into speech. "Are you all right?"

"It's the *Comedy*," he said. "I thought it was gone. And I'd half forgotten, but now it is here." He reached up and seized my head and brought it down so he could kiss my hair. "You have no idea what you and your Tio Teruccio have done," he said. "You and God."

My father did not often speak of God. "And God?"

He was paging through the manuscript with reverent hands. "I didn't tell anyone," he said absently. "How were they to know?"

He glanced up at me, then down again at the closely written words. Then he slowly closed the pages and held them as gently as if they were an infant, stroking the smooth, springy parchment from time to time as though he could not help himself. "Well, Antonia, this is a very great gift you have given me."

"I'm glad," I said. His open display of emotion disoriented me so much that even that conventional response took effort.

He looked around, as if to see that we were alone, and cleared his throat. "You have some time?" he asked me. "There is no bread that must be taken from the oven or laundry that must be hung?"

"I have some time."

"I wonder if you would like to hear a story," he said. "A very long story, actually."

"I'd like that very much."

We settled ourselves on the outcropping. My father looked past me to the Apennines and Pisan mountains aflame in the late afternoon sun. Lavender-gray thunderheads bloomed behind them, and the wind was picking up. We'd have rain before nightfall.

"You know how hurt your mother was when I published the *Vita Nuova*," he said abruptly.

"Yes."

"She was angry, of course, and not always kind to me. And in return I behaved very badly, far worse than she had. It didn't seem so bad at the time—my friends joined me in my debauchery—but later, when I became a politician and began to consider the implications of men's actions, I understood the evil that I had done. Then my friend Forese died, and I considered what my own legacy would be. It was not a comforting prospect. A wife all but abandoned, some poetry that I would not wish my own children to read—I don't mind telling you that I felt myself to be thoroughly chastened."

He cleared his throat. "You were too young to remember this, but just before we left Florence I achieved some political prominence. I was anxious to do better by my city than I had for myself. Forese's brother Corso, an evil-hearted man—"

"The Black Baron," I said. "I remember."

"He was causing trouble, and his principal opponent was Farinata's father, Guido, my best friend in the world now that Forese was dead. I had, in fact, dedicated the infamous *Vita Nuova* to Guido, if you will remember. Anyway, the priory decided that both Guido and Corso would have to go if Florence was to have any chance of maintaining the peace. I agreed with the others, and they were exiled. Almost immediately, word came that Guido had caught malaria in his new home at Sarzana. He was very ill, probably mortally ill, and it was my decision that had made him so. The question of my personal worthiness became more and more urgent. I couldn't eat, couldn't sleep, until finally your mother told me to go to Rome, where Boniface had just proclaimed a jubilee. If you heard mass at fifteen of Rome's most important pilgrimage churches, all your sins were forgiven. So I went, and wept, and bloodied my knees climbing the sacred stairs, and fasted and didn't change my linen and in general behaved like a pilgrim." He smiled at me. "I thought myself very devout, and very fine."

He sighed. "Anyway, I was staying in a little room near the Piazza Navona, and it was my last night in Rome. I was returning the next day to my family and to my political responsibilities, and for the first time it occurred to me that, no matter how hard I tried, I might discharge them imperfectly. I was a very proud young man," he said softly. "I took one last long walk around the city—through Saint Peter's and the Castel Sant'Angelo, down the river all the way to the Colosseum and back again. I was determined to find a sign of God's grace, or at least his mindfulness of me. I don't think I've ever felt quite so alone. Anyway, there was nothing. No sign, no enigmatic stranger, certainly no holy apparition. I went back to my little room and prayed harder than I ever had in my life. I wanted to do good, I wanted to be good, and I was afraid I would achieve neither."

"So what happened?" I asked.

"Nothing," he said. "Absolutely nothing. I cried myself to sleep as I hadn't done since your Nonna Bella died when I was a boy. And then I had a dream." His voice died.

"What kind of dream?" I prompted.

"A very special dream," he said. "So vivid that I am not sure to this day whether I was in or out of my body. I found myself lost and starving in a wood. It was a huge wood, with large, dark, menacing trees, and I was terrified. I remembered my mother's dream when she was pregnant with me—you know the story?"

I nodded. Shortly before my father's birth, my Nonna Bella had had a dream in which she had found herself under a laurel tree in a green meadow near a sparkling fountain. She had been delivered of a son, who had fed himself with the berries from the laurel and drunk of the fountain. As he grew, he became a shepherd, and tried to reach the leaves of the tree that had nourished him. But he fell, and when he arose he had become a peacock, the wise bird with a hundred eyes in his angelic feathers.

"I looked for the laurel tree and the meadow with the fountain, but I could not find them. A dark mist arose, and a noise, lots of noises—groans and whispers and creakings—but no words. Nothing you could hold on to. I felt the earth falling away from me, and in the moment when I was sure I would be swallowed up by a chaos that was so profound that I could not see or hear or touch or name it, I called out to God."

"You called to God?" It would never have occurred to me to call to God. The Virgin, maybe, but not to God himself.

He looked at me, surprised. "Who else?"

"Your birth saint, Santa Lucia," I said. "Maybe the Virgin. But God seems so far away."

"Well," he said. "Well. Just as this chaos was undoing me, I called out with my last breath to God. And the tentacles of darkness that seemed to be growing over me fell away like dried husks from the vine, and I found myself on a mountain with a woman dressed in white. She asked me what I wanted, and I said to see the tree of my mother's dream. She pointed, and there it was, and I ate of the fruit, and drank of the fountain next to it, and I was filled."

He looked down at me, his eyes bright. "When I say I was filled, Antonia, I mean that in that moment, all yearning, all striving slipped away, and it was as if my bones and blood existed for no other purpose than to support the joy of my spirit. My companion asked me if I knew what I was feasting on. 'Yes,' I said. 'It is the love of God, shedding itself abroad in the hearts of men.' Then she asked me again what I desired, and I told her I wanted to share the sweetness of the fruit with the people I loved. When I said it, I meant you and your mother and your brothers, but then she said, 'Look!' and I saw crowds of people, all looking for the tree, and I realized I loved them all. I called to them, but a mist of darkness arose and a Babel of voices, and I could be neither heard nor seen. Then she said again, 'Look!' and I looked, and I saw angels writing the book of heaven and earth, and prophets writing the book of God. My guide reached into her robe and took out a book, smaller and shabbier than the rest, and somehow I knew it was mine.

"'What is that book?' I asked my companion. She handed it to me and said, 'It has not been written, yet it is written.' Then I swallowed the book, and awoke."

My father sat back, his animation quenched. The wind had

come up, and scudding clouds raced over our heads, turning the landscape from golds and blues to dun and then back. Papa pulled his cape around him with a fretful little motion, an old man once again.

I didn't know what to make of the story he had told me. "Was it real?" I asked him. "Or was it a dream?"

"It was more than a dream," he said without hesitation. "That I would swear. But when God speaks to you, it is too much—" He waved his hands. "I didn't know what it meant, you see. I still don't. I was vouchsafed a vision and given a task, but how to accomplish it? I tried—oh, how I tried! But the words I wrote were dead and lifeless on the page. They lacked all spirit, all humanity."

"Like the *Banquet*," I said without thinking, and wished the words back.

"Just so," he said, looking down at the bundle in his lap and adjusting it so that the pages lay square. "You are a little too quick for comfort, my Antonia."

I started to apologize, but he waved it away.

"No, no, it was not a complaint. Indeed, I believe that was my error, to believe that I could write such a book without discomfort to myself. Of course that was not true. My soul needed to be enlarged until it was big enough to see, and that I could not do for myself. But it wasn't until Guido Cavalcante, your fiancé's father, died at my hands that I was willing to ask God how this task was to be done."

"You didn't kill him," I said. "The malaria did. And it was he who made the decisions that led to his exile. You were merely administering the natural consequences of his intemperate behavior."

"You are generous to your old father," he said. "Come, we should start back. It grows cold."

"So what did you do?" I pressed him as I got to my feet and shook out my skirts.

"I decided to tell the story that I wish someone had told me when I was at the beginning of all my strivings, the story that might have directed my feet toward God. I started by writing what I knew about hell, because I could not describe the journey to God's love unless I showed first the consequences of a life without it. It was an excruciating experience, I must say, imagining the hell that my actions might yet lead me to. It is not a comfortable thing, Antonia, to compare the life you live with life as it should be, and I suppose I was more grateful than anything else when the poem was lost."

His words distressed me. I wrapped my arms around myself as thunder rumbled in the distance. "So you just stopped doing anything? After God told you what to do?"

"It wasn't that black and white," he said, a trace of defensiveness in his voice. "I kept hoping the poem had not truly been lost, that your mother had secreted it somewhere and would eventually return it to me. In its absence I started to write the *Banquet,* and by the time I realized that the poem was unlikely to turn up, the urgency of the vision had faded. I told myself the *Banquet* would do as well, and then that my work for the emperor would do it, and perhaps the treatise on political philosophy I have been working on more recently." He laughed bitterly. "And when I realized the siege was failing, it occurred to me that I have been a Jonah, running away from the task God gave me, thinking that I needed only please myself."

He left the next day. I believed all the things he had told me. Of course I did. I was still just a girl and hoarded every word that fell from his lips like a miser. And my only prayer when he left us was for him, that his *ingegno* would be up to the task God had called him to do.

When my mother left, I stayed behind to help with the olive harvest. I am ashamed now to remember how relieved we all were to be rid of them both—my prickly, prideful parents with their little vanities and chronic dissatisfactions. The five of us—Gentucca, my three brothers, and I—were young, healthy, and strong, and it seemed to us then that my parents' disappointments were gossamer things that would dissipate in the face of the energy that sang through our veins like new wine. My mother left on a hot, sultry day that belonged to August rather than November, and while she and her traveling companions were still visible on the horizon Pietro turned to us and said, "I think it is time for a swim."

Jacopo and Gian grinned at him. "Amen to that, brother," Gian said.

I made a face at Gentucca that said clearly, "Boys get all the fun." She winked at me and stuck her arm through Gian's. "Gian," she said, pouting. "You surely are not going to leave Bice and me behind on a beautiful day like this one."

He looked at her in that besotted way of his, then beseechingly at the others.

Pietro was shaking his head no, but before he could say anything, Jacopo had interrupted in a scandalized voice. "No, really, Gian, it wouldn't be suitable. Men and women swimming together—why, that's positively indecent."

I could have kissed him. Pietro and Gian hated it when Jacopo sounded like a prosy old priest. "I wouldn't say that there's anything indecent about brothers and sisters swimming together in broad daylight, would you, Gian?" Pietro said meditatively. "Especially if, say, the women were doing laundry down at the river and one of them were to slip on the stones.

You couldn't just let her drown, now could you? You'd have to jump in and save her. And then it would only make sense to teach her how to swim so that if she were to fall in again ..."

"Weren't you saying just this morning how eager you were to do one more big wash before the winter set in?" Gian asked her.

"You know, I was," she said demurely. "But there really is too much for two young girls to carry by themselves."

"Allow me to assist you," Gian said.

As it transpired, Gentucca could swim like a fish, and I was the only one who needed teaching. I was not entirely happy about this state of affairs. I had been nervous around water ever since the storm on the way to Vernazza years before, when I had imagined myself washing off the back of my poor little Jennet, and I had hoped to splash about inconspicuously in the shallows and let it go at that. But my brothers would have none of it.

"Throw her in!" Gian bawled to Pietro from the middle of the river. "It's the only way to learn!"

My flaccid fingers grasped the edge of the footbridge more desperately than ever.

"Nonsense, Gian," Gentucca said, her dark head next to her husband's as sleek as an otter's. "You don't want her to fight the water. Bice, if you relax into it, the water will hold you up."

"But I won't be able to breathe!" I wailed as I felt Pietro move impatiently behind me.

Jacopo, who had been watching all this with ostentatiously pursed lips and his skirts held pointedly away from any possible contamination by the water, spoke up from his place on the shore. "We depend on God for every breath we take," he said. "Every breath is an act of faith."

I turned to look at him in astonishment, and he winked at me. Then I was in the water. I'd like to believe it was because I jumped, but I think it was mostly a slip I didn't try to stop. The water closed over my head, and I started to panic as I remembered the way it had plucked at me in my dream until I dissolved. Then Gentucca's words came back to me, and I stopped fighting it. I propelled myself upward with my arms and legs as I had seen boys do a thousand times in the river on a hot day, and felt my head break the surface. "I swam! I swam!" I exulted, or tried to, but Pietro jumped in beside me with a huge splash, and my nose and throat filled with water. I gasped and choked and flailed until he took pity on me and pulled me into the shallows. But for just a moment I'd been dancing with the water, and before the afternoon was over I was something of an otter myself.

THE NORTH KINGDOM

Lucca and Verona, 1312–1317

I do not like to dwell on the four years that followed, and as if in blessing God has left me little memory of them. Of course Farinata didn't want me once it was clear that the siege had failed and my family name would be a hindrance rather than a help to his future career. I was so naïve that I hadn't even considered the possibility, and ran back to Lucca to hide my shame amidst the familiar round of cooking, sewing, and cleaning for my brothers. But that haven proved illusory. Gentucca's parents were carried off by a fever the first winter of her marriage. At about the same time, my Tio Francesco, made leery by the conquest of Lucca by the Ghibelline tyrant Uguccione, closed his Lucca office and retreated to the property in Prato his sons had been managing for him. We could not follow, since my brothers shared my father's exile, and found ourselves alone.

It was not a good time to lose Francesco's financial backing. Uguccione, a capable enough leader but too ambitious for his people's good, soon declared war on Florence. It became difficult to get word to my mother, and impossible to visit her. Trade slowed, then ground to a halt. And there was no help from Siena. Margherita wrote to say that Duccio had fallen and hurt his back. He'd had to close his workshop and had sold most of his tools and supplies to Ambrogio, who was apparently newly engaged to a cousin of the Tolomei banking family and hence had a generous dowry at his disposal. He and his new bride were off to Rome, so that he could study with the great artist Giotto.

This news fell on me like a blow. Duccio's household had been my safe place, insurance that I would never again experience the raw, oozing pain of being ripped away from the security of a stable family. And Ambrogio—he was my *deus ex machina*, the friend who could be depended on to appear whenever he was needed and make my problems go away. How dare he leave my life without warning? How dare he betray our friendship and begin a new life that excluded me? I silenced the voice that reminded me that I had done the same to him. For all he knew, I was still betrothed to Farinata— maybe even married. But knowing I had no right to feel as I did only overlaid my fear with shame. I was like a soldier who looks down and sees that he has forgotten both his shield and his weapon.

If the five of us in the household snatched some moments of contentment, it was in large part due to Gentucca, who despite her grief for her parents did her best to care for all of us like the indulgent mother we had never had. She was a marvelous cook, concocting delicious soups and stews from a scrap of this and a dab of that, and kept a tidy, friendly house. She encouraged us four siblings to spend time together, and gradually we began to re-weave ourselves into a family.

But Gentucca's goodness was not enough to protect her from her own series of tragedies. She became pregnant a few months after her parents' death, and her pregnancies were the worst I have ever seen; to this day I can't think of her without remembering the sweet, pungent stink of vomit. She kept nothing down from virtually the moment of conception until the agonies of labor. How she kept herself alive and nourished another creature into being I don't know—the sheer bull-headedness that made her such a good match for Gian, I suppose. Their daughter, a sickly, colicky baby with her father's temper and her mother's smooth olive skin, was born a year after their wedding. I was the baby's godmother, and I named her Angela.

Gentucca's body, punished almost beyond endurance by the difficulty of her pregnancy, could not produce enough milk for the infant, and we had no money for a wet nurse. We had a goat, however, and Gentucca and I did all we could to get enough milk into that little scrap of humanity to sustain the spark of life. But it was no good. She was dead in a month. She would be the longest-lived of Gentucca's three children.

We each found our own way to keep the terror of impending poverty at bay. Gentucca was soon pregnant again, and I dedicated myself to becoming the best nurse and housemaid I could be. It took all my strength and ingenuity to keep us all fed and the linens clean, and I was grateful for the labor. Jacopo took to roaming the hills, singing to himself and sometimes coming home late at night smelling of cheap perfume. Pietro threw himself into the work; he was a good businessman, but as our capital dwindled there was less and less for him to do. He began to visit churches and listen to the preachers who entertained with sermons and gymnastics. He was not a particularly religious person, but it was something to do that offered at least a little stimulation for his restless mind.

Gian simply gave up. At first he behaved as men do when their lives disappoint them, drinking and fighting too much and sleeping late. But all too soon, he discovered the lure of gambling.

Gentucca tried to reason with him, but not even his love for her was enough to blunt the siren call of the dice. He had been cheated, and the riches he would accumulate on this throw or the next would make it up to him. In the face of such blinding possibilities, no trifling questions of honor or responsibility could be allowed to matter. Pietro installed new locks on the office doors, but he might have spared himself the trouble and expense; he could find no hiding place for the keys that Gian would not eventually discover. Small things came up missing— a horn cup here, a woven basket there. Then the linens that had been Gentucca's dowry—sheets, tablecloths, napkins— and even the little shirts she had sewn for Angela. By the time I thought to hide my painting things, it was too late; they, too, had been sold.

The nightmare of the years that followed closed in rapidly after that. I had never known the desperation of actual physical want before, nor had I borne responsibility for the well-being of others without sufficient resources to care for them. By the second spring we were starving and so desperate that I walked to Florence, had my mother sell the cornflower-blue silk gown she had made for me and which I had left unworn in one of her trunks, knotted the coins it brought into my tattered *camicia*, and walked back to Lucca. My mother fretted that I was a single woman traveling without escort, but I was far beyond worrying about anything except keeping Gentucca alive. Pietro and Jacopo could go back to the monastery if they had to, and Gian was lost to us one way or another, but Gentucca had no one but me. The money that it brought fed us until the harvest, when we heard that Florence had offered amnesty to her exiles if they came back and confessed their sins. I hoped briefly that it would be enough to bring my father home. But he refused to return under those humiliating conditions, so my mother sold her grandmother's silver mirror, which saw us through the winter, and in the spring, the Book of Hours I had made her.

They said it was a fever that carried Gentucca off in the end, but I knew it was the heaving waves of her constant pregnancies, seizing her and wringing out every bit of life until, in the spring of 1316, she had nothing left and slipped away. Three weeks later, Jacopo went on one of his all-day walks and found Gian's body floating in the Serchio.

Where was my father during that last bitter year? There were rumors that the eye trouble that had plagued him as a young man had returned, and that he had left Verona. But no one seemed to know exactly where he had gone. We discovered later that he had spent most of that year in seclusion at Fonte Avelda, Saint Peter Damian's hermitage overlooking Mount Catria, petitioning for God's assistance with the last half of the *Commedia* and pleading with Santa Lucia for the restoration of his sight. He left Fonte Avelda after Easter, when the thin track connecting it to the outside world was cleared of winter snow and spring mud, and arrived in Lucca without warning on the stormy April afternoon of Gian's funeral.

He came upon us huddled around the sad little plot of ground outside the city gates where the poor and those unworthy of Christian burial were laid without stone or memorial of any kind. I recognized him before he recognized us, and saw the moment at which he realized that the mourners were his kin. His eyes fastened desperately on my face, registered that I was still among the living, and then passed to the next. He was almost upon the grave before he realized Gian was missing. He wailed and fell to his knees, scrabbling in the cold spring mud for earth to sprinkle on his head and crying out the agony of his soul from Book IX of the *Aeneid*:

"Here is our helpless ritual and our sorrow,
I have outlived my time to linger on, survivor of my son."

I watched as though he were acting out a play, and when he was done I went home and set out our poor bread and sour wine, and then I went to bed. I took Gentucca's pillow in my arms and buried my face in it, breathing in the familiar sweet, pungent odor, and I wondered where she and her children were. There was no trace of her in the house, no trinket or gown she had used or worn, no physical evidence that a woman named Gentucca had lived and grown and labored for those she had loved. She existed only in my memory, and that was a broken and unreliable tool. I couldn't remember now, for example, what she had looked like when I had first met her, only at the end, when her wrists and ankles looked like swellings on a twig and her hair was thin and brittle.

People came and said things to me, but I didn't listen. It was hard work to make myself remember each task we had shared, each bitter discovery we had made, and I had no energy to spare for other pursuits. My father kept trying to talk to me, but I would none of it. Then recalling, I suppose, the comfort it had brought Claire, he read to me from the *Inferno* until I could not bear it any longer and asked him which circle of his hell he had reserved for his grandchildren, dead because their good mother had the misfortune to marry an Alighieri male, and that I hoped to God it was nowhere near their father, who had taught all of us more than we wanted to know about that place. But then I remembered holding on to Gian's square, powerful body as we rode through the spring fields, and the way his laughter pulsed through my arms into my heart, and I turned my back to all of them, even Gentucca and her poor babies. I lay in my bed and closed my eyes and took myself back to the *béguinage*, where Sagesse drew perfect lines and I made them beautiful.

My father finally took us away with him. What else could he do? There was nothing left for any of us in Lucca. We went to Verona, to the court of his friend Can Grande.

Only those who have borne crushing responsibility and then had it abruptly removed can understand the fierce, almost bitter joy I took in my freedom during those first few weeks in Verona. The Scaligeris were a noble family led by Can Grande, a warrior active in both mind and body, three or four years older than I. He was not a polished man, and I know my father often shrank from his crudity. But I liked him. He may have been rougher than the courtiers we had stayed with in Paris, but he was also more vital and genuine, insatiably curious and inventive and generous to those in whom he sensed a largeness of spirit or talent. My father was only one of a number of protégés whom he fed, clothed, and sheltered for the good of their art.

We were housed comfortably in two rooms. My father and the boys slept in the chamber that served as my father's study during the day. I slept in the other, which we called the "work-room," although no work was required of us. The palace kitchens cooked our food, and drudges and laundresses looked after the fire and our linen. For the first time in my life, I had no claims on my time.

I could not bear to remain inside, but left my bed as soon as I awoke, as desperate to escape any human claim as I was to learn my new city. The only companion I could tolerate was Jacopo, who had the twin virtues of a silent tongue and a girl in the kitchen who kept us well supplied with bread, cheese, and wine so that there was no need to appear at the formal meals in the castle. Instead we roamed the city and the coun-tryside, coming home so late at night that we were asleep almost before our heads touched the pillows. We inspected every inch of the city; no block of Roman marble lying askew in the ruins of the arena, no bit of carving or painted ornament in any of the basilicas that dotted the town, no tree planted along the riverbank or flower unfurling in a public square was unknown to us.

Verona was a peaceful and prosperous city, a Florence as she must have been before she was rent and distorted by the battles between Guelfs and Ghibellines. Like Florence, Verona lay on a river, but while Florence's Arno was clogged with mud and not navigable, the fast-moving Adige was dotted with boats and barges. Verona was also graced, as Florence no longer was, by relics of its ancient past. Some of these were obvious, like the huge arena and the Roman theater across the river, but some were not. You'd glance at a fountain or a piece of dressed stone built into the wall of a cathedral and suddenly notice a graceful line or smooth drape, and realize that skilled hands dead for more than a millennium had left you a gift of unexpected beauty. And the Romans weren't the only ones. Their barbarian successors had, after converting to Christianity, ornamented the city's basilicas with weird stone and bronze carvings that retold the familiar Bible stories with the power and strangeness of a more primitive time.

Who knows how long I would have spent my days in this half-wild fashion, throwing myself into a sensory and visual feast so that the moments of unavoidable human contact were so muffled as to scarcely register, if it hadn't been for my father filling Can Grande's head with stories about the Emperor Frederick II, *stupor mundi*, and his "Castel de Monte." Can Grande decided that his large, serviceable palace should be transformed into a haven of refined gentility. The first clue I had of this arrived on an insufferably oppressive July afternoon, so hot that even Jacopo and I could not ignore it. By noon we were drenched with sweat and irritable with each other. Jacopo announced that he was going for a swim, and I retreated to the coolness of my stone-walled room for a siesta.

But when I pushed the heavy oak door open, voices were audible from my father's studio. I groaned to myself. I had no wish to do the pretty with one of my father's friends. I turned to go, with some idea of the cool darkness of the chapel, but they must have heard something, because before I had gathered my wits their chairs were scraping against the stone floor. A second later my father's face appeared at the drapery that separated the two rooms. "Antonia," he said, beaming. "Look who's here."

An elderly and very ugly cherub stepped forward into the light, short and round with a sparse white beard, light blue eyes that bulged slightly, and spaces between the teeth that were too small for his mouth. I was surprised by the warmth with which my father, ordinarily fastidious about personal beauty, gripped this odd person's arm. The mystery was solved almost at once, however. "Antonia, it is my very great pleasure to present Ser Giotto Bondone."

The great painter Giotto bowed over my hand. "Donzelle Antonia, a pleasure," he said in a peculiar high, fluty voice that reminded me, absurdly, of Tia Lucrezia.

I curtsied. "The honor is mine, Ser Giotto."

He chuckled. "What nonsense have you been filling your daughter's head with, sirrah?" he asked my father, with the ease of an old friend.

My father put his hands up, smiling. "It wasn't me, although it probably should have been. I have said nothing to her about our friendship." He turned to me. "Giotto was working on a polyptych in the Badia in Florence when I was prior there. We met again in Padua during my exile." He pointed with his chin.

"Come and sit with us for a bit, Antonia."

"Where, if memory serves, we had several long conversations about the nature of hell," Giotto said. "A topic that preoccupied us both to an unhealthy degree at the time." He scratched energetically at one of his ears. "I haven't painted a Last Judgment since. Imagining my way into hell is something that I want to do only once. I am glad to hear that you finally are delivered of your *Inferno*, as I was of mine."

"No gladder than I am, I assure you. Although now that I am almost through with *Purgatory*, I am discovering that representing the glory of God's knowledge and power has its own share of perplexities and fears."

"I don't envy you, my friend, that is certain," said Giotto, stroking his short white beard. "That is certain."

The two of them sat there nodding, lost in their thoughts like two old women for five minutes or more before I finally became desperate enough to break the silence. "What brings you to Verona, Ser Giotto?"

The little man sat back in his seat and drummed his stubby fingers on his paunch. "Eh, Can Grande has a bug in his bonnet that Verona wants refinement. A bug I imagine your father bears some responsibility for. He wants the palace apartments frescoed. A small job, somewhat beneath the caliber of my recent commissions, but one does not like to say no to a young despot who is fortunate in war. So I told him I would come, fresco one room and design the others, train the local talent, that sort of thing."

"My daughter is a painter," my father said. "Quite a good one."

I knew I should look away and mumble something equivocal, but I didn't. I wanted to impress the man who had called Ambrogio—and his new bride—to Rome. "Ambrogio Lorenzetti and I worked together on Duccio's Maestà," I said with a lift of my chin—and almost honestly.

Giotto leaned forward, his face alight with interest. "Of course—I'd forgotten, Dante, that your sister is married to the man. So, tell me, Antonia, how experienced a painter are you?"

"I've mostly illuminated manuscripts," I said hastily, realizing where this might be going. "Gold-leafing. Some of the plain parts on painted panels. I was never a real apprentice. I have no experience with frescoes."

"And now you are doing—what, exactly?"

I looked to my father for help, but he only looked amused. "Getting to know the city, I suppose."

"Would you like to learn about fresco?" Giotto asked me.

"I'm not sure I'm up to your … your …" What was the word he had used a moment before? "Your caliber."

"We're in Verona," he said. "Not Rome. Not Florence. Anything will look good to these barbarians. At least you know how to paint, which is more than can be said of the boys from the village they'd find for me."

"Of course if you think it would be too much for you …" my father began.

"No, of course not," I said, a bit breathlessly.

"Good. We will begin in the morning."

In deference to the heat, Can Grande decided that dinner would be served outside that evening, on the largest of the bridges spanning the Adige. Jacopo and I had seen the servants erecting brightly colored awnings on our morning walk, and by the time the supper gong sounded they had carpeted the entire bridge with grasses and banks of wildflowers, the conceit being, I supposed, that we were dining in a meadow. Can Grande's newest courtesan, who had the misfortune to suffer from both hay fever and a new pale yellow silk gown, surveyed the ducal banquette, newly watered in a vain attempt to keep the wildflowers from wilting, with unmistakable horror.

At that moment, an alarm signaled the arrival of the ducal party, home from the hunt—a foolish way to spend a hot July afternoon, in my opinion. They had not paused to wash the dirt and blood from their persons, and as Can Grande bent forward to kiss his frozen-faced lady, Giotto's ugly face was split by a delighted grin. "Did I say they were barbarians? Hasn't the poor boy a bossy older sister or mother or someone who can tell him how it's done?"

"He is abler than he may appear," my father warned as the young duke caught sight of our party and came forward to greet us.

"Dante, my friend! And Ser Giotto! Is this not delightful? Just the right note of informality, I think, and such a nice change from the ordinary. Antonia, how splendid that you have joined us this evening." He turned behind him, signaling to one of his companions, a young blond man, powerfully built, whom I had not seen before. "Allow me to present my kinsman, Dino d'Alboino."

His companion was handsome in a Lombard sort of way, with blond hair and blue eyes and a stocky, powerful figure. He leaned over my hand and murmured in ungrammatical Latin spoken with a heavy northern accent, "She is as luscious as a peach, and ready to be plucked."

I was annoyed. "I am no piece of fruit, nor a drudge either, put here for your personal amusement," I snapped back in my best Latin, "but a woman of virtue and birth, who requires your respect and your protection."

"Oh, hoo, the kitten has claws," the blond said, and winked.

Can Grande clouted him on the ear, but he was hiding a smile, and they soon moved away.

"That was not wise, Antonia," my father reproved me. "Dino may be a bastard, but he is still a member of the court."

"He is a fool if he thinks to disguise his intentions by speaking bad Latin in front of a scholar," I said impatiently.

"What makes you think he didn't mean Papa to understand every word?" Pietro breathed in my ear as the conversation became general. "Be careful, Bice. Being the guest of a powerful man is a trickier proposition than you seem to understand."

I loved frescoing. I didn't have to do any of the hard, physical labor, of course—we had plasterers to put up the first rough layer of *arricio* and the final smooth coat of *intonaco*. But the scale of the thing meant that at the end of the day my body knew it had accomplished something. It tired me out, and for that I was grateful.

The subject of the painting—chosen, no doubt, in consultation with my father—was the romance of Tristan and Iseult. After years of painting God and his works, I must say that it felt rather odd, almost sacrilegious, to devote so many weeks to pondering a French romance that ended in tragedy. I knew the poetry was beautiful, but without the magic of the words I found the subject matter artificial, empty, and depressing, and I understood why my father had turned from the romantic poetry of the *Vita Nuova*—and perhaps a bit more about why we had left Les Baux so quickly.

But I did not have as much leisure to contemplate the character of my subject matter as was usually the case. For the first time in years, I was working under the guidance of a teacher, and a generous one at that. Giotto treated me more as a partner than an assistant, hiring paint grinders for each of us. Once the grid was on the *arricio*, we did the preliminary charcoal sketches together, brushed on the red sinopia over the sketches, and finally executed the painting itself on the wet *intonaco*. And unlike many of the artists I had spent time with, he enjoyed explaining exactly what he was doing and why he was doing it.

Although Giotto and Duccio had both trained in Cimabue's workshop, they had very different styles. Giotto's work lacked some of the sensitivity to color and lyricism of line that marked Sienese painting, emphasizing instead the volume and solidity—the physical reality—of his subjects. At first I found his figures coarse, even ugly, and his open portrayal of their real, recognizable responses unseemly, but over time his paintings came to seem truer and more compelling to me than Duccio's attenuated elegance.

He'd also begun to use space differently. His landscapes seemed empty, almost unfinished, to my illuminator's eye, but as I lived with those serene expanses of field or water or sky, I found myself falling into them in a way I did not with my own crowded scenes.

"Where did you learn to do that?" I finally asked one afternoon as I sat eating sausage and bread.

"Do what?" he asked absently. "Look, Bice, do you think that highlight is too orange?"

"No. It just looks that way because the light's shining on it. Where did you learn to leave space like that?" I gestured with my elbow toward a series of receding hills that seemed to drift off the wall altogether.

He stopped fussing with the hand he was painting and stood back from the wall, stretching his back as he surveyed the skyline he had completed the day before.

"Why?" he asked, putting his brush down and rinsing his hands perfunctorily before dropping into his folding chair, which gave an alarmed creak. I got up and took him his share of the lunch, and he peered up at me with his bright eyes. "Does it bother you?"

"It did at first," I admitted. "But not anymore."

He gave his delighted, childlike laugh. "You know who taught me that? Your friend Ambrogio Lorenzetti."

We had never spoken of Ambrogio since the first day when I had bragged about working with him. It was a shock to hear his name again. Even more shocking was the stab of loneliness and yearning that followed. I missed him. I missed him to death. And Margherita. And Segno. And Taviana and Feo and Duccio. I wanted to be home in Siena, where no one called me a luscious peach ready to be plucked and where if I was alone it was because I wanted to be. I was tired of being invisible, tired of being dependent, tired of being afraid and forgotten and a burden and a hanger-on. Even Giotto, my generous teacher, was just going through the motions. He would chatter like this no matter who was next to him—probably even if it was just to his brushes.

Giotto misunderstood the reason for my silence, and gave his high, affected little laugh again. "The difference between a good painter and a great one, my dear Bice, is that the great ones never stop learning. Even if it is from their apprentices. Look—here—see, without this space, there's no urgency, no wanting, no movement, no life. Your father discusses much the same idea in his *Purgatorio*, in fact."

I knew my father had been working on *Purgatorio*, the canticle of repentance, since he had finished the *Inferno* two years before, but after the shattering experience of hearing the *Inferno* recited after Gentucca's death I had not spoken to him about his work. "I haven't read it," I mumbled. What I was really interested in was more news about Ambrogio—how was he? What was his wife like? Were they happy?

"You haven't read it?" Giotto looked at me, scandalized. "That is a crime. No, put your paints away. I will finish this myself. *Madre di Dio*, what were you thinking? Your father sacrifices everything to pass on what he has learned to others, and his own daughter does not trouble herself to read it?"

Maybe that's because his own daughter is part of the sacrifice, I said grimly to myself. "He doesn't like to be disturbed when he is working."

But he would not be denied. "Nonsense. Go. I mean it. You should have done this long ago. Or he should have asked you. Shoo! Shoo!"

"Papa?"

"Antonia, is that you?" My father pulled back the curtain, his thin face alarmed. "Why aren't you painting? Is everything all right?"

"Yes, yes, everything's fine, why shouldn't it be?" I answered, obscurely annoyed by his solicitude. "Giotto sent me to ask you about *Purgatorio*."

"Ask me what?" He gestured to a chair beside him, and with a sigh I went to join him.

"Well, actually, he wants me to read it," I mumbled, my head down.

"Oh, he does, does he?" I could feel my father looking at me. "I was under the impression," he said, "that you were not interested in hearing any more of my poetry. Indeed, I was beginning to think that you were not interested in hearing anything from me at all. For two people who live in the same rooms, we seem to see remarkably little of each other."

I fidgeted uncomfortably. "Well, I am here now."

"Not that I blame you," he continued. "It takes time to find oneself again after a ... a ... period of difficulty."

I said nothing, just scraped at a bit of green paint on my arm.

"Difficulties that a father who spent less time with the children of his pen and more with the children of his body might have been able to at least partially spare you?" I lifted my eyes to his, and it was he who looked away. He rubbed at the gray bristles on his cheek. "There is only one Father who is perfect, and I am not he. I ask you only to remember that I am getting closer to him as quickly as I know how."

He turned his face to mine, unafraid to let me see the depth of his regret and shame, and I realized that if I wanted to, I could let go of the whole uncomfortable bundle of anger and fear and hurt between us. I fumbled for the words that would tell him that I knew this, that would soothe the almost unbearable poignancy of the moment. "Isn't that what purgatory is for?" I asked shakily. "Learning to make the journey from where one is to where one would like to be?"

"So it is," he said. He stood, paused for a second, then leaned forward and gave me a rough, clumsy hug. Then as I sat back and mopped at my eyes, he made rather a business of taking a bundle of parchment from the locked *cassone* at his feet. "I want you to know, Bice," he said, putting it into my arms very gently, "that I am interested in anything you have to say about this. Anything at all."

We both knew he was talking about more than the poem.

Others have written much more learnedly and lyrically than I can about my father's three-part *Divina Commedia*—the *Inferno*, which Tio Teruccio had saved for him, the *Purgatorio*, which I read in one sitting on that day Giotto ordered me to, and the *Paradiso*, not finished until some years later—and I will not repeat them except to say that it is the truest poem, the truest art, I have ever known. I wouldn't have thought that my father, or indeed any man or woman, was capable of such truth. It is not always pleasant to encounter the self you see reflected in the deep pools of its three canticles, but their very depths invite me to return to the poem again and again, hoping each time that my mind and heart have grown capable of grasping more of its beauty and its power. My father's passions cost both him and his family dearly, but I cannot deny that in the three canticles of the *Commedia* they bore sweet and nourishing fruit.

It was February before Giotto's last sinopia was completed and the replacement team deemed ready to execute the remainder of the frescoes in the guest chambers. I wasn't part of the team, of course—no woman was part of a workshop that was not led by a close male relative, and indeed I'd spent the last month or so frescoing our rooms with depictions of the muses while Giotto trained his team. But now our rooms were almost done and Giotto was leaving and the future wavered in front of me. By Shrove Tuesday, the day before the beginning of Lent and Giotto's departure, I was beginning to slip back into the gray place I'd been when we first arrived in Verona.

"What's the matter with you?" Pietro asked at supper while Papa read a book and I toasted my feet at the fire. "You used to look forward to Shrove pancakes all year and you haven't eaten a bite." Since it was forbidden to consume dairy products during the forty days of Lent, it was traditional to use up all the eggs, butter, and milk on the special pancakes that were eaten only on Fat Tuesday.

I poked at the delicate golden cakes on my plate and shrugged. "I'm just not hungry." I shivered and moved my feet closer to the fire. "It's so cold."

Jacopo came into the room, his cheeks red from the wind and rain. "It's a wild one," he said cheerfully.

"You're getting me all wet," I complained as he warmed his hands at the fire.

"So push over a bit."

"I was here first."

"My apologies, *principessa*," Jacopo said with an elaborate bow.

I felt them waiting for me to laugh. Instead, I shook my hair into my face and ignored them.

"She's moping again."

"Oh for the love of heaven, Bice, what's got your goat?"

I shrugged, suddenly close to tears. I hated behaving in this stupid, peevish way, but I couldn't seem to stop myself.

"You know what it is, of course," Pietro told Jacopo. "*Febbraietto, corto e maledetto*. Little February, short and cursed. The nights have been long forever," he complained in the wavery voice of a distraught old woman. "I can't remember what it's like not to have chilblains or to smell musty wet wool. If I could only see the sun! If only there were no mud! If only I could taste something green again! If only there were no cold drafts! If only spring would come! If only my beau were not leaving me! Ah, me, what am I to do?" He threw himself sobbing onto Jacopo's shoulder.

Despair that was creeping close to desperation had eroded my sense of humor, and the old joke about my supposed liaison with Giotto had worn especially thin. "*Diamine*, he's as old as Papa. It's not funny, Pietro."

Jacopo tut-tutted. "Language, my dear girl. Language. Where did a well-brought-up young lady like yourself pick up such evil words? It's disgusting."

"Well, it is such a trial to be a lady of leisure," Pietro

confided to him. "Oh, for the days when I was up before dawn in all kinds of weather, fetching water from the frozen well and baking bread from moldy old chestnuts, when my life had some purpose, some meaning—"

I reached for something to throw at him, but the dishes weren't mine to break, so I shouted instead, caught in the grip of unsuspected passion. "Go to hell, the pair of you! It's easy for you. Jacopo has his women and the canonry Can Grande gave him, you have your legal studies, and Papa has his great poem. But what about me? I have no husband, no child, no prospect of either, no work, no cause to throw myself into, and not even enough of a dowry to buy myself a place in a convent so I can be safely shut up for the rest of my life!" I reached for my wine, but my hands were trembling so badly I couldn't lift the cup to my mouth.

"Go back to Florence if you're so miserable," Jacopo said.

I was so infuriated by his casual dismissal of this cry from my heart that I gaped at him, speechless.

And Pietro's reaction was no better. "I very much doubt that Mother is interested in having another mouth to feed. You know how hard things are now that the farms are gone— Bice would just be a burden."

At that moment I think I would have tried anything to claw the smug expressions off their stupid faces. But before I could act, my father, usually totally oblivious to his surroundings when he was working, looked up from his parchment and cleared his throat. The three of us were instantly silent.

"I received a communication this afternoon from Guido da Polenta, the new ruler of Ravenna," he said. "As it happens, the archbishop of that city is an old friend of mine from Bologna. He made a pilgrimage to Fonte Aveda while I was there, and we renewed our friendship. Bishop Rainaldo mentioned the meeting to Ser Guido, who apparently knows of my work. At least, he's read the *Inferno*, which consigns his niece Francesca to the second circle of hell. Being a broad-minded gentleman, however, he has decided to overlook this blot on his family's honor."

He looked around at the ring of our faces in the flickering orange light of the fire. "The long and the short of all this is that I have been invited to serve as a sort of notable-in-residence in Ravenna, complete with generous allowance, servants, and a benefice for my oldest son—two livings, actually, Pietro, neither one requiring the taking of holy orders or distasteful vows of poverty or celibacy. Would that be of interest to you?"

"Two livings?" Pietro said in a dazed voice. "I'd have the income from two livings?"

"On the chance that these favors might not be sufficiently dazzling to lure us to his court," my father continued, "Ser Guido has also let drop that he would be willing to foot the bill for providing illuminated copies of the *Commedia* to my adoring public." He cleared his throat, not looking at me. "I had thought, Bice, that you might be willing to perform this office for me, although there is certainly no obligation for you to do so."

"No," I said. "I mean, yes. Of course I will. You mean I'd have something to do?"

"Something to do, and most probably a room of your own and assistants to help you do it." He glanced at all of us again, then away. I couldn't imagine what might be coming next. "Since you all seem to be of the opinion that a move would be a good thing," he said, "I should perhaps mention that Guido da Polenta was quite specific that we would be furnished with a house of our own." He picked up one of his quills, examined it, and put it down again. "Do you think she might still want to come?"

HOMECOMING

Ravenna, 1317–1320

And so my parents finally found their happy ending. My mother, secure at last in a home of her own and confident of her station, set about making my father's life comfortable. I thought that he had probably invited her to join us more out of obligation than affection, but once she was there, he took great pleasure in her management of their domestic affairs. She knew the foods he preferred, the way he liked his rooms arranged, the rhythm of his habits better than he did himself. And his surprised gratitude for her little services and pride in her skill were like dew in a desert to her after the long years of loneliness and worry.

It was a time of peace and abundance. My parents were together and financially secure. They were even, in a small way, celebrities. My father was teaching at Ravenna's university, and admiring students who hung on his every word often stopped by the house and made much of my pleased mother and her good cooking. My brothers were happy. And each time I reached for parchment that I hadn't had to prepare myself, each time I greeted a new passage of the *Commedia*, each time I went to bed with a full belly and no fears for the morrow, I knew myself blessed.

It should have been enough. But it wasn't. In vain I riffled through the evidence of my good fortune. My family was together. I had food to eat, clothes to wear, good work to do.

My mind was filled as it had not been for years with my father's poem and its rich associations with my earlier life, and my eyes and soul feasted on the beauty of my new city. In the years following the fall of Rome, Byzantine and barbarian emperors had built basilicas and baptisteries that, though plain on the outside, glowed on the inside with the quickened fire of brightly colored mosaics. When the light was right—whether daylight or candlelight—the individual tesserae glittered like living jewels, a new version of the stained glass I had loved in France. Quiet, perfect Ravenna, encircled by the arms of the Adriatic coast and the soul silence of the great *pineta*, and shot through with the great legacies of the late Roman empire and the Christian faith, seemed to me to be God's city on earth. Everywhere I turned, I saw dreams realized and aspirations fulfilled.

But they weren't my dreams and aspirations. I shared them, certainly—but only as a participant, a pebble, not as the mosaicist who assembled and organized the tesserae into a beautiful whole. And perhaps that was as it should be. Perhaps the value of my life, like the lives of so many women before me, lay in being a supporting player, invisible but necessary to lives larger than my own. Except that in the lives of my family, at least, I no longer seemed to be necessary at all.

I played with the old idea of returning to Siena and assisting Duccio with what remained of his business, and went so far as to send inquiries to Margherita in Assisi. But barring that unlikely possibility, the only course open to me in the aftermath of the Council of Vienne and papal proclamations against *béguinages* was to become a cloistered nun. I had the means—I was sure Guido da Polenta would provide Dante's daughter with the necessary dowry were he to be asked. And perhaps that was what God wanted me to do. Perhaps that was the payment he required for the peace and prosperity we had finally found; perhaps the gift of reading about my father's own journey to God in the *Commedia* was meant to prepare me to do the same in the more traditional form of the convent.

So I set myself toward preparing for the cloister. But I failed. Each time I walked through the *pineta*, each time I sat on the shore and read the stars, each time I visited the on-going mosaic restorations with my father's friend the archbishop, I remembered how much I loved the world. The smell of the pines and apple blossoms, the sea wind that tumbled my hair and enlivened my spirit—how could I say goodbye to all this? But surely, if that was God's plan for me, surely my life in the convent would blossom into something deep and living and good, much as the tragedy of my father's exile had been converted to the richness of a pilgrimage achieved. My solitary walks became longer and more prayerful, until I felt that my soul was stretched out naked in its yearning all the day long, until any decision, even the living death of a convent, seemed preferable to the gray uncertainty and lack of purpose that muffled every thought and deadened every emotion.

I reached bottom on the stormy August afternoon when Margherita's letter came at last and told me that Duccio was dead, carried off by another stroke on Saint Peter and Paul's feast day. I cried for him, of course, for the loss of his good-ness and the loss of his art, and for Taviana, who was no longer mistress of her own household but a dependent in the house of her married son Tommè. But mostly, I am ashamed to say, I cried for myself, in grief for the death of the happiness and security I had known in Siena, and in mingled dread and relief now that I knew the future that lay ahead of me. God had shut the last door in my face. My place was in the convent. That much was abundantly clear.

Without bothering to cap my inks or blot my parchment, I left the household sleeping through the afternoon siesta, desperate to be out in the world that I would be leaving so soon. I ran through the broad, deserted streets of the town and then the silent, dark ways of the *pineta* until I reached a bluff overlooking the sea. The rain had started, and in the distance came the occasional flash of lightning and the ominous rumbling of thunder. The storm was coming closer, and I didn't care—I welcomed it. "Is this what you want from me?" I shouted to heaven, my hair whipping my eyes and mouth. "Is that what all this has been for—shutting myself up in a convent, illuminating scriptures with scenes and places I will never see again?" Lightning crackled overhead. "Talk to me!" I cried. "Talk to me! I will make my life there, if that is what you need from me. But I need to know!"

I stood there staggering amidst the torrents of wind and rain me, willing myself to become open to the power that plowed the ocean waves, tossed the heavy, creaking trees, and furred the hair on my arms. "I don't know how to find You!" I cried again. "Show me how to find You!"

Eventually the thunder and lightning grew more distant and the sheets of rain softened, and the heat of my rage and frustration dissipated. I was cold, cold and numb, so cold despite the sultry August heat that my bones ached. By the time I got home, I was shaking uncontrollably and needed help to undress. Mother scolded me for dripping on her newly sanded floor and brewed tisanes and built up the fire. But by then I was tossing with a splitting headache and a fever so intense that I could not summon the energy to talk or move.

Hours or maybe days later when I came to myself, it was dark and I was drenched in sweat, my hair and the bedclothes clammy and matted to my skin. My mother was sitting next to me, her eyes puckered with worry. She offered me cool water, which I drank gratefully, and then some broth, but I couldn't face it.

"Maybe later," I said. "I'm just so tired ..."

She put the soup away, smoothed my hair back from my forehead, and hummed a psalm in her strong and beautiful voice until I drifted off into sweet sleep. By the time I awoke the next morning, I was hungry and ready for a bath. But while I still sat before the fire drying my hair, the shivering began again until I could no longer hold the comb in my hands. My mother entered the room with a tray just as it slipped from my shaking hands. She put down the tray with hands that suddenly were trembling nearly as badly as my own. We both knew the symptoms. I had malaria, the mosquito-borne disease that had killed Farinata's father, Guido, and there was no treatment.

Malaria is an odd disease, rendering its host deathly ill for hours at a time and then seeming to disappear until the cycle begins again two days later. In the beginning my mother joked that it was as if I were in labor, with eight-hour pains coming two days apart. After a week or so, however, no one was laughing. As my body wore out, the fever cycles began to bring on delirium and horrible, terrifying fever dreams peopled by sentient lumps of rotting flesh and swirling, threatening spirits of blackness.

The time came when I could no longer bear it, when the assault of the disease overpowered my physical self. So I left, shaking myself loose from my ravaged body with the same little click with which my father had surrendered his king to Tio Francesco during a chess game long ago.

I didn't hurt anymore, and I wasn't scared. It seemed I had left all my uncertainty and confusion behind in the sweaty, emaciated husk of a body I could see lying crumpled on the bed. I was several feet above it now, and I could see it from a hundred different angles at once, from inside and outside, on top and beneath, all without any loss of clarity or order. I knew I must be dead, but the knowledge did not worry me. I felt calm and whole, restored to the self I had always sensed I could be.

I heard some delicate chimes in the distance and noticed a light growing on the horizon. I felt drawn to the light and the music, and found myself passing through the wall of the house without effort and then rushing through the air faster and faster until suddenly I was standing in a meadow of flowers. The flowers were unlike any I had seen before—they shimmered, as though light didn't merely reflect off them but came from within, and there were thousands, millions of colors, brighter and more beautiful than anything I had ever imagined. A being was standing next to me, wearing a white hooded robe girdled with gold. She didn't frighten me—I knew she meant me no harm, just as I somehow knew she was a woman—and when she saw I loved the flowers she bent forward and picked one— a yellow rose—and handed it to me. I held it up to my face and breathed in its scent. It felt alive and vibrant in my hand, and I wanted to examine it more closely, and then I was somehow drawn into the flower, seeing it from within and without at the same time, feeling that as I did so we somehow joined each other and were one. And then I was myself again, and I turned to my companion to thank her.

Her hood fell back, and I saw that she was Gentucca. She smiled at me, and then indicated another woman I hadn't noticed. It was Sagesse, looking straight and tall and breath-takingly beautiful. She was weaving some wildflowers into a little girl's hair, and when she finished she turned the child to face me and I saw that the little girl had Gentucca's sweet eyes and Gian's square body and determined chin, and I realized I was looking at Angela, Gentucca's first child; I had imagined her lost to hellfire, since she had died before she could be baptized. Sagesse, who seemed to know what I was thinking, laughed at me, and then she and Angela began to sing the sweetest song I had ever heard, and while they sang they danced. Sagesse was as graceful as a bird, far more accomplished than any of the young Parisian girls she had wanted to be like on that holiday so long ago. I reached my hands to them and pleaded that they take me with them. But Sagesse shook her head, smiling, and said, "We can't come for you yet. But we will be here when you are finished with your work."

It wasn't speech, really—it was understanding more complete than words can communicate. "Is it you? Is it really you?" I wanted to know, and all three of them laughed and there was a burst of light and they were a thousand glowing particles dancing in the air around me. Then they were themselves again, or at least the selves I had known, and I realized that they were more than I had understood, and so was I. And then I knew it was time for me to return to Ravenna where my family prayed and grieved for me, so that they could have someone to love who loved them back. But it would be for just a while, a very little while. And then I would be back in the meadow of living light that was my real home.

Almost before I had completed the thought, I found myself on my bed, squeezing into my cramped, heavy, achy body, and the disappointment was almost more than I could bear. Then the door opened, and my mother looked in to see that I was awake. She came over to my bed and laid a cool hand on my forehead. "Your fever has broken, Bice. I think you are going to be all right." Her voice caught. "Your father and I have been so worried."

The fever had broken, but the illness still had to run its course. The attacks continued for another five or six months, but never with the virulence of the first weeks and never accompanied by black dreams of despair. And the terrible restlessness was gone. I did not know what path my life would take, but I knew now that I had not been forgotten.

I did not tell anyone about what had happened to me that afternoon. But I think my father may have known somehow. At any rate, he began to speak openly about what he had seen and experienced on the Easter of Gian's death as he walked among the beeches and oaks and clear, sparkling streams at the green feet of Mount Catria, the mountain of his consolation.

And so the world turned, and I wrote for my father when I could, and when I couldn't I sat wrapped in shawls dreaming of spring.

Spring came early that year—in December, in fact, on Santa Lucia's feast day, my birthday. I sat shivering in front of the fire, waiting with some impatience for the fever to come so that I could get back to work for a day or two before it struck again. There was a knock on the door, and then it opened and a powerfully built figure stepped in out of the darkness.

With a rush of heat, my body recognized him a split second before the rest of me did. It was Ambrogio, looking worn and travel-stained. I was both ridiculously pleased and embarrassed by the intensity of my unguarded reaction. "What are you doing here?" I asked him.

He laid his hat on the table next to me. "I heard that you'd been ill."

I laughed. "You're a little late."

He pulled a stool over to my settle, and sat down with his feet toward the fire. "It takes time for gossip to reach itinerant painters in small parish churches in Chianti."

"Well, you made a long trip for nothing," I said, a little nettled by his matter-of-fact manner. "I'm much better now."

"I can see that," he said, nodding gravely. "I can see that you are perfectly hale and hearty, except for a little uncontrollable palsy. Does that come before or after the fever?"

"Before," I said. "But don't worry. It's not contagious."

"I should hope it's not. Yes, I should hope it's not," he said. He slapped his gloves together and stared into the fire. "I should certainly hope not," he repeated absently.

I shot him a startled look. It was not like Ambrogio to be vague. And he didn't look well. His face was thinner, and there were lines around his mouth and eyes. "Is everything all right?" I ventured. "Is your family well?"

"Yes, yes, Pietro and Margherita are fine. She is expecting another baby sometime after Easter."

"No, I meant your family. Your—" Why was it so hard to say? "Your wife."

He looked at me as though I were delirious. "What wife? I don't have any wife."

"But I thought—I was sure—when Duccio had his first stroke—"

"Oh! You mean Carolina." His eyes slid away. "Our betrothal was of—short duration."

"Why?"

He shrugged. "I found a commission instead."

I was scandalized. "You were marrying her for her dowry?"

He looked embarrassed, but he brazened it out. "Why not? People do it all the time. Duccio needed the money, and there was Carolina—it seemed downright providential."

296

"Until the commission came along." I shook my head. "I wouldn't have thought it of you, Ambrogio."

"Why am I justifying myself to you?" he asked. "Weren't you engaged to Ser Pretension?"

"But Farinata never pretended to be a good man. You, on the other hand—"

"*Porca monda*, you are the most annoying—" He bit off whatever he was going to say and got up so that he could pace about the room. "You're the one who told me that I was like my mother, that I'd neglect my wife and think only of my work. And you were right—whenever I was five minutes late, Carolina would hang her head and look reproachful and generally droop around the premises as though I'd whipped her. And we weren't even married yet, we were just courting—"

"I never said any such thing!" I retorted. "You said that about me, remember? Every time I picked up a paintbrush you'd go on and on about how I was sure to break my poor husband's heart, and why didn't I go help Margherita in the kitchens, and then when I finally did the things a woman was supposed to do, you looked at me like I was an insect for walking away from painting like some simpering— Don't you dare laugh at me! Don't you dare!"

"I'm not laughing at you," he said, and then when he realized my shaking was not just from the illness, "Shh, shh. I'm just teasing you." He took me in his arms and began to stroke my hair. "Shh, shh, it's all right. I'm sorry. I didn't mean to upset you. Stop, stop. It's all right."

His gentleness undid me. "It's not me," I wept against him. "It's just the malaria."

"Of course it is." He pulled me down next to him on the settle. "I'm not sure why we're fighting. I've come to ask you to marry me, you silly girl."

I went absolutely still, then I pushed myself away and went to sit on the stool. He started to pull me back, then dropped his arms, looking puzzled and a little hurt. "I thought you'd want to," he said, his voice carefully neutral.

I knew my cool response had surprised and hurt him, which was the last thing I wanted to do. After a moment I went to kneel in front of him. I took his hands and before I could think better of it I told him what I really thought.

"I just don't think I can forgive anyone anymore. First it was my parents, then Farinata and Gian and Gentucca, and Claire and Sagesse—there are just so many sides," I said, not very coherently. "And I know you have to look at them all, and everyone's doing the best they can, but they don't know, they don't understand, that it doesn't just hurt them, it hurts everyone." I reached out and brushed back a lock of hair that fallen onto his forehead. "I don't want to have to forgive anymore. Especially you. I don't think I could bear to have to forgive you."

"You won't have to," he promised.

I looked at him, at the stubborn, little-boy jaw and steady hazel eyes I knew better than my own, and, despite myself, I believed him. He leaned forward, and I reached up to touch the hard, bristly line of his cheek. "I've always wanted to do that," I said.

He swallowed, then leaned a little farther to kiss the curve where my neck met my ear. It tickled, and I giggled and turned my head away, but he turned it back again and then his mouth was on mine, and his hands were hard against my back. I heard him make a noise in his throat, and then I stopped thinking at all.

Much later, he murmured something in Latin under his breath.

"What's that?"

"He ... tried to waken with new love, a living love, her long-settled mind and dormant heart."

"And he succeeded," I said.

Then we went to tell my mother and father.

EPILOGUE

Convent of San Stefano degli Ulivi,
Ravenna, 1350

I began this tale while I awaited the birth of our first child, Camilla, born not far from Siena while Ambrogio painted Madonnas for the monastery of San Galgano. We had waited for her for ten long years, happy years, but so incomplete without her that, like Soeur Claire before us, we went on a pilgrimage to find her. Her sisters followed quickly, and we had twenty years of perfect happiness before the Black Death ravaged our city, and I found myself alone once again.

Alone, but now not lonely. I have taken the veil in Ravenna, God's city, and have discovered that, as I hoped, a life of meditation and service is painted in brighter, warmer colors than I imagined possible. My life is not easy, but amidst its trials and tasks I take rest in the promise that the yearnings that possess me will someday be filled. When I reach for Ambrogio in the night or see my daughters' lovely faces in times of laughter or sadness, I remind myself that my longing is only the shadow of the joy we will know when we are together again.

So it does not matter that I, like Gentucca, am forgotten by the world. I have tended my little corner of it with love, and when it is my turn to leave this life I know my family will be waiting, and that God will transform the broken and scattered bits of our harvests into a garden of living light.

AUTHOR'S NOTE

We know very little about Antonia Alighieri, Dante's only daughter, except that she joined her father at Ravenna during the last three or four years of his life and that she became a Dominican nun called Suor Beatrice at the convent of San Stefano degli Ulivi in Ravenna, where the writer Boccaccio visited her in 1353 with a gift of ten gold ducats. Ambrogio Lorenzetti is also something of a mystery. We know that he was Pietro's younger brother, that he was unusually learned for a painter, and that he and his three daughters apparently died of the plague in Siena in 1348. The rest of this story is fiction, although I've worked hard to make it congruent with the historical record as I understand it, with one exception. Dante was scrupulous about peopling the *Commedia* with characters who had died prior to Easter week, 1300, the supposed date of his journey. For the purposes of the story, however, I have allowed Filippo Argenti and the models for Ciacco, Matelda, and Pietro the comb seller to live longer than they actually did.

I read neither Latin nor Italian, and have relied on Robert Fitzgerald's translation of the *Aeneid* and Barbara Reynolds' version of the *Vita Nuova* for the quotations you find here. Two especially good translations of the *Commedia* itself are those recently published by Robert and Jean Hollander and by Robert Durling and Ronald Martinez. You can find out more about Dante and his poetry at my Dante class's website: *www.waterfordschool.org/Dante/index.htm.*

This project began when the National Endowment for the

Humanities' Seminar for School Teachers program made it possible for me to spend six weeks studying Dante in the company of some of the finest people and scholars it has been my good fortune to meet. Ron Herzman and Bill Stephany, ably and memorably assisted by Lynn and Wes Kennison, Christie Fengler-Stephany, Bill Cook, Gary Towsley, and Ellen Herzman, taught me to love Dante, Siena, and the medieval world almost as much as they do. Nancy and Hilary Heuston, Pat Newberry, and the Waterford School made a second trip to Italy and France both possible and a cherished, if slightly hysterical, memory. Jan Kieckhofer hosted me with her customary generosity during a research trip to the Marion E. Wade Center at Wheaton College, whose staff was welcoming and professional. Despite heavy demands on his time, Professor Stanley Benfell graciously read the entire manuscript and saved me from many errors and omissions, as did Front Street's wonderful copy editor, Katya Rice. Helen Robinson designed the beautiful cover on short notice and under trying conditions. And of course none of this would exist without Stephen Roxburgh, who is not only a matchless, supportive editor but a skilled and exacting teacher. I am grateful to them all.